P9-DTV-234

WITHDRAWN
UTSA LIBRARIES

*Planned
Short-Term
Treatment*

Planned Short-Term Treatment

Second Edition

RICHARD A. WELLS

THE FREE PRESS

NEW YORK   LONDON   TORONTO   SYDNEY   TOKYO   SINGAPORE

Copyright © 1994 by Richard A. Wells
Copyright © 1982 by The Free Press
                    A Division of Macmillan, Inc.

The Free Press
A Division of Simon & Schuster Inc.
866 Third Avenue, New York, N.Y. 10022

Printed in the United States of America

printing number

1 2 3 4 5 6 7 8 9 10

Library of Congress Cataloging-in-Publication Data

Wells, Richard A.
    Planned short-term treatment / Richard A. Wells.—2nd ed.
       p.   cm.
    Includes bibliographical references and index.
    ISBN 0-02-934655-X
    1. Brief psychotherapy.   I. Title.
    RC480.55.W44   1994
616.89'14–dc20   94-13229
                                                            CIP

To my parents

Contents

Preface and Acknowledgments

There is no doubt that interest in short-term treatment has increased greatly since the original version of this book appeared in 1982. In the intervening years its overall effectiveness and applicability has been even more firmly established, and promising new variations in brief methodology have developed. A number of these innovations are incorporated into this revision, along with a continued exposition of the basic principles of a cognitively oriented, social-skill based, problem-solving approach to brief intervention.

At the same time, we are moving into an era when major changes in both the delivery of therapeutic services and the settings in which they occur are being contemplated and debated. It will be critical for clinical practitioners across all the helping professions to not only be knowledgeable about the most effective and efficient therapeutic methods but also to participate in the decisions being made about their implementation. These decisions are too important to be left entirely in the hands of politicians, third-party payers, and the like.

As in the first edition, my intent has been to present a model of planned short-term intervention that will be useful to the direct practitioner, in the front line of helping service, as well as to students and teachers of clinical practice. With the perspective of the clinician in mind, I have emphasized the immediate details of practice and attempted to illustrate the manner in which techniques and strategy must be adapted to the specific needs and unique characteristics of our clients. Two interrelated goals have influenced this new edition:

(1) to incorporate recent refinements and innovations in brief therapeutic practice and (2) to preserve the eclectic, empirically based foundation that was a major strength of the original version.

In preparing this revised edition of *Planned Short-Term Treatment*, I have had to look back over a career in mental health that began in 1954 and has coincided with some of the most impelling changes in the delivery of psychotherapeutic services. Over this period of time, psychotherapy has evolved from a long-term, psychoanalytically dominated method, available mainly to a socially privileged population, into a predominantly brief service, influenced by behavioral and family systems frameworks, and accessible to much wider and more diverse client populations. These changes herald a much needed democratization of therapeutic method and applicability, and the strong consumer orientation of short-term treatment has played an important role in this transformation.

From an epistemological viewpoint, the model of brief therapy advanced in this book falls into what Fishman and Franks (1992) have identified as the "pragmatic paradigm," where the concern is with *how* the therapy functions and *what* it accomplishes, rather than theoretical explanations of *why* it works. This framework is explicated in the opening chapter, along with discussion of the client populations best served by brief treatment and a review of its research base.

The succeeding chapters attempt three main tasks: (1) to outline a theoretical foundation for short-term treatment, (2) to examine the process and goals of the initial phase of brief intervention, and (3) to explore certain of the major strategies of change employed by the short-term therapist.

Thus, Chapters 2 and 3 can be seen as interrelated. In the first, I examine several theoretical frameworks that have proven useful in conceptualizing the process of short-term treatment and guiding its application. This chapter presents an eclectic approach to theory on the ground that there is no compelling reason to choose one theoretical orientation over another; all have their advantages and disadvantages for the practitioner. On the other hand, Chapter 3 takes a much more pragmatic stance and describes several short-term cases in detail, in order to give the reader a clearer picture of the characteristics and typical course of this form of therapeutic helping.

Chapters 4 and 5 then examine the initial interview in depth. The theme of engagement into treatment will be emphasized, and the active and directive role of the practitioner within this process is highlighted. Because of the brief therapist's deliberate restriction of time, and selection of a limited focus, the skillful management of the first contact is critical to effective brief therapy.

Following this emphasis on achieving a good beginning, Chapters 6, 7, 8, 9, and 10 are concerned with the implementation of change. The clinical application of behavior enactment (or rehearsal) methods and various types of task assignment are examined and clinically illustrated. These change strategies are particularly useful in short-term treatment because of their active nature and immediate application to problems in living. Chapters in this section also discuss social skill training approaches and the increasingly influential cognitive restructuring methods. Skill training, derived from behaviorally oriented sources, emphasizes the step-by-step acquisition of facility in such socially important areas as communication, affiliation, assertion, and the management of stress. Cognitive restructuring, which has burgeoned in popularity and sophistication during the 1980s, draws upon a number of theoretical sources and emphasizes a series of highly useful techniques for altering negative self-evaluations, excessively high performance standards, irrational beliefs, and, of course, the debilitating effects of anxiety and depression. Finally, although clinical examples of family and couple intervention appear in many of the earlier chapters, Chapter 10 describes and illustrates specific applications of brief psychotherapy in these important areas of public and private practice.

The concluding chapter discusses the innovative work being done with single-session psychotherapy, and draws from this practice a number of principles critical to all brief intervention. In addition, Chapter 11 examines the technical and ethical issues in employing outcome and follow-up evaluations in practice, and concludes with a discussion of the future of short-term treatment.

Any author must acknowledge multiple influences and, in the end, hope that these many debts are adequately documented in the citations and references. Certain writers and researchers stand out, however, as enduring sources of knowledge and inspiration. Jerome Frank's seminal contributions to the psychotherapy literature have played a major role in shaping my thinking and practice. Social learning theory, particularly as explicated by Albert Bandura, has provided an integrative framework for my view of the principles of clinical assessment and intervention. Finally, William Reid's pioneering development of task-centered casework and his persistent labors in examining and validating many aspects of brief therapeutic practice have been yet another significant influence.

My clinical work and teaching have been both supported and enriched by the influence of a number of friends and colleagues. Mary Page, Larry Pacoe, Patrick McNamee, Phillip Phelps, and Vincent Giannetti have all contributed in meaningful ways; the dean and faculty of the School of Social Work at the University of Pittsburgh have collectively offered a congenial atmosphere in which to teach and practice. My students have been receptive and stimulating in their interest in short-term methods and have kept me alert to the need to present theory and method in a form that responds to the immediate demands of clinical practice. The many individuals, couples, and families with whom I have worked have taught me to respect the strength of the human spirit, both for its resiliency and for its ability to endure.

1

Short-Term Treatment: Overview and Evidence

If it were done when 'tis done, then 'twere well it were done quickly.

—Shakespeare, *Macbeth*

It is only in very recent years that the *efficiency* of therapeutic service has become an issue in mental health circles. The question of whether one or another of the many helping approaches can deliver relief from suffering or restore function more promptly than others has not been a historic concern of the field. Effectiveness, of course, *has* been an issue. Does psychotherapy work? is the broad question. Despite some strident voices to the contrary (Eysenck, 1952; Fischer, 1976), most clinicians have maintained that it does, and a series of reviews of the research literature (Andrews & Harvey, 1981; Bloom, 1992; Lambert et al., 1986) now support this position. The dilemma facing the present-day practitioner, across all the mental health professions, is one of how to combine these dual imperatives of effectiveness and efficiency. Garfield (1980) clearly states the issue when he notes that "from any vantage point . . . a brief but effective therapy would be much more utilitarian than an equally effective therapy which requires a much longer period of time" (p. 277).

As a consequence, there is no doubt that practitioner interest in short-term treatment has greatly increased in recent years (Bolter et al., 1990). Following a definition of brief intervention, this chapter examines the various factors that have promoted the present heightened interest in short-term methods and presents an overview of the

1

principles of such clinical practice. Additional sections explicate certain theoretical and philosophical issues related to its use and discuss the particular clientele most suited to brief therapeutic approaches. A final section reviews the substantial body of research evidence supporting the effectiveness of short-term treatment, as well as data on the prevalence of brief intervention in the daily realities of clinical practice.

SHORT-TERM TREATMENT: A DEFINITION

Throughout this book, the terms *short-term treatment* or *brief psychotherapy* will be used interchangeably to refer to a form of therapeutic practice that can be defined as follows:

> Short-term treatment, as I shall use this term, refers to a family of therapeutic interventions in which the practitioner deliberately limits both the goals and the duration of the contact.

The goals of brief therapy are almost always mutually contracted by therapist and client and are directly related to the specific life difficulties the client wishes to solve. The length of intervention is determined by the clinical judgment of the therapist and may be anywhere from one to fifteen (occasionally as many as twenty) sessions. Interviews are usually hour-long and are typically scheduled on a weekly basis. Within these parameters of focus and time, many variations are possible, and these, of course, will be the continuing subject matter of this book. At this point, however, this definition will serve as a rough guideline to the most distinctive characteristics of short-term methodology.

LEGITIMIZING SHORT-TERM TREATMENT

The origins of brief psychotherapy can be traced back to the beginning of this century (Wells & Phelps, 1990), but it did not emerge as a recognized methodology until the 1960s and 1970s. Contributions have come from all the major helping professions; such authors as Parad and Parad (1968) and Reid and Epstein (1972) in social work, Langsley and Kaplan (1968) and Barten (1969) in psychiatry, and Cummings (1977b) and Shelton and Ackerman (1974) in clinical psychology have significantly participated in its early development. Clinicians and theorists such as de Shazer (1985), Budman and Gurman (1988), Edelstein (1990), and many others, have contributed to its continuing growth and vitality during the past decade. Indeed, my own most recent works (Wells & Giannetti, 1990, 1993) bring together a multidisciplinary group of clinical practitioners who are actively practicing various forms of brief psychotherapy in both public and private settings across this continent. A number of key factors have contributed to the resurgence and growth of short-term treatment:

INSTITUTIONAL AND ECONOMIC PRESSURES. The development of community mental health facilities, during the late 1960s, placed enormous pressure on the helping professions to meet expanding demands for service. These pressures continue to this day. In addition, the 1980s has been marked by the steady growth of health maintenance organizations (HMOs) and employee assistance programs (EAPs), both of which emphasize brief, highly focused therapeutic services.

The community mental health centers have suffered from declining governmental funding but must still strive to meet expanded client loads despite depleted staffs. The HMOs and EAPs, on the other hand, have profilerated across the country but are under constant pressure to contain the costs of care. Thus, interest has become more and more directed toward finding interventive methods requiring less staff time yet still offering satisfactory standards of service. At the same time, an increasing number of the third-party payers represented by private and public insurance plans have placed strict limitations on the duration of the therapy they will fund.

It may be overly simplistic to assert that mental health practitioners are only adopting brief therapeutic methods because this is what third-party payers demand, but there is no doubt that this is an important factor. For example, Marmor's (1979) discussion of short-term dynamic psychotherapy not only describes the intellectual ferment that has been a catalyst in the development of this form of brief treatment but, perhaps even more compellingly, also identifies some cogent economic factors related to its growth.

At the same time the development of third-party payers, together with the imminence of some form of national health insurance, places psychiatrists under pressure to find shorter, more broadly applicable, and more efficient techniques of therapy or risk exclusion from these programs for fiscal reasons. As a consequence, we can anticipate that the briefer techniques of group therapy, behavioral therapy, and family therapy will emerge more strongly in the years ahead. (p. 149)

We are still awaiting, at this writing, the emergence of a national health insurance scheme, but Marmor's other predictions accurately reflect much of the present state of therapeutic practice.

In their review of the burgeoning development of managed health care programs, Austad and Berman (1991) point out that as much as 25 percent of health care costs are consumed by mental health services. They identify three major trends in the field of health care: (1) dramatically increased overall costs have led to an emphasis on close review and accountability of all services; (2) growing recognition of the reciprocal influence of physical and psychological factors has underscored the importance of mental health services within an adequate health care package; (3) both of these trends have led to an emphasis on active, short-term approaches sharply focused on the interplay between the somatic and psychological factors facing the typical patient or client (cf. Hoyt, 1993).

A DIFFERENT CLIENTELE. As a further consequence of the movement into community mental health and the various forms of managed health care, another factor has become increasingly evident: not only do the traditional methods not meet the need for effectiveness and efficiency, but in many instances the clients do not want the methods. Thus, as service has been increasingly offered to lower socioeconomic and working-class groups, it has been found that their concern is with the reduction of current social and interpersonal stress—with ridding themselves of distressing and incapacitating difficulties in daily living. Such problems may, at times, appear mundane but can represent very real dilemmas for the prospective client.

Alice Martin, a nineteen-year-old single woman, was referred to a community mental health center by the nurse practitioner who was caring for her during her second pregnancy. The nurse expressed concern that Miss Martin, who was six months pregnant, was having difficulty in managing her day-by-day activities, since her boyfriend, on whom she depended a great deal, had recently been sent to prison. An initial interview with Miss Martin revealed that she saw herself experiencing problems in two areas: first, she was receiving welfare payments and was finding it difficult to budget her money; and second, she was worried about child care and transportation arrangements at the time of labor and delivery but was reluctant to approach her family for help.

Traditional approaches based on Rogerian client-centered principles, or psychodynamic theory, emphasize personal growth or intrapsychic exploration and lack the methods specific to such immediate goals. In addition, conventional clinical philosophy has either disparaged such problems as unimportant or, at best, regarded them as mere "symptoms." While middle-class clients have often been willing to accept this view, lower socioeconomic clients have been notoriously reluctant to do so and typically "drop out" upon encountering this sort of attitude.

UNPLANNED BRIEF TREATMENT. There is a good deal of empirical evidence, moreover, that whatever the modality of intervention, many clients do not stay in treatment if emphasis is placed on such broad concepts as personality reorganization or overall personal growth in the context of long-term contact. Where systematic studies have been conducted, it has been found that mental health clinics and family service agencies have surprisingly high drop-out rates. As many as 80 percent of cases are seen for six or fewer interviews. Garfield (1986), for example, has reviewed the numerous studies substantiating this finding across all settings, while Beck and Jones (1973), Parad and Parad (1968), and Sledge and his colleagues (1990) offer data on family service, child guidance, and mental health clinics, respectively.

The large percentage of cases involving six or fewer interviews suggests that, in the day-by-day reality of practice, a great deal of *unplanned* short-term treatment takes place. On the one hand, contact between helper and client may be brief simply because the process founders; however good the intentions of the therapist, nothing really helpful transpires and the client withdraws from the relationship. On the other hand, it may well be that the client has benefited from even this short encounter and has therefore chosen, unilaterally, to terminate active treatment. In either case, there is no doubt that most therapeutic contact is relatively brief, and it behooves us to examine the meaning of this phenomenon.

In this regard, Gerald Zuk (1978) has emphasized that one of the significant changes in the practice of family therapy was a movement toward short-term contact and Haley (1963, 1991) has persistently sounded this same theme. Both contend that the majority of families are prepared to allow therapeutic access for only a limited period of time and that the therapist must capitalize on this apparent restriction by utilizing an appropriate methodology. As Zuk (1978) notes, this places considerable emphasis on the importance of engagement into therapy, especially where motivation is weak or ambivalent.

CRISIS AS AN ENTRY POINT. Research on crisis (Ewing, 1990; Hansell, 1975) has strongly suggested that many people only come for help at a point when they are in severe distress. Because a crisis tends to resolve itself, for better or worse, within a relatively short period of time, it is apparent that helping services must be devised that work effectively within this natural time limit. Once again, access to many clients is comparatively brief, and the therapist must be prepared to work in the most helpful manner possible within these limitations rather than futilely wish there was more time.

EQUALITY OF OUTCOME. Finally, where short-term and long-term approaches have been empirically compared, there has been a consistent finding with significant client populations that they are equal in result. Short-term treatment, in other words, is not necessarily a second-rate substitute for long-term treatment but is, in many instances, capable of delivering as much service in less time. This, of course, has many implications for practitioners, agencies, and funding sources. Third-party payers, for example, have become aware of these findings and are not willing to underwrite long-term intervention.

Clients, on the other hand, have a right to both effective and efficient service, and "Do not treat unnecessarily" has long been an ethical principle in the helping professions. Austad and Berman (1991) underscore yet another ethical imperative when they point out that, especially in contexts such as managed health care where large populations must be served, short-term therapy approaches "encourage the fair and equitable distribution of services to the greatest number of people" (p. 7).

AN OVERVIEW OF SHORT-TERM TREATMENT

As there are a variety of brief therapeutic approaches now available, I will attempt to specifically identify the theoretical base and overall strategies of the integrated model presented in this book.

Theoretical Influences

The theoretical base of the model of planned short-term treatment I will describe represents an integration of three major influences in the helping field: (1) the behavior modification methods deriving from social theory; (2) the time-limited approaches stemming from the study of crisis; and (3) the strategic/structural methods of family therapy based, in large part, on interpersonal relationship theory.* Although brief therapy has sometimes been mistakenly considered synonymous with crisis intervention, in fact both behavior therapy and key aspects of strategic/structural family therapy have played a critical role in its development (Wells & Phelps, 1990). In this overview I will identify selected aspects of these three important frameworks of clinical thought and identify how each theoretical framework makes a distinct contribution to the practice of short-term intervention.

1. Behavior therapy (and its many cognitive infusions), for example, has shown that people can achieve meaningful change in their lives through structured methods that emphasize the identification of desired behaviors, the step-by-step acquisition of change through observation, imitation and practice, and the generalization of such change into real life via homework tasks and assignments.

2. Crisis theory and intervention, on the other hand, have not only identified the stressful life events that frequently motivate people to seek help but have also highlighted the significance of time in the process of change. That is to say, a crisis can be seen as a time-limited event in the life of its victim, which will resolve itself (for better or worse) unless effective help is received within its natural life span.

---

*For the sake of brevity, I will refer to strategic/structural family therapy simply as "family therapy." Its theoretical principles and therapeutic strategies will be described in Chapters 2 and 10.

3. Family therapy not only offers a highly useful series of techniques and strategies for therapeutic intervention in parent-child and marital problems but, from its base in interpersonal relationship theory, directs the therapist's attention to the critical importance of the individual's current social networks in both creating and relieving problems in living.

Both behavior therapy and crisis intervention, along with family therapy, are aimed at instigating change in the current life and key interpersonal relationships of the individual seeking help. They share the common assumption that human difficulties are most usefully conceptualized as problems in living—disruptions in the person's daily life or emotional equilibrium, dissatisfaction with the quality or quantity of interpersonal relationships, deficits in the essential social skills needed to manage one's life—and that the focus of treatment should be on remedying these gaps. Short-term treatment is a deliberate and concentrated method of meeting such goals and is intended to be a practical and accessible means of helping large groups of people who otherwise would have little suitable therapeutic service at their command.

RELATIONSHIP TO CRISIS INTERVENTION

It should be noted, however, that although it is influenced by certain aspects of crisis theory, the short-term therapy model described in this volume is not identical with crisis intervention. The various short-term approaches can be seen as a related family of interventions, incorporating crisis intervention as an important subtype but including techniques, strategies, and goals that move well beyond the crisis formulation. These include interventions aimed at promoting change in specific areas of personal and interpersonal functioning (including, of course, both marital and parent-child relationships), methods of imparting important social knowledge and skills, and, in other instances, approaches designed to assist an individual in solving a particularly difficult life problem.

Crisis intervention typically aims at restoring the precrisis equilibrium of the sufferer. Brief treatment, in contrast, often attempts to develop new learning and skills that will enable the individual to progress beyond his or her original status. Crisis work is primarily supportive and ameliorative—and highly valuable within these parameters. Short-term treatment, in the broader dimensions that will be presented in this work, is designed to engage the client in problem resolution or change efforts with wider-ranging implications. A further important distinction is that crisis intervention emphasizes the individual or family in acute emotional distress, whereas short-term treatment is suitable for a range of clients whose affective state may be much less profoundly disturbed.

THE BASIC MODEL

In practice, short-term intervention involves the employment of specific personal and behavioral change methods, over a defined period of time, with the objective of bringing about positive changes in the client's current life. In addition, the helping process is intended to relieve the often painful stress and demoralization that accompany disruptions and difficulties in the client's intimate interpersonal relationships, important social roles, and significant areas of personal functioning. Dropouts and unplanned terminations decrease markedly with this dual emphasis on time and reality (Beck & Jones, 1973; Leventhal & Weinberger, 1975; Sledge et al., 1990).

The therapist and client jointly select one or two major areas of difficulty as the target of the helping intervention and agree to work on these problems for a planned period of time (Hoyt, 1990). It is usually the responsibility of the therapist to choose the particular change techniques that are judged to be most pertinent to achieving the desired goal and to guide and encourage the client in their application. The change methods employed are structured, in the sense of comprising a series of steps (or phases) that break down the process of change into component parts and guide the activities of both helper and client. Many such techniques are now available in the clinical literature, covering a wide range of common social and interpersonal situations.

The therapist's activities throughout the helping process are directed toward three major goals:

1. Making problem and goal definitions as clear as possible
2. Assisting and supporting the client in systematic, step-by-step problem solving

3. Using the pressures of an explicit time limit as a key factor toward change

In carrying out these activities, the clinician becomes in many instances an *educator* (Becker et al., 1987; Guerney et al., 1971), providing important information and teaching needed skills in living or, in other instances, an expert *problem solver* (Haley, 1976; Nezu, 1989), guiding clients in systematic ways of dealing with the intricacies and frustrations of the human condition.

PHASES OF INTERVENTION

Looking upon time as a critical element in the process of short-term intervention, it is possible to conceptualize the contact between helper and client as comprising three distinct phases, each with distinct temporal boundaries:

1. The first phase consists of one or two interviews in which problems and goals are defined and an explicit contract negotiated.
2. This is followed by the main period of intervention (which may be one to as many as fifteen sessions in length), in which selected change strategies are utilized and which concludes with an evaluative termination interview.
3. The third phase involves a follow-up contact two to four months later. This interview or telephone conversation, initiated by the therapist, is for the purpose of reviewing the client's current status.

The time durations suggested for each of the phases noted above should not be regarded as inviolable and may vary, depending on the clinical judgment of the practitioner. In any case, it is important to stress that the therapist not only spells out the time dimensions of each of these phases to the client but also adjusts the therapeutic effort to fit within the defined boundaries. This results in highly positive pressures on both therapist and client to identify the most pressing problem(s) and to work productively to bring about the desired changes. Implicit in the short-term helping process is the belief that change is most likely to ensue from a concentrated focus on a single but significant problem in living (and, conversely, the belief that much natural problem solving is weakened by attempting to deal with too many problems simultaneously). In order to emphasize this process, the helper will insist that the client with multiple problems choose the one or two of highest priority for intervention.

TERMINATING OR RECONTRACTING

Most short-term work terminates at the end of the contracted period (plus the designated follow-up), but it should be noted that it is always possible for therapist and client to negotiate, at the end of a particular helping sequence, an agreement to concentrate on a new problem area. Additionally, if short-term treatment does not achieve its goals within the expected time, therapist and client may agree to move into further time-limited contact or, in some cases, extended treatment. Further variations in time usage are possible, including single-session therapy (Bloom, 1981, 1992; Rosenbaum et al., 1990; Talmon, 1990), where contact is deliberately limited to a single interview, and intermittent time-limited treatment (Budman & Gurman, 1988; Cummings, 1991), where periodic short-term contacts are offered.

A PROSPECTIVE CLIENTELE

Many helping methods have unfortunately based their techniques and strategies on clinical experience and research with a socially and emotionally advantaged clientele. Indeed, by their very nature, a number of therapies either directly or indirectly screen out prospective clients who are not intelligent, highly motivated, relatively affluent, and managing their current lives well enough that they are willing to enter a lengthy therapeutic experience with little immediate hope of benefit.

Yet there is no doubt that a great many very ordinary people seek help only when emotional stress and interpersonal difficulties have assumed major proportions. Such a clientele has become much more evident as community mental health centers, HMOs, and EAPs have made therapeutic services increasingly available to the general public. Such potential clients have little concept of therapy as a process aimed at wide-ranging personality change over a period of years but, as research studies of client expectation make clear, typically anticipate that contact will last about six sessions (Budman & Gurman,

1988). Such individuals tend to drop out of treatment rather rapidly when its goals appear vague or irrelevant and the expected time commitment seems endless. Other clients become dependent on the helping process and stay within its protective confines long past any point of real gain (Howard et al., 1986).

There are large numbers of people to whom the services of private practitioners—whatever their discipline—are simply not accessible. This is partly a question of money: many struggling middle-class, lower-middle-class, or blue-collar clients (to say nothing of the poor) cannot afford the fee of the private practitioner. Yet even among those fortunate enough to have health-care benefits that include mental health services, Giannetti (1990) notes that for 49 percent of the population, such coverage is inadequate. Furthermore, the expectations that these clients bring into the therapeutic situation are frequently far different from the conventional therapist. They do not want to change their total personality; rather, they want to learn how to consistently discipline and nurture a difficult child. They do not want to expand their intellectual and emotional awareness, but instead are concerned with how to reduce the quarreling and dissatisfaction of a painful marriage. These are legitimate requests—not "symptoms" of something else—and need to be met with respect, concern, and effective helping from the clinical practitioner. This pragmatic, consumer-oriented stance can be seen in the following case vignette:

> Mrs. Antonini phoned a family service agency to request help for her husband, whom she described as extremely upset and anxious about difficulties he was encountering at work. She accompanied him to the initial interview and they were seen together.
>
> A neatly dressed, rather conventional working-class couple in their middle twenties, both were ill at ease as the session began. Finally, with obvious discomfort and embarrassment, Mr. Antonini described how his co-workers at the factory where he was employed had been verbally harassing him for the past year or two. The harassment consisted mainly of remarks and innuendos to the effect that he was effeminate or even homosexual. These stemmed, Mr. Antonini said, from an incident where he believed he had been overheard masturbating in the company washroom. Mr. Antonini had been able to make only the most ineffectual responses to these sallies; his major

coping device was to avoid contact with the chief instigators of the ridicule. He had become increasingly upset about the situation, but only recently had he been able to confide these difficulties to his wife. He felt some relief from having shared his feelings but at the same time expressed an almost desperate concern to find some way of managing the continuing harassment.

I will return to this case in greater detail in a later chapter. At this point it will be sufficient to note that although a complex of psychological, emotional, and social factors are evident in the difficult situation facing Mr. Antonini, the focus of brief therapy was on responding to his urgent request for some tangible ways of coping with a situation that was both deeply troubling to him and threatening his ability to continue to earn a living.

EMPIRICAL BASE OF SHORT-TERM TREATMENT

Reid (1978) has argued that one of the essential values in a client-oriented approach to clinical practice is "the supremacy of research-based knowledge over knowledge acquired from other sources, such as practice wisdom or untested theory" (p. 5). In examining the empirical base of short-term therapy, I will not attempt to survey the total array of research studies supporting its efectiveness. Drawing on earlier writing (Wells & Phelps, 1990), the major findings can be summarized as follows:

1. The duration of most therapeutic contact, whatever the intentions or orientation of the practitioners, is relatively brief, averaging 6 to 8 sessions. . . .
2. When clients benefit from psychotherapy, of whatever kind, these positive changes occur relatively early, with 75% of clients being improved within 6 months. . . .
3. Finally, comparative studies have consistently found that explicitly time-limited treatments deliver results that are equivalent to those of open-ended or long-term therapies. (p. 8)

Indeed, in relation to this last point, Bloom (1992) comments that "perhaps no other finding has been reported with greater regularity in the mental health literature than the equivalence of the effect of time-limited and time-unlimited psychotherapy" (p. 9). This finding does not mean that extended treatment should not be practiced, but emphasizes that there is a need to identify those individuals or problems requiring lengthy intervention, since the majority of clients benefit as much from a time-limited intervention.

MAJOR OUTCOME STUDIES

There are a number of areas in which the evidence for the effectiveness of brief therapy is especially strong. These include conflicted marital relationships, the emotional and social problems of children and adolescents, crises of individuals and families, and such critical mental health problems as depression and anxiety.

Several major studies will be described in this section in order to provide the reader with some picture of the supporting evidence available and, in particular, to highlight the problems and client populations of relevance to clinical practice in mental health, family service, health care, and child guidance settings. It should be noted that all of these large-scale studies were conducted during the 1960s and 1970s, when brief psychotherapy was emerging as a distinct method, but subsequent research has affirmed their continuing validity (Bloom, 1992; Koss & Butcher, 1986).

For example, in one of the landmark studies of time-limited approaches, Howard and Libbie Parad (1968) examined the results of 1,656 cases seen in planned short-term treatment in a nationwide sample drawn from family service agencies and child guidance clinics. The problems dealt with ranged over the wide spectrum of marital, family, parent-child, interpersonal, and behavioral problems common to such agencies. The Parads note that 86 percent of the cases were handled within the planned time limits and only a minority of clients (14 percent) required lengthier treatment.

From evaluations completed by both therapists and clients, it was found that the target problem improved in 65 to 75 percent of the cases (with the clients giving the higher rating). Similarly, better coping with stress was reported in identical percentages of therapist and client ratings.

In a study of more than 1,000 cases of brief therapy with children (and their families) in a child guidance clinic, Leventhal and Weinberger (1975) found that short-term treatment produced improvement rates equal to (or better than) the long-term treatment approaches the clinic had previously employed. As in the Beck and Jones (1973) study noted earlier, this large-scale study also reported that dropout rates were greatly reduced.

In another important study, Sloane and his associates (1975) compared the outcome of both behavioral and psychodynamic short-term approaches (each employing a three-month time limit) with the changes occurring in a wait-list control group. The ninety patients in this study were moderately to severely disturbed adults seen as outpatients in a community mental health center. Results were evaluated using therapist, patient, and significant other (spouse, family member, etc.) ratings of change. In addition, a comprehensive evaluation interview was conducted by an independent clinician. All of these assessments were carried out before and after treatment and at one- and two-year follow-up points. Highly experienced therapists were employed in both treatment conditions.

Significant and substantial levels of improvement were found in both treated groups at termination in comparison with the nontreated clients, indicating that therapeutic intervention can induce meaningful change within a relatively brief time span. The behavioral and psychodynamic approaches were equally effective, although, contrary to popular opinion, the behavioral approach was effective across a wider range of client disturbance. The psychodynamic intervention was most effective with mildly disturbed individuals, whereas the behavioral methods helped those with both mild and severe dysfunction.

These results must be tempered, however, by the finding that by the one- and two-year follow-ups, all patients, whether treated or untreated, were substantially improved. This supports the general viewpoint noted earlier (Howard et al., 1986; Lambert et al., 1986) that any psychotherapeutic intervention operates most effectively in the early phases of contact and that, beyond this point, natural remedial factors will promote positive change whether or not the individual is treated.

Finally, a cluster of studies (Cummings, 1977a, VandenBos 1977b; Cummings & Follette, 1968, 1976; Cummings & VandenBos, 1979; Follette & Cummings, 1967; Rosen & Wiens, 1979) have examined the role of very brief psychotherapy in managed health care settings. A central concern for Cummings and his associates was whether a psychotherapeutic intervention would reduce the patient's need for such other services as physician visits, pharmaceutical prescriptions, emergency room visits, diagnostic tests, and so on.

Their overall finding was that brief intervention played a significant role in alleviating the emotional distress that for many patients was being reflected through physical symptoms and did, in fact, reduce medical services. Moreover, in one of their studies they found that a single psychotherapy session was sufficient to reduce medical intervention by 60 percent over a five-year follow-up period, a startling finding that had already been suggested by earlier studies (Goldberg et al., 1970) in the managed health care area. These are important findings in relation both to the rapidly expanding utilization of managed health care throughout this continent, and the pressing need to contain the escalating costs of health care generally.

FOLLOW-UP STUDIES

Clinicians have been understandably concerned about the durability of the effects of time-limited intervention. Are gains from brief therapy ephemeral and liable to dissipate rapidly once therapeutic contact ends? A number of studies of short-term treatment (e.g., Cummings & Follette, 1976; Keilson et al., 1979; Langsley et al., 1971; Reid & Shyne, 1969; Sloane et al., 1975; Wells et al., 1977) have included follow-up evaluations in their research design. Thus, client status has been assessed anywhere from four months to five years after the conclusion of treatment. The consistent finding has been that the gains from short-term treatment show little or no decline at follow-up, an effect consonant with follow-up findings for all therapeutic approaches (Nicholas & Berman, 1983). Once again, the empirical data emphasize *equality* of outcome for brief and long-term approaches.

TREATMENT DURATION: LONG OR SHORT?

A pervasive belief in clinical circles has been that most psychotherapists prefer and, indeed, actually practice long-term treatment. Despite this enduring piece of clinical mythology, several large-scale studies of clinical practice provide strong support for the position that the duration of most client-therapist contact, across all of the major helping professions, is relatively brief, whatever the preference or intentions of the therapist. The major study by Beck and Jones (1973) offers such a picture of clinical practice in social work, while Langsley (1978) and Koss (1979) offer similar reports on the clinical work of psychiatrists and psychologists, respectively. More recent studies confirming these findings will also be noted.

The study of social work practice conducted by Beck and Jones (1973) was based on an examination of more than 3,000 cases from a nationwide sample of family service agencies, gathered in 1970. The authors compared these findings with a similar study conducted in 1960 and found that for interventions with relationship and personality problems (77 percent of the agencies' caseload) there was a marked trend toward increased use of short-term treatment, particularly with child-related problems. The most startling finding, however, is their report (1973, p. 188, n. 30) that the short-term cases in their sample averaged *five* sessions, whereas long-term cases ("continued service" in their terminology) averaged *nine* interviews! That a nationwide sample of "continued service" cases falls squarely within what can only be considered short-term time limits certainly reinforces the notion that a good deal of brief treatment is being given in an unacknowledged manner.

The same phenomenon is present in the other major helping professions, as Langsley (1978) describes the results of a survey of psychiatric practice conducted over a six-month period in 1974. In this study both private and clinic-based psychiatrists reported on the diagnosis and treatment of all cases where intervention was considered complete and was terminated with the practitioner's agreement. A total of 4,072 cases were reported by 147 private practitioners and 51 clinic-based psychiatrists. It is important to note that these were all cases in which treatment had been concluded; the study did not include consultations, incomplete treatment, or unplanned dropouts.*

Within this sizable sample it was found that the median number of

---

*It should also be noted that Langsley's major purpose in conducting the survey was not to document the prevalence of short-term treatment, but to ease the worries of third-party payers who thought that private psychiatric treatment was predominantly long term. As the earlier quotation from Marmor indicated, a recurring fear among psychiatrists is the notion that they may be excluded from the rich lode of a national health insurance, if such legislation is ever passed.

office visits, across all diagnoses, was 12.8 for private psychiatrists and 10.3 for the clinic-based practitioners. Thus, in terms of length of treatment, there was little difference between private and institutional practice; therapists in both settings were obviously conducting a fair amount of relatively brief treatment. As Langsley points out, contrary to popular belief, psychiatrists as a group do not predominantly practice long-term treatment. Private psychiatrists, in particular, frequently utilize brief interventions, and even the more severe disorders do not necessarily receive lengthy treatment. If anything, the trend was for such milder diagnostic categories as "situational disturbance of childhood and adolescence" to receive longer contact.

Finally, Koss (1979) examined the characteristics of all the cases seen over a year's time at a private clinic staffed by seven psychologists. The 100 subjects included in the study comprised all persons who requested and attended at least one psychotherapeutic session during the time period. The central finding was that the length of completed treatment for 79 percent of the sample was twenty interviews or fewer. Koss points out that this pattern is not too different from that of clients in public agencies, and it underscores the need to "continue to develop and evaluate treatment approaches designed to utilize effectively the brief time clients—even the most socially advantaged—will remain in psychotherapy" (p. 211).

These three large-scale studies were conducted during the 1970s, but Garfield (1986) finds the same trend continuing when he reports that the average length of therapy reported across a wide range of outpatient settings was between six and eight sessions. Indeed, writing in 1989, Garfield unequivocally states:

> Most of the psychotherapy that is conducted in the United States, at least, is brief therapy, and there is no basis for expecting any change in the immediate future. There are still opportunities for those individuals who want to enter psychoanalysis or receive some other type of long-term psychotherapy as a means of personal self-exploration in terms of a specific theory of personality. However, such therapy is clearly for the very few who desire such an experience and can afford to pay for it. For the rest of the population, brief psychotherapy remains the treatment of choice. (p. 156)

It appears unnecessary, then, to try to persuade practitioners to do more short-term treatment when, in fact, the bulk of actual practice is already relatively brief. The real difficulty may lie in the cognitive dissonance this creates for the therapist who, on the one hand, has been taught to believe in the superiority of extended treatment and yet must grapple with the reality of a practice that is largely brief contact. The purpose of examining the principles and techniques of short-term intervention in this work is not to change practice in any major way; this has apparently already taken place. The need, rather, is to explicate the empirical, theoretical, and technological foundations of time-limited intervention so as to improve the quality of such practice and reinforce its *explicit* acceptability among practitioners.

IMPLICATIONS FOR PRACTICE

It is thus apparent that brief psychotherapy has been widely tested with large numbers of cases in a variety of therapeutic settings. The approach can be as readily employed with the problems of children and their parents as it can with the difficulties of individual adults. Within health care settings, brief interventions not only benefit the patient but also help reduce the overall cost of the program. In both public and private practice contexts, brief therapy can be adapted to the interpersonal complexities of family and marital conflict as well as to the more individually focused problems of people in severe distress.

All of this establishes, moreover, that planned short-term treatment is not a passing fad, but a serious and purposeful therapeutic endeavour. On the basis of the accumulated evidence available, I believe that the following position is empirically justified:

> Planned short-term treatment should be considered the treatment of choice in such settings as mental health clinics, managed health care programs, and child guidance and family service agencies except where there is specific empirical evidence that a particular client group or presenting problem requires lengthier treatment.

This, of course, does not preclude the possibility that certain individuals, couples, or families will need more extended treatment, but it suggests that the way to find this out is after a trial of brief intervention has not achieved the desired results. Practitioners should not routinely enter into long-term treatment, since the research evidence strongly supports the position that, in a great many instances, brief intervention will bring about as much change as a longer intervention. Moreover, the equality of outcome that has been demonstrated is being achieved in less time, and with less cost, not only for the client but in relation to scarce personnel resources.

2

An Eclectic Framework: Theoretical Influences

Everybody has won, and all must have prizes.
—Lewis Carroll, *Alice's Adventures in Wonderland*

Practitioners easily become impatient with theory and tend, at times, to reject it out of hand as unrelated to the immediate necessities of practice. Yet no one can function without a "theory" of some sort, even if it is only the loosest collection of commonsensical notions about why people experience difficulties (or live successfully), and what they might do to overcome a problem in living.

This chapter advances the thesis that no *one* theoretical framework is sufficiently comprehensive to meet the demands of short-term practice and that the helper must necessarily adopt some form of eclecticism. The growing acceptance of such eclectic practice is discussed, along with a brief examination of the overall relationship of theory to practice.

The bulk of the chapter, however, consists of a proposed eclectic framework for brief psychotherapy integrating key concepts from (1) social learning theory, (2) crisis theory, and (3) interpersonal relationship theory. The essential theoretical principles of each of these three major frameworks is examined, and treatment implications of particular relevance to brief intervention is identified. A concluding section discusses commonalities between the three theories.

THE NEED FOR ECLECTICISM

The most important practical question for the clinician is how to bring about tangible and beneficial change in the client's life. In contrast to the pure scientist or the academician, the helping professional operates with the clear-cut expectation and, indeed, the societal mandate that her or his efforts will make such a difference. To attain these goals, clinical practitioners in the helping professions must answer three essential questions about human behavior:

1. How do problems in living develop? Why does one individual become embroiled in difficulties while another, often apparently similar in most respects, copes quite successfully?
2. Once a problem in living has developed, what maintains its existence? Given that such difficulties are by their very nature emotionally stressful and frequently impede individuals in the realization of important goals, what tends to support their continuance?
3. How does an individual change from a problematic to a nonproblematic status? Even more specifically, what part can a helping professional play in stimulating such processes of positive change?

The accepted response has been to turn to theory of some kind—or to devise a new theory—and there has been no lack of theoretical frameworks purporting to answer these central questions. In the face of the competing demands of so many viewpoints, it is becoming increasingly common for practitioners to describe themselves as "eclectic." Jayarante's 1978 survey of a large sample of clinical social work practitioners found that 55 percent identified themselves as eclectic. Another 25 percent reported that they employed more than one theoretical framework and, under a broad definition, could also be considered eclectic. Among those self-identified as eclectic, nearly 20 percent reported the use of *five or more* conceptual frameworks in their practice. Garfield and Kurtz (1977) have reported similar findings among psychologists. Indeed, with the publication of such works as Norcross's (1986) *Handbook of Eclectic Psychotherapy*, or Patterson's (1989) articulate discussion of a systematic foundation for eclectic psychotherapy, it is evident that eclecticism is becoming increasingly respectable and accepted across all of the helping professions.

The trend toward eclecticism appears to be especially the case where brief psychotherapy is the major mode of treatment and may well represent a process of adaptation to the demands of practice. Thus, Austad and Sherman (1992) report on a group of forty-three clinical practitioners—mainly psychologists and social workers—almost all of whom had been trained in a single theoretical framework (usually psychodynamic), and found that after several years of practice in a managed care setting they had become predominantly eclectic.

This predominance of eclecticism among clinicians has been criticized, usually by those advocating strict adherence to a single theory (Greene, 1978; Wolpe, 1969). Yet there is little doubt that the frontline practitioner has scant opportunity to reflectively weigh the merits of a plethora of competing theories. The clinician is constantly confronted by the need to act, and through action to promote positive change in clients who all too often do not fit the cleaner categories of any *single* theoretical framework.

Much of my consideration of the theoretical literature will be from this perspective. I will not regard the generalizations of any theory as true or false in an absolute sense, but will attempt to probe their usefulness in this vital task of preparing, motivating, and supporting clients toward the successful utilization of short-term helping processes.

SOCIAL LEARNING THEORY INFLUENCES

In his brilliant overview of the then-current status of social learning theory, Albert Bandura (1977b) points out that the most popular theories of human development and behavior have focused on the individual and have emphasized such motivational forces as needs, drives, and impulses. Bandura believes that this approach to psychological theory is inadequate and is now being challenged, particularly by the comprehensive viewpoint espoused by social learning theory. He has continued his integration of both theory and research in succeeding publications (Bandura, 1986).*

---

*In this last volume Bandura suggests that the conceptual framework is more accurately titled "social cognitive theory" but, as this new designation is still not in general use, I will continue to employ the familiar terminology of "social learning theory."

In the social learning viewpoint, an adequate explanation of behavior must include the antecedent inducements that may stimulate it; the expected benefits it will produce; and such cognitive factors as "anticipations, intentions, and self-evaluations" (Bandura, 1977b, p. 3.). It is in the area of cognitive factors that current social learning theory has significantly expanded upon previous behavioral theories. Additionally, in important relationship to the optimistic and positive outlook of brief psychotherapy, the theory places no specific emphasis on pathology; from the social learning perspective, there is no qualitative or etiological difference between prosocial or deviant behavior. The distinction is one of social norm or cultural evaluation, and all behaviors are acquired and maintained on the basis of three regulatory systems:

STIMULUS CONTROL. Certain human responses are primarily affected by external environmental events. For example, Pavlov's experiments demonstrated that the salivary responses of his dogs could come under the control of an external stimulus—in this case, the ringing of a bell. On the other hand, external stimuli may less directly control behavior by virtue of their association with previously rewarding events. In this instance, the external stimulus acts as a *signal* to the individual that behaving in a particular way is likely to bring reward or satisfaction. Thus, recently developed weight reduction programs have enhanced their effectiveness by teaching the dieter to identify and deliberately alter the physical settings in which overeating has commonly occurred. By consistently reducing exposure to these previously stimulating circumstances, the effects of other aspects of the program—reduced food intake, exercise, and so on—can be considerably enhanced.

REINFORCEMENT. A second major regulatory system lies in the feedback received, usually in the form of reinforcing consequences, for a behavior. What will be reinforcing, of course, is unique to each individual, but may include satisfying experiences from the behavior itself (sexual orgasm, for example), tangible objects of meaning to the client (food or money), or the person's own self-evaluative comments. In contrast to the stereotyped image of the behavior modifier as confined to doling out M&M's, many recent behavioral approaches have utilized this last reinforcement category; that is, clients have been taught to selectively increase their own rate of self-reinforcement as a potent change strategy. In any event, there is no doubt that consequences powerfully affect human functioning, both eliciting and maintaining behavior, and must be appropriately modified if change is to take place.

COGNITIVE MEDIATORS. Finally, social learning theory has emphasized the influence of what Bandura (1997b) calls "central mediating processes" as a third, and perhaps most influential, regulatory system. These are the complex of cognitive processes through which human beings organize, codify, and symbolically store their daily experiences. Over time these cognitive factors become stabilized into attitudes, beliefs, and values and consequently play a critical role in governing behavior. Using this vantage point, clients are trained to identify the cognitive patterns that may be operating to arouse uncomfortable and unwanted emotions or to inhibit or weaken desired behaviors.

This last facet of social learning theory has had an immense impact on the practice of psychotherapy, and most current behavioral approaches are more accurately characterized as cognitive-behavioral. Beginning with such pioneers as Mahoney (1974), Meichenbaum (1974), and Lazarus and Fay (1975), and continuing with the highly influential writings of Aaron Beck and his associates (Beck, 1976; Beck & Emery, 1985; Beck et al., 1979; Moretti et al., 1990), the cognitive-behavioral approaches have come to dominate much of contemporary psychotherapeutic practice.

In summary, social learning theory contributes several important theoretical concepts to the practice of brief therapy. First, it suggests a nonpathological viewpoint of human functioning in which certain behaviors or emotions may be unwanted by, or detrimental to, the prospective client yet are governed by the same regulatory systems that govern the entire range of human behavior. Second, as these systems operate in the current personal and social environment of the troubled individual, they are both identifiable and accessible to change. Third, it explicates a series of empirically substantiated strategies for specifying and altering the behaviors and cognitions that are currently maintaining the problematic situation. Fourth, it emphasizes here-and-now exploration and action, rather than protracted discussion of past history, thus making its strategies compatible with time-limited intervention. Finally, it views clients as active participants in the therapeutic process who can be taught and encouraged to self-manage the aspects of their lives—both current and future—that cause difficulties for them.

Implications for Treatment

Several other important guidelines for short-term therapy can be drawn from social learning theory, in addition to the various change strategies noted above. These will be briefly reviewed here.

1. *The principle of specificity* suggests that learning takes place most efficiently when its target and goals are clearly and concretely identified by both therapist and client. This not only makes the process of change more readily apparent to both participants, but also offers the client a modicum of protection against change efforts that he or she might not regard as desirable. For a number of clients, simply becoming more specific about their problem (and their desired goals) is a meaningfully helpful contrast to an initial state of confusion and turmoil.

2. *The principle of successive approximations* (or shaping) emphasizes that change takes place most easily in a series of steps or phases. A common frustration for disturbed individuals results from their thwarted attempts to change "at a blow," so to speak. Much of the skill of the therapist lies in an ability to break down a desired-goal state into the constituent elements or steps needed to achieve it, and to encourage the client in the systematic use of such a process. In contrast to theories that emphasize exploration of past history or "pathological" states within the individual, both specification and shaping call for an assessment of current behavior and related factors in the immediate environment, and active steps to achieve desired change.

3. *The principle of modeling* is based on the extensive research findings that a great deal of complex human learning takes place through observing the behavior of others. Again, a part of the expertise of the therapist lies in arranging and encouraging the use of needed modeling experiences.

Therapists of many orientations have characterized the helper and the helping process as a type of modeling experience for the client.

However, it must be remembered that modeling is a very literal process: what is observed is what is learned. If, for example, the client only observes the therapist asking questions or making brief, noncommital replies, then it is doubtful if any tangible skills for living can be learned from this example. Useful learning can take place, however, if the therapist, through her or his behavior, offers the model of an active, vital, striving individual to the client.

At the same time, many positive changes can be stimulated through having the client observe the actions of successfully functioning peers, or watch *in vivo* enactments and videotapes of individuals exhibiting desired levels of social skills.

4. *The principle of performance* emphasizes that change takes place most readily when the individual tests out the new behavior through actual activity. Even such obviously cognitive factors as expectations and attitudes, as well as specific motoric behaviors, are most significantly influenced in situations where the person can be induced to act (Bandura, 1977a; Bandura et al., 1980). This important principle underlies the stress placed in brief psychotherapy on such active change strategies as behavioral rehearsal and task assignment.

CRISIS THEORY AND CRISIS INTERVENTION

Perhaps because of its apparent simplicity, and undoubtedly because of its great utility, crisis theory and its practice counterpart of crisis intervention have been readily assimilated into the practice of most clinicians. In his discussion of the history of crisis intervention, Ewing (1990) draws upon the seminal writing of Caplan (1964) to summarize the most common formulation of the crisis state:

> crisis theory is grounded in the concept of homeostasis. People are continually confronted with situations that threaten to upset the consistent pattern and balance of their emotional functioning. Ordinarily these threats are short lived; the threatening situation is mastered by habitual problem-solving activity. Although the person is in a state of tension during the period prior to successful mastery, this tension is generally minimal because the period is relatively brief and the person knows from past experience that mastery is forthcoming. In some instances, however, the threat is such that it cannot be readily mastered by resort to habitual problem-solving methods. It is then,

according to Caplan, that the person begins to experience "crisis." (pp. 278–279)

Crisis intervention was in particular vogue during the 1960s and, along with Gerald Caplan, such writers as Howard Parad (1965) and Lydia Rapoport (1970) have discussed its theory and practice extensively. It has continued to be popular, and current innovations include (1) Ewing's (1978, 1990) suggestion that crisis intervention be viewed as simply one of the forms of brief psychotherapy, often complete in itself; (2) the development of strategies of brief family and marital therapy based on a combination of crisis and systems theory (Pittman, 1987; Pittman et al., 1990); and (3) Imber and Evanczuk's (1990) utilization of brief crisis therapy groups as an alternative treatment in community mental health centers.

The explanatory principles of the theory emphasize several key points:

NORMAL AND SITUATIONAL CRISES. Life is commonly characterized by any number of events, anticipated or unanticpated, that have the capacity to induce stress. Certain of these stress-inducing situations, such as beginning school, entering adolescence, getting married, or growing old, are almost inevitable happenings in the lives of most people. Others, such as divorce, life-threatening illness, or natural disasters, are products of unique sets of circumstances. However, both the "normal" crises of unfolding life and the "situational" crises of unexpected events can induce acute stress in the vulnerable individual or family.

VULNERABILITY TO STRESS. People vary in their ability to withstand or cope with stress. Whether any set of circumstances, normal or situational, induces a full-blown crisis state is a function of this individually determined capacity. It is important to note, however, that the precipitating stimuli for crisis are not uncommon events, but are frequent occurrences in the life of everyone. Haley (1973), for example, has extended the notion of normal crisis in his discussion of the family life cycle. In this description of family living, he points out how the progression from family of origin through courtship, marriage, the arrival of children, and so on, places increasingly complex demands upon the coping abilities of the family members. From this perspective, many family problems can be seen as the consequences of an accumulated crisis in living, when the solutions that are functional at one stage of life become dysfunctional in a succeeding stage.

CRISIS SIGNALS. Once an individual or family has moved into crisis, a characteristic set of affective, cognitive, and behavioral manifestations are triggered that typify the crisis state. Although these reactions mimic many of the manifestations of emotional disturbance or even psychotic states, crisis theory has emphasized that they are not pathological, but the expected and normal reactions to crisis. Indeed, Hansell (1973, 1975) has integrated crisis theory with the findings of social psychology and social anthropology to suggest that an individual's behaviors in crisis not only represent personal stress reactions but also serve as signals, to family and friends, of an urgent need for help.

DURATION OF CRISIS. Both crisis theory and the practice of crisis intervention emphasize that the crisis state is temporary and, within a relatively short time, its acute manifestations will abate. It has usually been proposed that the actual crisis state persists for six to eight weeks, and consequently the need for rapid intervention has been stressed. This has been seen as necessary in order to intervene at a stage where the individual or family, because of heightened emotional discomfort, is most accessible to help. In addition, however, rapid intervention has been conceptualized as important in preventing the crisis victim from setting into a regressed and dysfunctional resolution of the crisis state.*

Treatment Strategies

Crisis intervention has developed a number of interventive strategies that have strongly influenced the practice of all forms of brief

---

*An empirical study by Lewis et al. (1978) suggests that the duration of crisis, although still time-limited, may be somewhat longer than the commonly accepted six- to eight-week limit. Their comparative examination of hospitalized patients found that such cognitive manifestations as helplessness or lowered self-esteem persisted as long as twenty-seven weeks.

treatment. As Rapoport (1970) has suggested, the treatment offered by the crisis worker must maintain a strong orientation to the present and, in order to emphasize this focus, is characterized by a deliberate use of such active and direct techniques as advice, suggestion, and education. All of this thrust is based on the view that crisis is a temporary state and that the objective of intervention is to restore the client to independent functioning in a relatively brief time.

PROMOTING FUNCTION. Some clinicians (cf. Pittman, 1987) have compared crisis intervention to the directive approaches successfuly utilized with "school phobic" children and have suggested that the central emphasis should be on a rapid return to function. For example, in the family crisis therapy described in detail in such works as Haley and Hoffman (1967) and Pittman et al. (1990), the crisis team gives explicit tasks and assignments to the family in a planned effort to stimulate at least the rudiments of social functioning. As Pittman and his colleagues point out:

> The prescription may be quite simple: "Stop drinking. If you're not an alcoholic, it should be easy. If you are, Antabuse will help." "Stop the affair, at least for now. You can call him from here. I'll call if you're embarrassed to." "Do not commit suicide tonight. We'll find other alternatives tomorrow." "Go on to school/work, they'll help you if you need it." "Stay home tonight. The family needs to be together." (p. 320)

ACTIVE THERAPIST ROLE. Twenty years ago Golan (1974) highlighted the distinctive features of the initial contact in crisis intervention:

> On the one hand, the practitioner needs to establish quick rapport, both in order to elicit needed information quickly and to inspire confidence that he can help; on the other, the traditional concept of a "meaningful relationship" largely based on a leisurely exploration and testing over time and which often deepens into a regressive transference, has little place in this form of treatment. (p. 434)

More recently, Pittman and his associates (1990) described the therapeutic stance even more vividly:

> The therapist should enter the situation with an air of calmness but urgency, convey a clear sense of how things work, be impatient but

not unkind with people who seem to prefer chaos to change, and be optimistic that obstacles can be hurdled if one knows what is going on. Sympathy is out of place, as is a passive interest in understanding people's feelings better, disapproval of behavior on moral rather than practical grounds, or a protective willingness to join in conspiracies. (p. 317)

A pervasive theme in almost all the writings on crisis intervention is this emphasis on the active and direct role played by the therapist. Indeed, this theme is a common one throughout the entire family of brief therapies. Even the psychodynamically influenced short-term methods contain a similar stress, as the interview transcripts by Davenloo (1978) or Worchel (1990, 1993) clearly illustrate. Since neither activity nor directionality has especially characterized the traditional role of the helping person, much of the material in succeeding chapters of this book will attempt to illuminate this key aspect of short-term practice.

INTERPERSONAL RELATIONSHIP AND FAMILY THEORY

Like both social learning and crisis theory, the principles of Harry Stack Sullivan's (1953, 1954) interpersonal relationship theory have profoundly influenced psychotherapeutic thought. But unlike these other theories, the interpersonal relationship framework has often been relegated to a covert and unacknowledged place in theoretical discussions. Many clinicians are quite unaware of the the impact of this conceptual framework on their practice. For example, a good deal of contemporary family and marital theory and practice has been strongly influenced by the interpersonal viewpoint. This is particularly evident in the highly popular strategic/structural approach espoused by Haley (1963), Jackson (1965), and Satir (1964) and later refined and expanded by Salvador Minuchin and his co-workers (1974, 1978, 1981), all of whom owe a heavy debt to Sullivan. The present discussion, however, will focus on Sullivan's initial formulations, which are still of great relevance to the practice of brief psychotherapy.

A PSYCHOLOGY OF PEOPLE. The theoretical viewpoint that Sullivan developed is a psychology of people—their immediate effects upon one another and the critical role interpersonal relationships play in forming and maintaining individual response. Indeed, for interpersonal relationship theory, the notion of personality as an individual entity is truly an abstraction, a conceptual convenience. A person is not simply a product of prior experiences or a collection of traits, but is, within the flexible boundaries of her or his behavioral and physiological repertoire, constantly shaped and influenced by the promises and demands of the interpersonal environment.

Thus, the interplay between the budding individual and the various people in his or her life is seen not simply as a matter of adjustment or coping, but as formative of the essential patterns that we call personality. Moreover, this interpersonal influence continues throughout life, and from a totally consistent interpersonal perspective, it would be inaccurate to characterize a person as, for example, "suspicious" or "angry," as if this were a static or enduring aspect of character. Instead, such characterizations only assume real meaning when we can specify the interpersonal situations in which the emotions occur—"suspicious when her employer praises her" or "angry when his wife is uninterested in sex."

THE ROLE OF ANXIETY. The human organism must, of course, meet certain essential biological needs, but even these, in many respects, are qualified and mediated by interpersonal relationships. Sullivan believed that the capacity for anxiety is uniquely human, first experienced in relationship to the mothering person, but continuing throughout life in varying shapes and manifestations. Anxiety, in interpersonal relationship theory, is an experience between people, and the unit of analysis, in understanding any aspect of this phenomenon, must include at least two persons. More specifically, anxiety is the affective or emotional component of the perception that one's status with another person is diminished. This experience involves some degree of threat to self, and as Sullivan (1954) points out, "any lowering of self-esteem is experienced as anxiety" (p. 96).

THE IMPACT OF LONELINESS. At the same time that people experience anxiety in their immediate relationships with others, there is also, in the absence of human intercourse, the powerful experience of loneliness. Sullivan (1954) postulated that loneliness, as the felt component of a lack of any close human relationship, was as potent a motivating force in personal interaction as the avoidance of anxiety. He makes a telling comparison between the two experiences:

> Under no conceivable circumstances has it ever occurred to me that anyone sought and valued the experience of anxiety. . . . No one wants to experience it. Only one other experience—that of loneliness—is in this special class of being totally unwanted. (pp. 94–95)

DEVELOPING SECURITY. A good deal of human interaction, then, involves a delicate balancing of the need to avoid anxiety and the need to reduce loneliness. Certainly one can avoid anxiety entirely—since it is transmitted through relationships with other people—by simply eliminating all personal contacts. But this solution, the hermit's choice, inexorably propels the individual into the countervailing experience of loneliness. It would be inaccurate, however, to convey the notion that interpersonal relationship theory pictures life as a precariously uncomfortable process of balancing anxiety and loneliness, or as a painful series of choices between one or the other. Human relationships can also offer security, the felt experience of heightened self-esteem, and, through intimacy, the satisfying rewards of close personal association. These positive aspects of human interaction can promote growth and satisfaction in any of us and at the same time enhance our ability to cope with the exigencies of life.

DEVELOPING LIFE SKILLS. Finally, Sullivan (1953) spelled out, in considerable detail, a series of stages in human life through which skill in interpersonal relationships is developed. Throughout this schema of development, considerable emphasis is placed on the interpersonal context in which such learning takes place. Initially, of course, the child learns in relationship to the mother (or mothering person), but as life unfolds, increasingly complex and demanding social situations appear. More and more people play a part in the individual's life, and what we loosely refer to as "the environment" becomes increasingly populated. The family, of course, represents an especially important context for learning to manage this myriad of interpersonal transactions, and family systems theory has considerably expanded upon Sullivan's basic formulations, as previously mentioned.

Treatment Implications

In its translation into the principles of family theory, the interpersonal focus on relationships among groups of people has singled out the family as a key factor in both eliciting and relieving dysfunction (Langsley & Kaplan, 1968; Pittman et al., 1990). Thus, family relationships can constitute a potent source of stress and anxiety. At the same time, the family can offer its members a highly meaningful refuge from the everyday pressures of living. The practitioners of family treatment have gone far beyond this simple position, of course, in developing a complex of theoretical statements concerning the processes governing family structure and interaction. From this has evolved a series of techniques and strategies for intervention with critical relationships within the family, which will be described in detail in the chapter on brief family and couple intervention.

A FAMILY ORIENTATION. At this point it will be sufficient to note that the family orientation of interpersonal relationship theory— the belief that immediate family relationships can significantly affect individual behavior—has been a major influence in a number of brief therapy approaches. This influence is apparent whether or not the modality of treatment actually involves direct family interviews.

A clinical example of this can be seen in the case of Mr. Antonini, whose pressing difficulties with ridicule and harassment from his co-workers were described in the Chapter 1. The family orientation of the therapist played a significant role in the intervention. Initially, this point of view influenced the clinician to invite both Mr. and Mrs. Antonini to the first session and see them together to discuss the difficulties Mr. Antonini was experiencing. The actual intervention involved work on sexual reeducation and assertion training for Mr. Antonini, and again both spouses were seen throughout the sessions. This approach was helpful, not because the focus was on marital conflict, but because Mr. Antonini, as a frightened, dispirited individual, needed all the effective support that could be mobilized at this critical point in his life. His wife was available and receptive to this role—a natural helping resource (Maguire, 1991)—and engaging her active participation also had the effect of demystifying the helping process and reducing much of the stigma her husband felt.

FACILITY IN SOCIAL SKILLS. Both interpersonal relationship theory and social learning theory emphasize the critical importance of the individual gaining skill in managing the many personal interactions that pervade his or her life. From this common base, the two theoretical frameworks have mutually supported the development of a series of social skill training approaches that assist clients in attaining or enhancing their ability to function within their social milieu. Much of the technology for this training comes from the modeling, shaping, and performance-focused methods of social learning theory but, from an interpersonal perspective, such skills are essential if anxiety is to be reduced and opportunity for intimacy increased.

PARTICIPANT OBSERVATION. Perhaps the major contribution of interpersonal relationship theory to the practice of brief psychotherapy lies in its emphasis on the therapist as both observer and participant in the helping process. From the beginning of the therapeutic relationship, the therapist must be aware of how he or she affects, and is affected by, this immediate interaction. This refers to much more than one's general level of awareness of attitudes toward certain types of people or one's overall values about such important issues in living as intimate relationships, child-rearing practices, divorce, abortion, and the like.

From the outset, the therapist and client are inextricably caught up in a process of mutual influence within the interview situation (Beutler, 1984; Strong & Claiborn, 1982). The very words that the therapist uses, the phrasing or emphasis of questions or responses, the gestures, voice tone, physical distance, and so on, all have their impact on the client. The client's complex of behaviors have a similar effect upon the clinician, and these mutual reactions intertwine to form a process of reciprocal influence throughout a given session. Indeed, Sullivan's (1954) perceptive analysis of the intricacies of therapeutic interviewing has proven especially useful, as we shall see, in understanding the management of the initial interview in short-term practice.

COMMONALITY AMONG THEORIES

The several theoretical frameworks reviewed in this chapter have some distinct differences. Each posits a series of concepts to catego-

rize and explain human behavior, or selected aspects of social functioning, and these terms certainly differ. There are obviously varied
perspectives and philosophies influencing each theory. Comparatively speaking, some offer a panoramic explanation of human functioning, while others concentrate on only a selected aspect of the whole.
Beyond these global differences, however, there are a number of
common characteristics worth enumerating because of their immediate relevance to short-term intervention:

EMPHASIZING NORMAL HUMAN FUNCTION. Theorists from each of
these perspectives have been concerned primarily with explicating
the major characteristics of *normal* human functioning as these
unfold over the life cycle or are manifested under certain circumstances common to all human living. Thus, there is a central emphasis on how people generally develop or respond to common life
events rather than a focus on pathology per se.

ADAPTATING TO THE SOCIAL MILIEU. All of the frameworks have suggested that the essential task of the individual is one of adaptation to
the unique demands of his or her personal heritage—biolological
and cultural—and the immediate social milieu. The concept of adaptation, it should be noted, is an active one. It does not necessarily
imply a passive acceptance of one's circumstances, but can include
the possibility of highly creative responses. Moreverer, adaptation
can also be seen as a *process* rather than a goal, including both successful and unsuccessful efforts, as in instances where the individual
learns through successive approximations.

ENHANCING COPING SKILLS. This emphasis on adaptation, whether
accepting or innovative, is especially appropriate to the task of the
brief therapist. Many of the difficulties that come to the attention of
the members of the helping professions represent junctures where
social adaptation has failed or where the individual's ability to cope
has weakened. In other words, people seek help at the point at
which problems in living have developed. As a whole, these theories
offer the brief psychotherapist a comprehensive framework for
understanding the places where functioning may typically falter, as
well as potential guidelines for mobilizing constructive change
efforts.

AN ACTIVE THERAPIST ROLE. From each theoretical framework there is a heightened interest in the immediate activities of therapist and client within the therapeutic interaction. Each of these participants is seen as an active participant in the change process, and, particularly in respect to the clinician's role, attempts to influence the client directly are viewed as not only helpful but unavoidable. The emphasis and value placed on an active and immediate therapeutic stance makes this cluster of theoretical frameworks especially suitable in articulating the process of short-term therapy.

A GROUNDED OPTIMISM. Finally, the underlying philosophical tenents of each of these theories suggest an optimistic view of humanity. Directly or implicitly, each theory stresses the interplay between person and environment that can foster the development of personal and social capacities. In each instance the individual is seen as playing an important governing role in his or her fate rather than as subject to uncontrollable forces, inner or outer. At the same time, this optimistic outlook does not ignore or minimize the realistic threats and limitations to human attainment that can be contained in the environment or that may arise from unfortunate personal choices of the individual. Such a balanced emphasis between optimism and reality can be seen as central to the entire short-term treatment endeavor.

3

Scenarios for Practice

Write the vision, and make it plain upon tables, so that a
man may read it easily.

—Habakkuk, II, 2

Practitioners are often enough given an exposition of the theoretical
principles underlying an approach to clinical practice, or descriptions of the research studies substantiating the effectiveness of a particular change strategy, but little notion of how the theory or
empirical data are actually applied. This chapter describes several
short-term cases following the model outlined in the preceding
chapters. Sufficient details are given concerning the characteristics
of the clients, their life problems, and the interventions employed
that the practitioner will be able to form at least a rough cognitive
map of the implementation of brief therapy. Many of the distinctive
features of short-term intervention that these case descriptions highlight will be considered in greater depth in later chapters. The
immediate objective is to give the clinician an overall view of the
short-term treatment process in action.

VARIATIONS IN BRIEF TREATMENT

The most important facets of the brief treatment model are the specificity of objectives, the emphasis on current problems in living, the
frequent employment of structured change procedures, and the

deliberate setting of a time limit for intervention. Within these parameters, however, a number of variations are possible.

BRIEF TREATMENT WITHIN TIME LIMITS. The course of treatment may involve a planned number of interviews followed by termination of contact and, at the end of a designated interval, a follow-up assessment. This, of course, is the basic model of brief psychotherapy and perhaps its most common form. Its effectiveness is supported by a now sizeable body of clinical research, which was reviewed in Chapter 1. Further illustration of the versatility of this form of brief therapy include, for example, Gibbons and her colleagues (1979), who found time-limited intervention (averaging nine sessions) both feasible and effective for 54 percent of a group of 200 persons following their emergency hospitalization for a suicide attempt. With depressed individuals, both interpersonal psychotherapy (Klerman et al., 1984) and cognitive therapy (Dobson, 1989; Moretti et al., 1990) provide clear evidence for the effectiveness of time-limited interventions. Similarly, short-term family approaches as diverse as the McMaster group's problem-centered systems therapy (Epstein et al., 1990) or the one-person family therapy developed by Szapocznik and his colleagues (1989, 1990) have received substantial empirical support.

Over the past decade there has been increasing interest in very brief episodes of therapy, often no more than a session or two, and Bloom (1992) reviews the effectiveness of such interventions, especially in managed health care settings. Hoyt (1993) and Talmon (1990) both offer clinical illustrations of single-session intervention and their work will be discussed in succeeding chapters of this book.

RECONTRACTING FOLLOWING AN INITIAL TIME-LIMITED INTERVENTION. In some cases it is necessary that an additional period of contact be negotiated at the usual termination point and intervention continued for a further time-limited period. This may occur where client and practitioner agree that goal achievement is insufficient and additional work is needed. Recontracting may also be necessary in those instances where the client wishes to work on a problem that was of lower priority at the initial contracting point but continues to be troublesome.

The clinical research also offers some guidelines regarding the frequency with which recontracting occurs in practice. A study by Gibbons et al. (1979) of brief therapy with suicide attempters, for example, found that 17 percent were seen beyond the contracted time limits. The report does not say whether this extension of time involved continued work on the initially contracted problems or focus on another area of difficulty. However, it is interesting to note that this study reports a finding very close to that reported by Parad and Parad (1968), where 14 percent of their client population required further treatment.

GOAL-ORIENTED EXTENDED TREATMENT. In some instances therapist and client may decide that a series of interventions are needed, each planned within explicit time limits and evaluated at the end of each segment (Pacoe & Greenwald, 1993). In this more extended type of contact there is still a high degree of goal specificity, and treatment does not continue from one segment to the next unless client and therapist agree that the projected objectives have been reasonably achieved and, furthermore, that continued help is needed.

INTERMITTENT BRIEF TREATMENT. Brief therapy may consist of a series of discrete episodes of intervention, occurring over an indeterminant period of calendar time (Budman & Gurman, 1983; Cummings, 1991). In such a model the psychotherapist's relationship to the client is analogous to that of many other professionals—attorneys, family physicians, accountants—whose services are sought out intermittently by the client. Like these other professionals, the clinician must be readily assessible at the points where the individual experiences normal or unanticipated difficulties in living. Two case vignettes will illustrate this important type of brief intervention:

> Mrs. Altman, age forty-one, was initially seen for six sessions with the goal of assisting her in deciding whether she should seek a divorce from her estranged husband. This was a particularly difficult decision for her to make because of her Middle Eastern cultural background, which had emphasized a subservient and submissive role for women. She requested therapy again eighteen months later and by this time had obtained a divorce and established herself in the teaching profession. However, she was fearful and guilty about resuming social and sexual relationships with men and was now seeking help with this

dilemma. A twelve-session contract was negotiated and proved helpful in resolving these further difficulties.

Mrs. Altman's problems at this latter point were not unanticipated by the therapist but were neither accessible nor relevant during the earlier contact. At that time her energies were necessarily devoted to making an important and difficult life decision and living out its consequences. Phelps (1993), on the other hand, describes intermittent brief therapy where an initially helpful intervention needed supplementation at a later point:

> Jay, a six-year-old boy, was seen because of his parent's concern about behavior problems and hyperactivity he was exhibiting at home and school. Following a battery of assessment interviews and tests, he was diagnosed with attention-deficit hyperactivity disorder (American Psychiatric Association, 1987) and behavior management training for the parents was recommended. Following four sessions of parental training, and appropriate consultation with the school, Jay was responding positively and treatment concluded. A follow-up interview, three months later, revealed continued improvement, and the parents were advised to contact the therapist if any problems resurfaced.
>
> A little more than a year later, the parents reported a return of the behavioral problems with Jay, now eight years old, and that, furthermore, the previously successful management methods were no longer effective. As anger and frustration with Jay was much more apparent at this point, the therapist suggested twelve sessions of family therapy, which would include Jay's sixteen-year-old sister. These sessions revealed a family structure in which Jay served as a scapegoat who deflected unacknowledged anger between the parents. As Mr. and Mrs B. were able to work through this anger in a more direct manner, they were also able to reinstitute the behavioral management methods with Jay, and the family stabilized. Periodic follow-up sessions over a two-year period found this resolution being maintained.

The therapeutic contact described by Phelps took place in a private practice context and is certainly illustrative of the effective and responsive employment of intermittent time-limited treatment in such a setting.

In the remainder of this chapter I will offer several extended descriptions of short-term treatment that will illustrate the various forms in action. Emphasis will be placed on the initial negotiations with the client regarding goals and time limits, the identification of appropriate structured interventive strategies, and the implementation of these change methods through a variety of enactive and action-oriented procedures.

BRIEF TREATMENT WITHIN TIME LIMITS

Earlier I pointed out that surveys of clinical practice tend to substantiate that client contact in most instances is relatively brief and that truly lengthy treatment (whatever the intentions of the practitioner) is the exception. This suggests that much helping practice consists of *unplanned* brief treatment. Many of these brief contacts appear to involve a process in which helper and client work together for a certain number of sessions but without any agreed-upon time limit. Treatment terminates after several sessions, perhaps because the goals of intervention have been realized or, as often, because the client simply stops coming. Unless the client spontaneously returns for help at some later time, there is no further contact. This rather haphazard process is what many practitioners believe to be short-term treatment.

I have emphasized in the introductory chapter my conviction that this is an incomplete model for short-term therapy. Even in its most basic form, short-term helping should include both an explicit time limit for intervention and, after a designated interval, a planned follow-up session. Furthermore, the client should be aware that a follow-up session is planned and know its intended purpose, although I believe that the therapist should take the responsibility of arranging for the actual face-to-face interview.

Short-term intervention utilizing this basic model can be helpful in treating a wide variety of the personal, interpersonal, and social problems that concern many of the clients seen in such settings as family service agencies, mental health centers, general hospitals, and child guidance clinics. In conjunction with other modes of intervention the brief treatment model of engagement-intervention-follow-up can be utilized even in instances of severe dysfunction. Goldstein and his colleagues (1978), for example, describe a six-session family-oriented approach, utilized with schizophrenics and their families, that was significantly effective in reducing relapse and rehospitalization rates. The brief therapeutic intervention was highly structured and heavily oriented toward the realistic social pressures commonly faced by ex-mental patients and their families. A sequence of closely related objectives were emphasized:

> (1) The patient and his family are able to accept the fact that he has had a psychosis, (2) they are willing to identify some of the probable precipitating stresses in his life at the time the psychosis occurred, (3) they attempt to generalize from that to identification of future stresses to which the patient and his family are likely to be vulnerable, and (4) they attempt to do some planning on how to minimize or avoid these future stresses. (p. 1170)

In this study, it should be noted, the brief intervention was initiated at discharge from the hospital and combined with administration of the appropriate psychotropic medication to the schizophrenic family member.

The following cases are drawn from family service and mental health settings. Both illustrate the willingness of the helper to establish a helping contract in an area of the client's choosing and, further, to design an intervention that would specifically address this area of major concern—and no more. In other words, the therapeutic ambitions of the helper were disciplined by the limits defined by the clients.

Case Illustration: Controlling Anger

A physically handicapped, mildly retarded man in his late thirties, Mr. Jurecko reluctantly approached a family service agency for help with the temper outbursts toward co-workers that were jeopardizing his job in a large industrial firm. Both sensitive to his limitations and highly conscientious in his work, he had become increasingly vulnerable to the rowdy give-and-take of the working world. Mr. Jurecko's employer had stipulated that he must "get counseling" or risk losing his job.

It would have been all too easy to become overly absorbed in the implicit array of psychological, social, physical, and emotional complications suggested by even this sketchy vignette of Mr. Jurecko and his difficulties. The essence of helping, as Rabkin (1977) emphasizes, lay in responding to Mr. Jurecko's request for some immediately usable ways of controlling his temper, thus meeting his employer's concerns and, most important, preserving his job.

It was apparent during the initial interview that Mr. Jurecko's difficulties on the job were arising from a number of sources. He had a moderately impairing handicap, which placed some restriction on his physical capacities and made his speech heavily slurred and difficult to understand. His education had been mainly in "special class" settings in the public school system and had given him only the most rudimentary of academic skills. Even after several attempts at vocational training (sponsored by various rehabilitation agencies) he had not been able to gain any marketable technical skill.

He took his job as operator of a freight elevator very seriously and showed an almost fierce pride in his reliable and responsible performance of his duties. In the insensitive atmosphere of the working-class world, he sometimes encountered teasing and deprecating remarks from his fellow workers. This rough bantering created some stress, but additionally he described himself as often becoming extremely upset over what he viewed as the lazy and slipshod work attitudes of certain of his co-workers. Brief behavior rehearsals during the initial interview suggested that Mr. Jurecko possessed reasonably adequate assertive ability in situations where tension had not risen to too high a level. However, tension had been building over many months, and the two angry incidents that had precipitated his referral occurred on days when his dissatisfaction with himself, his job, and his co-workers had become particularly acute.

In both of these episodes Mr. Jurecko had become verbally abusive and shouted threats at other employees, and in one instance he had thrown a heavy piece of equipment across the room. Mr. Jurecko was realistically afraid that he might lose his job if he was not able to convince the management of the firm that he could control his temper in the future. He expressed discouragement about his handicaps and the restrictions they placed upon him but viewed them as limitations within which he had learned to live.

A contract was negotiated with Mr. Jurecko to concentrate on developing workable methods of temper control, and the therapist suggested that this goal was manageable within six sessions. It was explained to him that his angry outbursts could be seen as accumulated reactions to the stress he was encountering on a daily basis. This rationale was discussed with him and illustrated through references to the various situational and attitudinal factors he had described. He was told that the method of intervention would involve teaching him several ways of reducing stress in order to keep it from building up to unmanageable proportions. He was also informed that this approach would require that he practice the stress management techniques at home so as to gain proficiency, test them out and refine them in the actual work setting, and, finally, keep a daily record of tension-producing situations in order to follow his progress.

Intervention utilized an adaptation of the stress management model developed by Meichenbaum (1975) and, following these guidelines, emphasized (1) the development of behavioral skills in relaxation, and (2) attention to any cognitive cues that were engendering tension. Relaxation techniques involving muscular release and deep breathing were taught during the first three sessions, and Mr. Jurecko practiced these daily at home. He was asked to keep a very simple diary noting the occurrence and nature of any troublesome incidents at work.

The clinician's overall strategy was to provide Mr. Jurecko as quickly as possible with some tangible methods of reducing stress. It was felt that once his general tension level was diminished, he would be better able to look at how some of his own attitudes might be contributing to his stress. Perhaps fortuitously, a minor incident came up on his job during the second week of treatment. As this situation was not too demanding, Mr. Jurecko was able to handle the pressures quite well, and this bolstered his confidence in himself and, implicitly, in the treatment approach. Fortified by his developing skills and this beginning success, he coped with some further difficult incidents over the following week with equal aplomb.

Work on stress reduction techniques continued over the final three weeks of the contact. This focused particularly on developing such key words as "relax" or "calm" as relaxation signals that could be utilized unobtrusively in public situations. In these final sessions the focus also incorporated general discussion of the realistic pressures of factory work. Additionally, Mr. Jurecko's demands upon himself to perform, as well as his feeling of being trapped in a dead-end job, were identified as factors contributing to his general level of stress. Within the context of short-term treatment, the therapist's effort was to make Mr. Jurecko more aware of the impact of his own attitudes upon his difficulties rather than to resolve them.

A follow-up session with Mr. Jurecko three months later found him coping well with the day-by-day pressures of his job. He described a few episodes that had been upsetting to him, but he had been able to handle each of these without any undue outburst of anger. Although he was not using the stress management techniques consistently, it was apparent that he was able to call upon them as needed to reduce or control immediate tensions.*

Case Illustration: Leaving Home

In some instances the therapist may employ a straightforward problem-solving model in short-term intervention. The following case example, drawn from a community mental health setting, will illustrate the adaptation of this "commonsense" approach to therapeutic practice.

Mrs. Lorenson, a woman in her late twenties, was referred to counseling by a friend who had noticed her increasing preoccupation and apparent depression. She pictured herself in the initial interview as considerably upset about difficulties in two major areas of her life but unable to come to grips with either of these problems.

First, she had married about a year earlier, and, following a short honeymoon, her husband had been posted overseas by the multinational corporation by which he was employed. For various realistic reasons, it had not been possible for Mrs. Lorenson to accompany him on the assignment. Throughout this enforced separation, Mrs. Lorenson had been experiencing many misgivings about her marriage, which had been preceded by only a brief courtship, yet felt guilty and troubled about harboring such thoughts. Second, she was continuing to live at home with her elderly parents despite having quite adequate income to live elsewhere. Mrs. Lorenson was fearful

---

*A chance encounter with Mr. Jurecko three years later provided further follow-up data. At that time he volunteered that he was maintaining his job without any major difficulty and was still using the tension reduction procedures at appropriate moments.

of offending her parents by suggesting that she would feel happier and more comfortable in her own apartment.

Discussion and exploration of these two problems occupied the greater part of the first interview. Although her uncertainties about her marriage were most pressing and were causing the greater portion of her unhappiness. Mrs. Lorenson did not believe that she could reach any resolution of these feelings as long as her husband was out of the country. Until he returned and she could directly experience the relationship again, Mrs. Lorenson did not feel she could arrive at a realistic solution. On the other hand, despite its secondary status, her discontent with continuing to live at home was sufficiently strong that she wanted to do something about this quandary. It was agreed that six to eight sessions would be spent working on this problem.

The therapist followed a very simple problem-solving model over the sessions that followed. This model (D'Zurilla & Goldfried, 1971; Goldfried & Goldfried, 1975) suggests that once a problem is specifically identified, the first (and most critical) step is to translate it into a description of a desired goal. The goal statement may be thought of as a statement of how the client would want to be feeling, thinking, or acting if he or she no longer had the problem. In this case Mrs. Lorenson's problem of being discontented with living at home was transformed into the goal of moving into an apartment of her own. Other goals, such as gaining an understanding of why she was so deferential toward her parents, learning how she might live more comfortably in the parental home, or even the objective of moving to an entirely different city, might have been negotiated, but this was the goal that was most meaningful to Mrs. Lorenson. Achieving it became the purpose of counseling.

After the problem and goal statements have been sufficiently specified, then the problem-solving model stipulates that the necessary changes, leading from problem state to goal achievement, must be identified. These are usually visualized as a series of steps, or consecutive tasks, that will enable the client to progress from the present problematic situation toward the selected goal. Where the goal involves developing such social skills as assertive behavior, improved sexual functioning, or interpersonal communication, there may be a validated procedure in the clinical literature. Where this is the case, the function of the therapist would be to identify this change procedure, explain its expectations and limitations, and guide the client through the intricacies of its process. With many life situations, however, a unique series of steps need to be generated.

Brainstorming was used as a method of identifying the various steps that Mrs. Lorenson needed to take to reach her goal of independent living. In the brainstorming process both client and helper attempt to identify, in as imaginative and uncensored a way as possible, all of the elements that might be involved in moving toward the desired goal. Once a list of many such potential components has been generated, it is possible to eliminate the unfeasible or unnecessary steps and to arrange the remainder into a sequence leading to the desired goal. With Mrs. Lorenson the major steps included:

1. Decision making about the type, cost, and location of a suitable apartment
2. Searching for such accommodation through newspaper advertisements and real estate firms
3. Selecting an apartment and signing a lease
4. Informing her parents of her decision to move
5. Making the physical arrangements for the actual move

During the intervention, all of these steps were more specifically defined, broken into component parts where necessary, and accompanied by pertinent task assignments. Arranging the steps of the implementation phase in a suitable progression may at times require some sensitivity and skill. The needed sequence of steps can be seen as following either a *logical* or an *emotional* hierarchy or, in some cases, aspects of both. In the problem-solving intervention with Mrs. Lorenson, both logical and emotional considerations were utilized.

The logical hierarchy is based on the notion that a complex goal can be broken down into a series of simpler elements, each of which in turn will contribute to the ultimate attainment of the desired goal. In job finding, for example, assessing one's strengths, skills, and relevant experience is almost always a necessary beginning point in the sequence. Thus, in Mrs. Lorenson's case it was necessary to decide where she wanted to live and to determine whether suitable apartments were available in this area before further steps could be taken.

The concept of an emotional hierarchy recognizes that certain steps in a goal-attainment sequence are more anxiety-provoking than others and attempts to place the less fearful steps at the beginning of the implementation process. In assertion training, for example, the earliest steps are usually concerned with relatively simple assertions in the context of relationships of only minor emotional significance to the trainee. It is usually much less anxiety-provoking to deal with a clerk in a department store than to be assertive toward one's supervisor or spouse. Thus, in work with Mrs. Lorenson one aspect of the problem-solving sequence was deliberately placed further into the sequence in order to avoid her having to confront an emotionally demanding step too soon. Specifically, Mrs. Lorenson might have informed her parents of her decision to move as an initial step in the problem-solving sequence. However, this step, at the therapist's suggestion, was not undertaken until several other steps had been accomplished. Mastering these easier tasks first not only increased Mrs. Lorenson's confidence in herself but also had the effect of increasing her sense of commitment to her goal before she even approached her parents.

The necessary steps in the problem-solving process were clearly identified within an interview or two, and by the sixth session Mrs. Lorenson was concluding arrangements to move into her own apartment. Homework assignments in the earlier phases had been helpful in mobilizing and focusing her energies, and some brief behavior rehearsal had prepared her for the step of informing her parents of the move. Like many feared encounters, this latter task was managed relatively easily, with Mrs. Lorenson's parents showing little of the emotional upset she had anticipated.

At a follow-up interview a few months later, Mrs. Lorenson was comfortably settled in her new apartment, and her relationship with her parents continued to be amicable. She had still had no opportunity to confront her misgivings about her marriage and looked forward to her husband's eventual return to the country with some understandable apprehension.

Treatment Considerations

Aside from following the general engagement-intervention-follow-up paradigm, both of these case illustrations incorporate a number of features typical of short-term treatment that are worth reviewing:

1. The focus of intervention was on responding directly to the immediate request of the client. In one instance this request was

concerned with reducing the danger of losing a job; in the other illustration the client's concern was to be relieved of the discomfort of an undesired living situation. Although neither of these goals called for profound changes in the client, it was apparent that for both individuals a genuine problem existed that was beyond their immediate coping abilities.

2. Therapeutic intervention was designed to impact directly upon this request. A specific change method (stress management training) was utilized with Mr. Jurecko, while a more general problem-solving procedure was employed with Mrs. Lorenson. The clinician's responsibility was to identify an appropriate change strategy, guide and motivate the client in its application, and, as needed, assist in its adaptation to the particular needs of the client.

3. Although there were other areas of difficulty evident with both clients, the therapist did not attempt to intervene in these aspects of their lives. Mrs. Lorenson was quite clear that she did not believe she could resolve her doubts about her marriage until she had the opportunity for face-to-face discussion with her husband. Mr. Jurecko was less explicit about the other problems he was experiencing, but since the initial exploration revealed that his most heightened concern was about the possibility of losing his job, the therapist concentrated attention on this expressed difficulty.

There may be times when another problem directly interferes with or prevents resolution of the targeted problem. In such cases it is obviously the therapist's prerogative to point out this connection to the client, and work on the client's request may only be possible in conjunction with attention to this related difficulty. Clinicians should be cautious, however, in too quickly concluding that other considerations, of whatever theoretical variety, will block problem resolution. It should be remembered that a broad implication of the empirical evidence for the effectiveness of brief intervention is the strong suggestion that many difficulties can indeed be satisfactorily resolved despite the existence of concurrent problems in other aspects of the client's functioning. Thus, the belief that understanding must be attained before behavior can be altered or that certain behaviors represent "symptoms" of more deep-seated difficulties, and so on, may be more a purely theoretical conviction than a compelling reason to defer attempts to induce specific change.

4. Finally, in both cases the therapist demonstrated a willingness

to terminate work with the client at the projected ending point rather than look for reasons to continue. Haley (1967) identifies what he calls the "willingness to release patients" as a predominant characteristic of the provocative approaches to brief therapy practiced by Milton Erickson. He makes the following comments in relation to this aspect of Erickson's work:

> The framework he establishes in the therapeutic relationship has built into it the idea that the relationship is temporary to achieve particular ends. . . . Because of his positive view and his respect for patients. Erickson is willing to start a change and then release the patient to let the change develop further. He does not allow the needs of the treatment setting to perpetuate the patient's distress, as can happen in long term therapy. Since he does not see therapy as a total clearance, or cure, of all the patient's present and future problems, he is willing to give patients up. His approach is to remove the obstacles which, once removed, allow the patient to develop his career in his own way. (pp. 541–542)

As I shall point out later in this chapter, the decision to terminate can sometimes be difficult, particularly if the client has not clearly achieved the goal of the intervention. However, the follow-up session offers some safeguard against the dangers of "abandoning" a client who still needs help. This consideration underscores the necessity of a planned follow-up contact and, furthermore, the need for the practitioner to be particularly conscientious in arranging this interview at its appropriate time.

RECONTRACTING FOLLOWING AN INITIAL INTERVENTION

The short-term therapist may find it necessary in certain cases to renegotiate the length of the intervention. A rough guideline, based on the data from the Gibbons et al. (1979) and Parad and Parad (1968) studies cited earlier, as well as on my own clinical experience, suggests that this contingency may arise in perhaps one of every five or six short-term cases. The need for further time may become apparent at the termination session of the original series of sessions or at the follow-up interview. In either case, the decision to continue (or to extend the original contract) should be a mutual agreement between helper and client and, most important, based upon clear indications that the goals of intervention have not been reached. Alternatively, it is sometimes possible to find that the immediate intervention, though quite successful, has revealed a need to work on another area of difficulty.

Case Illustration: Coping with Sexual Fears

Recurrent chest pains had impelled a twenty-six-year-old unmarried man, Dennis Faber, to visit several physicians and hospital outpatient clinics. Following the fifth such consultation, which had confirmed the previous findings that there was no physical basis for his pains, Mr. Faber was referred to a family service agency for counseling.

He was a friendly, talkative young man, somewhat disheveled in appearance, who anxiously described a series of immediate difficulties in his life. A high school graduate with some sporadic technical training, he had recently been fired from his job (for "inattention") and was considering going into business for himself as a TV and radio repairman. He was excited about this prospect but apprehensive, since he had few financial resources except his unemployment compensation benefits and a battered old car.

At the same time, he felt dissatisfied and discouraged about his social relationships, particularly with women. Mr. Faber seldom dated, described himself as awkward and clumsy in even casual conversation with women, and was especially depressed about his lack of sexual experience. He saw himself as a sexual failure. Much of his difficulty, he believed, was due to his parents' extremely moralistic and inhibiting views in regard to dating and sexuality.

The initial interview with Mr. Faber was complicated by his voluble and anxious manner—he was an almost nonstop talker. Although a high degree of concern about his social and sexual competency was readily apparent, it was difficult to arrive at a definite contract to work on this area. Rather than move ahead into treatment without a firm agreement about its goals, the therapist is well advised in such situations to arrange only a minimal contract entailing further problem exploration. In this case the helper suggested that one or two further sessions could be spent in considering how therapy might be most helpful to Mr. Faber.

These interviews were spent in exploring the several areas described above, and by the third session a positive agreement had been negotiated to work on increasing Mr. Faber's comfort and ability in social and sexual relationships with women. A time limit of ten to twelve sessions was stipulated by the therapist, and Mr. Faber was given some material on human sexuality to read (selected chapters from James McCary's [1973] Human Sexuality: A Brief Edition) as his first task.

The first six sessions with Mr. Faber had two major purposes. One objective was to assess his social skill level in heterosexual relationships and, if necessary, employ systematic behavioral training to increase his facility in this area. The other major goal was to reduce his obvious anxiety about sexuality. In the initial interviews he had shown a great deal of discomfort and embarrassment about even discussing sex, and it was quite apparent that his prudish and moralistic family background had significantly contributed to this difficulty. However, the approach to inducing change in this area was not historical. A variation of cognitive restructuring was employed in which reading assignments on sexual matters increased his factual knowledge. Simultaneously, direct discussion of his immediate doubts and curiosity, in the accepting atmosphere of the therapeutic relationship, consolidated this new knowledge and alleviated many of his concerns.

Training in heterosexual skills proved necessary. This training was not as basic as some socially awkward individuals require but did include important work on such areas as initiating conversations, asking for dates, expressing feelings, and, broadly speaking, ways of developing a personal and potentially intimate relationship with women. In addition, some direct discussion on how to improve and maintain his personal appearance and hygiene was necessary. (These training methods are described in more detail in Chapter 8 on social skills.) During this period the interviews were typically divided between social skill training (and the behavior rehearsal methods used in its implementation) and more general reflective discussion of his reactions to the reading assignments on sexuality.

During the final six weeks of contact Mr. Faber's confidence in himself had increased sufficiently that the therapist encouraged him to begin active dating. He began rather hesitantly, but within a few weeks had successfully managed to take out several young women.

Although he felt awkward at times, he was pleased to find that the women he dated seemed quite satisfied with his company. As one might expect, the dates involved some of the kissing and fondling typical of beginning relationships and, on one occasion, sexual intercourse. These personal and sexual experiences provided further opportunity to refine the social skills developed in the earlier sessions and to support Mr. Faber's growing realization that he could be quite attractive to women.

Although Mr. Faber's experience was still limited, it appeared reasonable at the twelfth session to strongly emphasize his positive gains and to terminate active intervention. The therapist arranged to contact him for a follow-up session in three to four months. The decision to terminate at this point, rather than negotiate an extension of treatment, was influenced by the practitioner's conviction that Mr. Faber was moving forward in a positive way. It is often better to encourage this type of independent growth, by the very act of termination, than to foster uncertainty or dependency by continuing treatment.

The follow-up session, however, proved this clinical judgment to be wrong, because Mr. Faber was quite discouraged and bogged down. He had dated only sporadically since last seen and had lost most of the self-confidence that he had developed earlier. Mr. Faber felt baffled by his lack of progress, and a further series of sessions was negotiated. The therapist suggested that this second contact should be limited to eight sessions and should concentrate on remedying whatever was impeding Mr. Faber in utilizing his previously developed skills.

As there was good evidence that Mr. Faber's heterosexual skills were now adequate and that in general he was less anxious about sexuality, this continued intervention was much more cognitively oriented. Early exploration, both in the interview and through task assignment, attempted to identify any motivational or attitudinal factors that might be operative. Exploration of his self-dialogues when he was in the company of women suggested that certain of Mr. Faber's own expectations and beliefs were setting him up for failure. In addition, these same factors were creating considerable internal stress during any dating situation. For example, as he approached an attractive young woman, he often found himself thinking, "She won't want to talk to me" or "She'll laugh in my face if I ask her for a date."

Similar ruminations were affecting him during the course of a date. Some of these cognitive cues were identified by asking him to imagine himself in conversation with a woman. Others became apparent, since he kept a daily log of his reactions.

As this mixture of self-deprecation and internally stimulated anxiety became evident, the difficulty Mr. Faber was meeting in utilizing the skill learning from the previous sessions became understandable. The therapist thereupon initiated training in cognitively oriented self-management methods, emphasizing to Mr. Faber that this would give him an active means of coping with the anxieties and uncertainties he was experiencing. It was pointed out, however, that self-management techniques of this sort would have little effect unless he deliberately employed them in the appropriate situations. In large part the first three sessions were devoted to basic relaxation training and, following the clinical guidelines suggested by Mahoney (1974), Meichenbaum (1975), and others, guiding Mr. Faber in learning how to use cue words and unobtrusive physical techniques in stressful situations. Homework assignments during this phase concentrated on practicing these techniques and refining their application in real life. Additionally, he was asked to mentally rehearse successful encounters with women in order to check his prevalent tendency to dwell upon negative anticipations.

This cognitive behavioral approach was helpful in offering Mr. Faber some tangible ways of managing himself, but was not sufficient in stimulating him to move forward again. For two or three weeks he remained blocked and found various reasons to defer any serious attempts at resuming dating. He spoke of how busy he was in developing his new business and found minor flaws in all the women he met. The therapist attempted to respond to the genuine anxiety that was implicit in this impasse, but by the sixth of the eight sessions decided that Mr. Faber must be confronted with the need to act despite his fears. The confrontation had the desired effect of energizing Mr. Faber, and through the final weeks of counseling he began dating relationships with two women he had recently met. A good level of emotional comfort and social ease was evident in both these relationships, and active treatment was concluded at the eighth session.

A formal follow-up interview with Mr. Faber was delayed by vacation schedules and other contingencies until almost seven months after this final session. Telephone contact, however, had affirmed that he was quite satisfied with his social life and experiencing no obvious difficulties. This picture was even more positive when he was seen in a face-to-face follow-up session. By this time he was dating frequently and in the previous two or three months had become quite close to one young woman. They were enjoying a regular sexual relationship, and Mr. Faber no longer saw himself as the sexual failure he had once described. As a matter of fact, he was mildly perturbed by his girlfriend's hints that they should begin thinking of marriage or at least start living together. Although Mr. Faber did not think he was ready for marriage, he was also aware of the irony in now having to face an issue that had never confronted him as a "sexual failure."

Some Generalizations

Many of the same factors that characterized the two cases described earlier are also evident in the case of Mr. Faber:

1. Again it is evident that the practitioner of brief therapy takes an active and direct role in the process of specifying the major problems and goals of treatment, although the content of these goals is largely governed by the wishes of the client. That is to say, the therapist's insistence is upon the necessity of arriving at clearly understood objectives before beginning intervention, not upon the nature of these goals.

2. The course of treatment with Mr. Faber also demonstrates the short-term therapist's propensity for utilizing structured change methods in which a sequence of steps or stages guide both helper and client activity. Although stress management techniques played a part in therapy with Mr. Faber, as with Mr. Jurecko earlier, this similarity is coincidental. The strategy of change could easily have been assertion training or some other structured technique if this had been responsive to the client's needs.

3. The work with Mr. Faber over the course of the two segments of treatment additionally illustrates the frequent need for a *package* of interventions. At various points, not only stress management but social skill training and cognitive restructuring methods were combined with more conventional reflective discussion methods. The art of therapy often lies not only in the knowledgeable selection of a

cluster of strategies but also in their skillful integration in actual practice. My intent, however, is not to advocate a shotgun-like blast of technological virtuosity, but a sensitive adaptation of disparate inducements to change.

4. It will also be evident that brief therapy frequently takes a very literal approach to bringing about change in the client's daily life. Such an approach can seem almost embarrassingly direct and in many instances may involve nothing more or less than a concentrated effort to increase the activities or behaviors that will constitute goal attainment for the client. Thus, when Mr. Faber wished to date more often, the most straightforward approach to this goal was to teach him the interpersonal skills most likely to increase his chances of obtaining dates with women. Once these skills became established, then the therapist became as direct in encouraging him to use them. Indeed, in the second segment of contact the therapist did not hesitate to confront Mr. Faber with the need for action.

5. At the same time, it would be inaccurate to suggest that short-term therapy is little more than a routinized and insensitive application of mechanical procedures. As I will discuss later at some length, the influence of the therapist is possible and meaningful only within the context of a warm and emotionally responsive relationship. In addition, carefully graduated task assignments, consistent reinforcement and support, and watchful attention to adverse client reactions all play an integral part in the management of any change process, structured or otherwise.

6. Finally, throughout the intervention the therapist is alert to the immediate effects of the helping process. Are the strategies employed enabling the client to progress toward his or her desired goals? This does not necessarily require elaborate testing or monitoring devices, but in large part is managed through two features of brief intervention: First, the frequent tasks carried out by clients serve as probes, not only of their capacity and willingness to change, but of the direction this change is taking. Second, the goals of intervention should be so clearly defined in the initial phase of contact that it will be quite apparent when they have been met, or at least reasonably approximated. Clients may be asked to keep diaries or charts that record aspects of their daily life, but these are more in the nature of information-gathering devices than precise evaluative instruments.

GOAL-ORIENTED EXTENDED TREATMENT

There is no doubt that there are times when it is necessary, in the considered judgment of the clinician, to work with a client over a period of time that falls beyond the usual three- to fifteen-session boundaries of short-term treatment. This contingency may arise at the beginning of therapy, or it may become apparent after a brief intervention has proved unsuccessful. In such instances it is possible to adapt a number of the guiding principles of short-term intervention to the lengthier treatment. The extended contact can be broken down, for example, into a series of time-limited periods each of which concentrates on an identified problem or on a major component of the overall goal of treatment. Within these stages, structured techniques can be used, client participation encouraged, and various devices utilized to evaluate the process of change. A case from a family service agency will illustrate this approach.

Case Illustration: Becoming Uncoupled

Unlike many other conflicted couples, Mr. and Mrs. Toman entered marriage counseling at the instigation of the husband. They were a rather unexceptional lower-middle-class couple, both high school–educated. Mrs. Toman was now training as a medical technician at the local community college, while Mr. Toman worked at a minor clerical job in a large manufacturing firm. Both were in their late forties, and they had been married for more than twenty-five years. Although they had never been especially happy together, the past several years had been markedly difficult. Their two oldest children were now adults and on their own, while the two younger children were in college and, through scholarships, loans, and part-time work, essentially independent. Mr. and Mrs. Toman were finding themselves confronted with a decision about whether to continue a chronically dissatisfying marriage now that family responsibilities no longer bound them together.

Mrs. Toman described her husband as having been both dominating and unloving throughout their marriage and felt she had continued in the relationship only in order to provide a home for the children. Mr. Toman acknowledged many of the difficulties his wife recounted and agreed that he had been responsible for much of their estrangement. However, he thought that the problems had been exacerbated by the two serious heart attacks he had sustained about seven years earlier. Moreover, he was highly concerned to maintain the marriage as, from his strongly religious perspective, neither separation nor divorce was a viable alternative.

A six-session contract to explore the marital relationship and determine if it could be strengthened was agreed upon by both Mr. and Mrs. Toman. Even at this early stage, however, Mrs. Toman was a reluctant participant, and her reluctance became even clearer as the sessions proceeded. The tasks typical of short-term treatment served to highlight her almost total emotional disengagement from her husband, since she either did not carry them out or did so in only the most perfunctory manner. Within three or four weeks it was apparent that there was little possibility of fruitful marriage counseling. The therapist used the remaining time, in both individual and conjoint sessions, to confront the couple with this bleak predicament.

The sixth session brought out Mrs. Toman's firm conviction that the marriage was utterly hopeless. She was only deferring divorce proceedings until she finished her technical training and could become self-supporting. This abrupt termination of marriage counseling and the prospect of a lengthy marriage coming to an end were a considerable shock to Mr. Toman. Hearing his wife speak so bluntly of her intention to divorce him evoked a great deal of immediate emotional turmoil. He readily accepted the therapist's offer of individual counseling. Mrs. Toman was not interested in any individual contact because she had a counselor, whom she had seen a year or two earlier, to whom she could turn.

The intervention with Mr. Toman continued over the next twelve months and involved more than forty interviews. It was not visualized as an extended contact at the beginning of treatment but evolved into this form, since the evaluative work at the end of each segment indicated a strong need to continue counseling. It will be described in relation to the several goal-oriented phases, each of about eight to ten weeks' duration, into which it fell.

DEALING WITH CRISIS. Although he had been quite aware for several years that his marriage was failing, it was still a distinct shock to Mr. Toman to hear his wife openly declare her intention to divorce him.

The fact that this had been not been said in the heat of a quarrel but announced in the relative calm of the final conjoint session added to its impact. A confusing welter of feelings and thoughts fueled his sense of crisis.

Initially, he felt strong anxiety about what his life would be like outside the familiar confines of even an unsatisfactory marriage. At the same time, he was experiencing periodic surges of the almost formless but potent anger that grips one who must grapple with the realization that a central relationship has failed. These strong feelings were combined with a pervading sense of guilt stemming from his religious convictions and, at a less easily verbalized level, fear about his physical health and the possibility of further serious illness. This latter apprehension was by no means unrealistic. Brown (1976) points out that the many change events almost inevitably associated with divorce total "an ominous 258 [points]" on the stress scale developed by Holmes and Rahe (1967) and notes that "80% of those who scored above 300 on this scale became pathologically depressed, had heart attacks, and developed other ailments" (p. 407). Brown considers the reduction of the attendant stress to be a primary objective of divorce counseling.

Treatment in this first phase was essentially crisis intervention, and the active techniques typical of this approach were utilized. Mr. Toman was encouraged to ventilate the turbulent feelings he was experiencing, and the helper, in addition to serving as a strongly empathic listener, offered explanatory comments that placed many of these reactions within the understandable framework of crisis. In order to increase Mr. Toman's knowledge of the normalcy of much of his turmoil, he was supplied with reading material on common fears and attitudes toward divorce. Finally, some simple relaxation exercises were practiced in the treatment session and utilized by Mr. Toman as a means of reducing some of the stress he was experiencing and consequently giving him a tangible method of coping with his fear of a further heart attack.

ACCEPTING MAJOR LIFE CHANGE. As the crisis subsided, Mr. Toman became more comfortable in facing the fact that within a few months his life was to undergo a major change. Although he was no longer acutely uncomfortable, he still had many questions about how he would be able to cope with the divorce and his unwilling return to a single life. He and the clinician agreed to work together for another two or three months with the goal of preparing him for this transition. In a certain sense he was already alone even though he and his wife were still living in the same house. Despite this nominal proximity, they followed entirely different schedules, occupied separate bedrooms, seldom had a meal together, and talked only when absolutely necessary.

The major theme of therapy during this phase was one of accepting and coping with the major life change that was about to be thrust upon him. As this focus was more specifically examined, some of its goals became extremely practical. For example, how could Mr. Toman increase his ability to take care of his own needs in anticipation of the time when he would be living alone? In tasks related to this, he began to wash his own laundry, shop for groceries, and cook more of his meals at home. Similarly, almost all of his social life for more than twenty years had revolved around his role as father, husband, and family member. Again, discussion and task assignments centered on identifying interests and activities that he could develop and actively locating new friends and social contexts where he could share these interests. Finally, although he was convinced that because of his religious convictions he himself could take no initiative in seeking divorce, Mr. Toman began to reflect on some of the ways in which his personal values would be challenged. At the urging of the therapist, he arranged an interview with his clergyman to discuss his religious status and to seek out information on his church's current views on such questions as sexuality and remarriage.

DEALING WITH IMPENDING SEPARATION. As work concluded on the previous phase and Mr. Toman saw himself as at least moderately ready to reenter the single life, it became apparent that his wife was about to initiate divorce proceedings. In one of their rare conversations she told him that she had consulted an attorney and expected that a divorce petition would be filed within a few weeks. Despite having anticipated the divorce for some time, Mr. Toman felt a renewed surge of the anger and anxiety that had troubled him at the very beginning of treatment. It became necessary to reapply, in milder form, the crisis intervention procedures that had characterized this first phase. Thus, Mr. Toman was again supported in openly expressing his aroused emotions, and the therapist encouraged him to resume the relaxation exercises that had been helpful earlier.

By this point it was apparent that treatment was no longer explicitly short term and that contact with Mr. Toman would most likely continue for some time. However, the therapist deliberately kept the intervention goal-oriented, in the conviction that this not only would provide an effective form of service but also would avoid encouraging undue dependency on Mr. Toman's part. A new contract was negotiated, aimed at supporting Mr. Toman through the physical separation from his wife. Three main goals were important to him: (1) coping with his renewed anger and stress, (2) working on the altered relationship with his children that would be necessary as divorce became a reality, (3) helping him to deal with certain of the concrete aspects of negotiating a divorce settlement and moving to new living quarters.

Perhaps the simplest aspect of this phase was that of reducing Mr. Toman's renewed stress to manageable proportions. The other areas of concern progressed more slowly, and in major respects the therapeutic stance during this phase was markedly different. That is to say, the earlier phases of counseling had involved a rather behavioral orientation in which general concerns were translated into concrete objectives and related tasks. By contrast, many of Mr. Toman's tangible worries in these sessions—"What can I tell the children about the divorce?" "Should I accept my wife's ideas about dividing the property?" —were discussed in relation to such major themes as personal integrity, aspirations, and values, and the feelings of competency and self-worth these engendered. The helping strategy thus became one of examining the specific questions confronting Mr. Toman as aspects of broader psychological and emotional issues—a process, of course, much more reminiscent of psychodynamically oriented therapy than the behavioral methods previously employed. This shift in emphasis was influenced by the clinician's perception that at this point Mr. Toman was not in need of specific direction in his life, but was attempting to place particular elements of the ongoing experience of separation and divorce into a comprehensible framework of value and belief.

REACTING TO LIFE ALONE. The final segment of counseling with Mr. Toman took place over a two-month period following the physical

separation of the couple. Mr. Toman had moved into his own apartment, but almost immediately began to find himself lonely and
depressed. Two major goals were negotiated for this concluding
phase of therapy: (1) to continue the build-up of social interests and
new friendships he had begun much earlier, and (2) to start looking at
himself as a single person and, particularly, considering what this
meant to him in terms of relationships with women.

The focus on expanding his social activities was handled through a
combination of reflective discussion of his needs and periodic task
assignments directed at an identified area of interest. Some of this
reflection and activity was no different from that engaged in by all
persons attempting to expand their social and recreational network,
but other aspects were peculiarly related to the divorce experience.
Emily Brown (1976), in her highly informative discussion of divorce
counseling, speaks of the "rapid and massive change which is triggered by the physical separation" (p. 400) and reviews research findings that identify this juncture as the point of greatest trauma. For
Mr. Toman the physical transition provoked two central emotional
issues: he worried about the possibility of mounting loneliness and
isolation if he were unable to continue his efforts to seek new affilia-
tions, and, perhaps even more strongly, he feared that in any intimate
relationship, his sexual functioning (long abandoned with his wife)
would fail. The major goals of this final phase tended to be interrelated. Considering his role as a single person, for example, faced Mr.
Toman with attitudinal and value issues related to intimacy, sexuality,
and so on, that in turn played an essential part in how he would
choose to develop new relationships. Once again, the task assignments served to direct him firmly to the interpersonal milieu where
these choices had to be made.

A follow-up interview four months later found Mr. Toman functioning reasonably well. His overall adjustment was good and his
social life relatively active. He found himself experiencing occasional
episodes of loneliness or boredom, but he was generally optimistic
about his ability to cope with his new life. He had begun some very
tentative dating, but his apprehension that he would be unable to
achieve satisfactory sexual functioning in a new relationship was still
untested. He contacted the therapist a year after this follow-up session and was seen for two interviews. By this time he had moved into

a close relationship with a middle-aged widow and was seriously contemplating remarriage. His description of this budding relationship was highly positive, and, contrary to his fears, its sexual aspects were very rewarding to him. Because his essential dilemma was around the conflict between his religious beliefs and the question of remarriage, he was referred to a religious counselor to pursue these issues.

Some Final Considerations

It will be apparent that many of the same principles, techniques, and strategies that govern regular brief treatment are also employed in what I have called goal-oriented extended treatment. The major difference, of course, lies in the lengthier period of contact between therapist and client. Yet, even within this larger span of time, goals are specified for each distinct segment of treatment, and care is exercised to stipulate reassessment points that are sufficiently close that both client and clinician remain aware of the approaching evaluation. It would be highly detrimental to this process if the time limits of a given segment were ignored and treatment allowed to assume an entirely open-ended character. Thus, in many respects adherence to time constraints is even more important in this type of extended treatment. Further, as in the briefer time-limited variants, it is the helper who must assume the major responsibility to maintain this central aspect of the treatment structure.

The description of goal-oriented extended treatment and the examples of brief intervention given earlier in this chapter can be viewed as representative of the process of short-term therapy but are by no means intended to exhaust its complexities or possibilities. Other illustrations will be offered in succeeding chapters, and I will return to some of the examples given in this chapter to illustrate certain specific details of the interventive process. Before concluding this expository examination of brief (or goal-oriented) treatment, however, several general features require attention.

For instance, evident throughout the illustration of goal-oriented extended treatment—and perhaps even more apparent in the briefer variations described earlier—is the influence of what Kanfer (1979) has called the *instigative* approach to therapy:

This strategy presumes that behavior change occurs *between* therapy sessions and that the "talk sessions" serve mainly to explore objectives, train the client in methods, and motivate him to modify his extra-therapeutic environment and to apply learning principles to his own behavior. In this sense the patient learns to become his own therapist. During sessions, assigned tasks are practiced, tactics are discussed, and a favorable orientation toward change is created. (p. 189)

Kanfer contends that an instigative approach can avoid many of the difficulties with generalization that have plagued therapeutic practice. That is to say, all therapies have wrestled with the problem of ensuring that the changes that may take place within the therapeutic session are paralleled by similar changes in the client's daily life. Practically speaking, it has simply been assumed that if the client becomes more open and self-disclosing, let us say, within the therapeutic relationship, then identical movement is taking place in other relationships. The instigative strategy of viewing the therapy sessions as secondary to a primary emphasis on planned changes outside the session is a deliberate attempt to bypass the generalization dilemma by focusing directly on the client's natural world.

Similarly running through all the variants of time-limited treatment that I have described is an underlying *educational* stance that, in many respects, is in opposition to the more prevalent philosophies of therapeutic helping. Quite aside from whether one subscribes to a disease model for explaining the development of emotional and social disturbance, most clinicians (whether psychodynamic, behavioral, or humanistic in theoretical orientation) have continued to utilize a medical model of practice. From this viewpoint the client is seen as a sufferer whose difficulties need to be individually diagnosed and treated by a professionally trained practitioner. Instead of following the medical paradigm of study, diagnosis, and treatment, the practitioner influenced by the educational model tends to see the therapeutic endeavor as fundamentally concerned with the *teaching* of the essential knowledge and interpersonal skills needed for effective living. Thus, the practitioner is primarily a provider of important information and skills to individuals, troubled or otherwise, who might wish to employ these learnings in better managing their lives. Guerney (1977) has extensively discussed this perspective on helping:

Viewing matters in this light, essentially as matters for educational effort, it seems far less important for the helper to discover what is wrong in a relationship, or why it went wrong, than to provide clients with appropriate knowledge, training and experience aimed at the future—that is, aimed at overcoming the difficulties or accomplishing the relationship goals in question. Usually, once one knows what clients wish to accomplish, not much time needs to be spent in finding out what makes them behave the way they do (diagnosis) and still less in finding out how they got the way they are (genesis). Rather, it is assumed that by far the most expeditious approach is immediately to begin: (1) teaching them what it is they need to know (providing the rationale); (2) establishing the appropriate life experience they need to elicit such behavior (providing practice); (3) helping them perfect their skills (providing supervision); and (4) increasing the use of skills in appropriate everyday situations (fostering generalization). (p. 20)

Although it shares some common ground with the instigative approach discussed earlier, the educational model of clinical practice carries other implications. It approaches the client as an individual in need of information or skill, as a student willing to learn, rather than as a patient who must be healed. The role of the helper is one of identifying the pertinent learnings that might be offered and, in conjunction with the client, deciding if these are suitable to the goals that the client wishes to achieve. As Guerney points out, such a stance reduces the need for a finely tuned diagnostic assessment and instead suggests that helpers must be able to clearly explain the benefits and limitations of their expertise so that the client can make a knowledgeable choice.

Finally, despite the obvious employment of a number of interventive strategies drawn from behavioral and social learning theory, it should be apparent that many of the techniques characteristic of the psychodynamic approaches can also be incorporated into brief intervention. In the work with Mr. Toman, for example, there were several points where major life themes were examined in a reflective and clarifying manner in order to enable him to thoughtfully consolidate his troubled value and belief system. Similarly, there were points with Mr. Jurecko where his attitudes toward himself and his work situation were carefully explored as a means of enhancing his awareness of their relationship to his anger outbursts.

Although later chapters will examine interventions such as behavior rehearsal and social skill training, techniques commonly considered behavioral, I think it is important to emphasize that this choice is entirely pragmatic rather than ideological. That is to say, any strategy for change must be evaluated in relation to the data supporting its usefulness in practice. Behavioral techniques have established a level of effectiveness that cannot be disregarded and are, additionally, often highly relevant to the limited and specific goals of short-term intervention. Yet at the same time there is at least broad substantiation for the effectiveness of psychodynamically influenced therapy. The study by Sloane and his colleagues (1975), for example, clearly establishes that short-term psychodynamic therapy benefits its recipients. Beyond the immediate question of outcome validation, there is no doubt that such techniques as reflection, clarification, and, in general, the attempt to insightfully examine important attitudinal and value themes must play a part in the repertoire of clinicians of all theoretical persuasions.

The issue becomes one of integrating a variety of strategies for inducing personal and behavioral change into a meaningful practice repertoire. This does not mean that one has to use all the techniques all the time, in some sort of "democratic" melange, but it definitely suggests that practice should not be confined within a narrow technical and theoretical range. The problem is one of selectivity. Perhaps the particular phase with Mr. Toman where reflective and clarifying techniques became predominant will illustrate this point. It will be remembered that this represented a stage in the contact where he was less concerned with what to do than with his need to understand the impinging effect of an unwanted event—the impending divorce—upon his existing value system. At this time, therefore, the therapeutic need was not for action but for reflection, and techniques pertinent to this latter goal became highly salient.

The synthesis required by a pluralistic approach, then, does not require that one regard the various theories and techniques as equivalent or interchangeable, but that the practitioner develop an appreciation of the differing purposes and goals that may be served by each approach or strategy. This allows for a knowledgeable and sensitive matching of client need and appropriate clinical knowledge and skill. An overriding concern, however, is that the clinician possess a sufficiently comprehensive range of interventive knowledge and skill that such selectivity is possible.

4

The Initial Interview: Basic Goals

> If therapy is to end properly, it must begin properly—by
> negotiating a solvable problem and discovering the social
> situation that makes the problem necessary.
>
> —Jay Haley, *Problem-Solving Therapy*

First impressions can be confusing and inaccurate, yet they can also be of immense importance in establishing the tone and character of a human encounter. The initial interview in clinical practice, a matter of one hour, perhaps less, can significantly shape the outcome of whatever counseling may follow. Budman and colleagues (1992) take a similar stance:

> The first encounter sets the tone, tenor, structure, direction, and
> foundation of the therapy. Obviously, corrections can be made and
> directions changed following this visit, as the patient/client . . .
> reveals additional information about his or her situation. However, it
> is often the quality of the initial meeting that has an enormous bear-
> ing on what comes later in treatment. (p. 4)

Indeed, for many clients the helping experience begins and ends at this point, because they are screened out by the therapist or, more often, screen themselves out (Garfield, 1986; Wells & Phelps, 1990). Like political refugees, unwilling to accept or endure the restrictions they perceive will be placed on their freedom, clients will exercise their option to "vote with their feet." It is therefore worthwhile to spend some time examining the initial interview in order to understand the essential elements needed at this vital entry point into short-term treatment.

Many therapists in private practice seem to have a finely tuned appreciation for the nuances of the initial interview. This is not necessarily due to a greater skill level in the private practitioner as compared with the agency-based clinician, but may be the function of an economic variable (Budman & Gurman, 1983). The private practitioner's livelihood is dependent on a refined ability to engage clients in an ongoing and workable relationship. The agency worker, on the other hand, can always turn to the agency's intake pool or waiting list for another case if the client drops out of treatment. Private practitioners, with the exception of a relatively few well-established individuals, do not have this luxury. Therefore, their skills in managing the initial engagement process—"hooking" the client—become quite polished.

THE DEMANDS OF TIME

There are time limitations from the first moment of contact with the potential client; therapists have about one hour—whether or not they are explicitly aware of this time constraint—to establish a relationship that can make helping possible. Within this limited period of time, a number of events must occur in the interchange between helper and client that will positively influence the projected venture of therapy. Thus, although the initial interview is inextricably bound to whatever may transpire in the future, it can be seen as having a reality of its own, as complete within itself and generating its own compelling demands. From this perspective, it is surprising that this aspect of clinical practice has been so little examined until recently (Budman et al., 1992; Morrison, 1993) and is so often regarded as simply a prelude to the more serious business that will follow.

The individual needing help, caught up in any of a range of troubling emotions or struggling and distracted by some problematic life situation, is hardly in a position to contribute greatly to the success of the first meeting. Clients are usually upset and distressed by their difficulties, infected with hopelessness about achieving any solution, sometimes reluctant to reveal the extent of their misery, and, as often as not, distrustful (even suspicious) of the therapist. Looking on the initial interview simply as an interpersonal encounter, it is remarkable enough that we can expect our clients, upon the briefest of acquaintance with the therapist—heretofore a complete stranger to them—to immediately reveal so many personal and private aspects of their lives.

THERAPIST'S ROLE

The major responsibility to create a positive atmosphere where learning, problem solving, or personal change can take place falls squarely upon the therapist. The initial interview, therefore, cannot be a random encounter, a social conversation, an inquiry into pathology, an exercise in "labeling," or a veiled interrogation in which the client must establish his or her "suitability" for service. Rather, it should be a process of dialogue and negotiation, aimed at discovering a mutually agreeable purpose for counseling, yet a process firmly guided by the professional competence and values of the practitioner.

This suggests quite strongly that the therapist should be active and direct in the initial interview and at the same time should maintain a careful respect for the perspective offered by the client. In most instances of short-term helping, the life problem of greatest concern to the client will become the goal of helping: parents who have difficulty in managing their children should learn more effective methods of discipline (Phelps, 1993), married couples who can't talk together need to develop meaningful ways of communicating (Snyder & Guerney, 1993), individuals who are discouraged about finding work need assistance in obtaining employment (Azrin & Besalel, 1980), and so on. These and many others are all legitimate and important problems that can profoundly affect the life of the client and those around him.

The brief therapist should not only be willing to grapple seriously with such common difficulties, but should also have a wide-ranging knowledge of the problem-solving and change methods in the clinical research literature pertinent to their resolution. The citations in the preceding paragraph, for example, each identify a well-substantiated method specific to the designated problem area and suggest the eclectic range of technical facility and knowledge the effective brief therapist must possess. Additionally, and just as important, the skilled helper has a highly developed ability to influence people to use such change methods toward the attainment of their chosen therapeutic goals. Skillful management of the initial interview is a critical first step in this process.

ESSENTIAL GOALS

As the first interview begins, the therapist must realize that, given the typical client's emotional distress, lack of skill in coping with problems, or fearfulness in facing intense personal difficulty, the likelihood of a successful beginning is poor. Unless the helper, in a planned and deliberate way, initiates activity directed toward several vital and basic goals, it is quite possible that this human encounter, like others the client has experienced, will end in failure and disappointment. This chapter will discuss in detail five essential goals of the initial interview:

1. Creating a hopeful atmosphere
2. Demonstrating explicit understanding of the client's emotional state
3. Identifying one or two major problems in living
4. Establishing a contract to work on a designated problem
5. Setting a time limit for service and assigning the client an initial task

As I examine the theoretical rationale for each of these goals and their relationship to each other and to the overall purposes of the initial interview, it will become apparent that there are a number of ways of accomplishing each goal, depending on the style and personal characteristics of the therapist. But each goal must be realized at least in part if the initial interview is to accomplish its major purpose: providing a sound beginning for effective helping.

It should be noted that throughout this and the next chapter, my assumption will be that the therapist who conducts the first session will also be the ongoing helper. Fortunately, the once prevalent practice of an "intake interview" conducted by a separate practitioner is becoming a relic of the past. The minority of agencies that still retain this anachronistic practice should realize that, despite some minor organizational convenience, it can seriously increase dropout and premature termination rates (Garfield, 1986).

CREATING HOPE

Clinicians should not be surprised to find that the client's sense of hope—in technical terms, motivation—is at a very low ebb as he or she enters the initial interview. The client would not be a client (a person in need of help) if her or his own reserves of hope were not drained. It falls upon the therapist, then, to contribute a different perspective in which the possibility of change is implicit and in which hope, at some level, can begin to emerge. Yapko (1992) emphasizes a similar dimension when he identifies one of his major goals during the first interview as being "a building of expectancy—a future orientation that lets the client know that the future will be different and better than the past or present has been in some way" (pp. 158–159).

THERAPEUTIC RESPONSIBILITY. This is not to say that the helper should be naively or blindly reassuring, but it does emphasize that some modicum of hope is essential. Unless this first encounter does something to enhance the client's belief that his or her situation can possibly be different—to give some flicker of hope, however slight—then the chances of successful helping are considerably diminished. As Sullivan (1954) has stressed, the client expects and must receive some benefit from the interview. Gaining a sense of hope is a particularly important kind of benefit, and although the helper often has to work on this facet of the therapeutic process with considerable delicacy, there is no goal in the initial interview with greater consequence.

SOURCES OF HOPE. To a considerable extent, the creation of hope, and the resulting enhancement of the client's willingness (and ability) to cope, flows from intangible aspects of the counselor's own belief system—both personal and professional—and the manner in which these beliefs are conveyed to the troubled individual. If the therapist is pessimistic about life or perfectionistic in attitude, or subscribes to theoretical frameworks that disparage human potentiality for change, little of a hopeful nature will be conveyed to the client. On the other hand, if the therapist has a personal outlook that is optimistic, a well-developed tolerance for human frailty, and theoretical beliefs that are supportive of such views, the intangible aspects of hope are much more likely to be conveyed.

The question, then, is how hope can best be enhanced within the context of the initial interview. As we are all aware, the conventional social response to the troubled person is reassurance—in effect, a direct attempt to counter the sufferer's prevailing belief system with new beliefs intended to restore hope. In its commonsense versions, such reassurance is often given in massive doses, accelerating in quantity and tempo if the recipient proves unresponsive. From a theoretical perspective, reassurance is essentially a cognitive intervention—an attempt to provide information and to change belief—and, as far as it goes, it does have some merit. In the hands of the overconcerned friend or a clumsy professional, however, it is all too frequently aimed at the least problematic aspect of the sufferer's belief system, and consequently has little effect.

ENHANCING EFFICACY. Social learning theory offers an important insight into this issue. Bandura (1977a, 1977b, 1986) identifies two major sets of beliefs governing much of human activity. In contemplating a particular decision or action or in the process of carrying out a series of steps toward a chosen goal, we must make two judgments almost simultaneously. We must decide what behaviors, broadly speaking, are likely to achieve the desired result, and we must estimate our ability to carry out these behaviors. The first of these cognitive events Bandura calls "outcome expectations," while the second he refers to as "efficacy expectations." He reviews a number of research studies that support the position that the inhibition of action or the arousal of debilitating emotion is more likely to be related to efficacy expectations—the judgment of personal capability—than to issues of outcome. More plainly, people often *know* what to do but seriously doubt that they *can* do it. From this perspective it is the weakened or inappropriate efficacy beliefs of the troubled person that are most potent in arousing negative affect—anxiety, tension, fear, and consequent hopelessness—which, in turn, inhibits the ability to act. Thus, the therapist's efforts to arouse hope must speak, directly or indirectly, to the client's lowered sense of self-efficacy.

MASTERY AND MORALE. Similar views have been advanced from other theoretical perspectives. For example, Jerome Frank's (1968; Frank & Frank, 1991) work on the concept of "mastery" and his discussion of the weakened morale characteristic of psychiatric patients, and Robert White's (1963) postulation of "effectance" and "competance" as independent ego energies concerned with "adaptation and with the governing of behavior by reality" (p. 24) both identify a similar theme. Ripple et al. (1964) also underscore the exquisite balance between hope and distress and the critical relationship of this balance to continuance in treatment in *Motivation, Capacity and Opportunity*, their classic study of the early phases of the helping process:

> The client's discomfort and his hope regarding a solution of the problems are in the foreground in his initial help-seeking. Regardless of the specifics of goal or service sought or the capacities available for use, it is the motivating pressure that provides the dynamic for engagement in problem solving or in using the helping offered. (p. 206)

THE THERAPIST'S TASK. This discussion emphasizes the therapist's responsibility to attempt deliberately to instill hopefulness in whatever manner is most pertinent and responsive to the client's struggle. At a minimum, the therapist's actions—in the spirit of the Hippocratic injunction "First do no harm"—should not contribute in any way to a decrease in the client's ability to cope. This can happen, however, if the therapist's activities, whether through incompetence or misdesign or benign neglect, significantly subtract from the client's morale.

Finally, while such issues as the therapist's theoretical beliefs and philosophical stance play an important role in enhancing the client's sense of hopefulness, there are many minor operations—redefining, relabeling, explanation, normative education, persuasion, and suggestion are examples—through which the helper can also augment hope. In these instances, a cumulative effect is intended. That is to say, through the repetition of such techniques, a gradual building of a hopeful atmosphere can occur, or at least the downward slide into discouragement and resignation will be halted.

DEMONSTRATING UNDERSTANDING

Almost without exception, theoretical and clinical descriptions of the therapeutic process have emphasized the importance of the helper's ability to empathize with the client's feelings. In addition to this consensus within the clinical literature, a substantial body of empirical research—beginning with Truax and Carkhuff (1967) and most recently reviewed by Hepworth and Larsen (1990)—has supported the position that empathic understanding (along with the accompanying facilitative qualities of respect and genuineness) is essential, though not sufficient, for successful helping. Schulman's (1981) large-scale study of client reactions to therapy found this skill one of the most highly rated, in regard to both relationship building and overall helpfulness. Like the arousal of hope, whether or not the client is openly expressing emotion, the therapist must look for opportunity to verbalize his or her recognition of this vital dimension of the engagement process.

OPERATIONALIZING EMPATHY. During the initial interview and especially in its early moments, the helper's demonstration of an understanding of the client's emotional state is especially critical. It cannot be overemphasized, however, that this understanding must be explicitly demonstrated, because therapists (even those of considerable experience) often mistake a sympathetic listening posture or an intellectual grasp of the client's emotions as representing accurate empathic response. Careful study of the definitions offered by Carkhuff (1969) or Hepworth and Larsen (1990) should be helpful in dispelling this notion.

Accurate empathy means that the therapist not only identifies the major emotion (or emotions) the client is expressing, but also clearly includes these in his or her response to the client. Thus, if the client is expressing considerable dissatisfaction and frustration about a job situation, the therapist's response might be as simple as "Your job is really bothering you, really getting you down." If the client, through words or nonverbal cues, is clearly expressing sadness or anger, then these emotions must be openly and specifically recognized by the clinician. This may sound obvious, yet it is amazing—even disconcerting—to observe how often helpers do not respond in this simple manner, but instead become caught up in such peripheral matters as information gathering or diagnostic evaluation. A short verbatim passage from an initial interview with a troubled young woman will further illustrate the therapist's efforts to establish emotional connection through response to feeling.

CLIENT: I don't know where to start really. It's just my whole life is such a mess now. I just really don't know where to start. It's everything.

THERAPIST: It's like a lousy, lousy feeling about yourself.

CLIENT: My job's a mess and I just—it's just everything. I don't—you know, I go to work but I just don't think I'm really catching on to what I'm supposed to be catching on to at work. I've been working there for six months but I just don't feel I'm learning what I should have learned. I still feel that I don't know what's going on and I just—

THERAPIST: (Interrupts) Am I following you? You're uncertain whether you're managing with work, keeping up with the job.

CLIENT: I just—I don't know if I can do the job. I don't know if I can learn it.

THERAPIST: You're really doubtful, really uncertain.

In this brief excerpt, occurring at the very beginning of the initial interview, the helper's almost exclusive effort is to establish emotional contact with the client through response to feeling. All matters of content are secondary to this goal. Where the client works, the nature of her job, her age and education, whether she lives alone or with her family, what events in her life have led her to her present dilemma, and any other of a multitude of facts do not matter at this point. The therapist concentrates on the emotional dimension—the person in pain—and consistently directs attention and response to this facet of the client's experience.

The client and helper are engaged in a truly human dialogue, with the helper taking an active role in understanding the problematic emotions the client is undergoing about herself and her immediate world. At first the therapist can make only a general response to the client's global statement of turmoil, but even this response is framed in words that attempt to capture the personal struggle of the client—"It's like a lousy, lousy feeling about yourself."

As the client becomes a little more specific about where the struggle is occurring, the helper does not hesitate to interrupt her in order to convey understanding and maintain an active participation in the dialogue. When the identification of a particular feeling proves too mild, the therapist intensifies the level of response—"really doubtful, really uncertain"—as the exchange continues. Duncan and his associates (1992) advocate a similar use of empathic response and characterize it as "attempting to understand and *work within* the expressed meaning system of the client" (p. 35, italics in original).

EMPATHY AND ENGAGEMENT. Accurate empathic understanding, carried out in this simple yet powerful manner, plays a key role in engaging the client into treatment. There is no doubt that people respond to a person whom they perceive as understanding of their feelings. They become more trusting of such a person, talk more about themselves, and in general are more likely to continue contact. Thus, Truax and Mitchell (1971) found in their review of the research in this area that clients will tend to increase their self-exploration—their revealing of self—in response to highly empathic counselors.

In relation to continuance in treatment, Waxenberg (1973) found that families were more likely to continue past the initial interview when they were offered high levels of accurate empathy in the first meeting. Waxenberg's findings are of particular interest because she found that nonwhite (Black and Chicano) families were as likely to remain in treatment, regardless of the ethnicity of the therapist, if the level of accurate empathy in the initial interview was sufficiently high. In light of the very high dropout rates often seen in minority populations (Lorion, 1978; Lorion & Felner, 1986), this is a critical finding.

EMPATHY AND HOPE AROUSAL. The need for empathic understanding may be especially acute in the person in crisis, the very sort of individual whose emotional disruption has provoked a request for help. Direct and accurate response to the feelings that are affecting such a person not only offers understanding but can also foster hope. For instance, discovery by a troubled young woman, such as the one in the preceding dialogue, that another human being is able to face her most frightening, disheartening, or angry feelings squarely can significantly influence her perception of her situation. This does not mean that the distressing emotions change, but the client is now able to see herself as less alone, less alienated from the world. Grier and Cobbs (1968), in their pioneering discussion of psychotherapy with African Americans, have poignantly captured this facet of the helping encounter:

The essential ingredient is the capacity of the therapist to love his patient—to say to him that here is a second chance to organize his inner life, to say that you have a listener and companion who wants you to make it. (p. 180)

EMPATHY AND INFLUENCE. The therapist in short-term treatment is particularly concerned with assuming a position of influence in the life of the client. Without such influence, the effects of the various strategies employed in time-limited treatment will be diluted and therefore less persuasive. This deliberate assumption of a position of influence is temporary and directed only toward the change goals that therapist and client negotiate, but it is essential to effective helping. The clinician's explicit demonstration of empathic understanding discussed in this section is a key ingredient in this needed process, since people are much more likely to be influenced by someone who they believe understands them. As painful and unwanted feelings tend to predominate at times when people need therapeutic help, this dimension of their life must be clearly understood. Yet we must never forget that empathic response builds both a human, intimate relationship and considerable power. The therapist should recognize and ethically manage not only the intimacy that is established but also the power that this can impart. Both are needed; neither can stand alone.

IDENTIFYING PROBLEMS IN LIVING

Short-term treatment is aimed at helping people make the immediate changes in their lives that will reduce emotional distress, improve their relationships with significant others, solve difficult personal problems, and, by doing so, enhance their capacity for more satisfying living. All of these very general goals must be reduced to the specific difficulties, the problems in living, that a particular client or family is experiencing as help is requested. Wood (1978) summarizes the benefits of such direct problem formulation:

Working with the client toward a simple and clear statement of the problem with which he or she wants help achieves two purposes: it helps the client to begin to comprehend what he or she needs and wants to change in his or her life situation and what he or she wants to work toward; and it helps the worker achieve clarity and focus about the purpose of the interaction with the client or client system. (p. 451)

Along with these considerations, there is also provocative research support for the power of specific problem identification. In the comparison by Sloane and his colleagues (1975) of the effect of two treatment approaches (behavioral and psychodynamic) with a wait-list control group, a major element in the initial assessment of all three groups was specification with the clients of the two to three major life problems confronting them—a process identical to what I am advocating here. At the termination evaluation, it was found that the *untreated* group, who had received no specific therapy beyond this assistance in more clearly identifying their problems, had made significant overall progress—equivalent, in fact, to those treated psychodynamically, though less than that achieved by the behavioral group.

Preliminary Problem Formulation

Problems in living may be simply defined: The client is seen as experiencing an undesirable emotional state in relation to a specific aspect of his or her current life. As Wood (1978) emphasizes, "The problem in living with which the client is struggling must be stated in clear and straightforward terms, preferably in plain English" (p. 451). This statement of the problem is developed as much as possible from the client's own description, although sometimes the therapist will have to guide and assist the process.

The following examples, drawn directly from practice, are typical problem formulations:

- Mrs. A., a single parent, felt angry and frustrated about her inability to control the behavior of her adolescent son.
- A young man was depressed and anxious about his lack of confidence in relationships with women.
- A middle-aged couple, Mr. and Mrs. M., were extremely upset by the problems the husband was experiencing with sexual arousal.
- Mr. P. was suffering marked physical and emotional tension in the everyday course of his busy life.
- Sally Q., a woman in her early thirties, was extremely upset by her

mother's frequent criticism of her and the marked favoritism the mother showed toward her younger sister.

- Mr. and Mrs. V. were contemplating divorce as a consequence of their inability to talk openly about an incident where Mr. V. believed his wife had been unfaithful to him.

Each of these brief examples could, of course, be much more explicitly defined, but they illustrate the kind of preliminary problem formulation that client and therapist will cooperatively develop in the initial interview.

Problem Categories

Reid and Epstein (1972) present a useful series of categories for conceptualizing the problems in living—in their terminology, "target problems"—that may confront people. These will be briefly summarized:

INTERPERSONAL CONFLICT. A difficulty or conflict occurring in the relationship between two (or more) individuals, with particular reference to a situation in which neither feels free to withdraw from the relationship. This problem in living is, of course, most commonly seen in families, between husband and wife or parents and children, but can also occur in teacher-pupil, boss-worker, and other such relationships.

DISSATISFACTIONS WITH SOCIAL RELATIONSHIPS. This refers to situations in which an individual client feels distressed about his or her interaction with others, although these significant others may not see the relationship as unsatisfactory, nor will there necessarily be conflict. Thus, the client may picture his or her behavior as unassertive or overdependent or, in more general terms, may feel lonely and distant from others.

DIFFICULTIES IN ROLE PERFORMANCE. The client perceives a gap between his or her actual performance of an important role and the manner in which he or she would like to act. For example, a mother may see herself as too demanding of her children, or a student may not be able to involve herself in study.

REACTIVE EMOTIONAL DISTRESS. Here, the client's major concern is with the pronounced negative feelings that he or she is currently experiencing in life, rather than the situation that provoked them. The situation itself may be in the past, or it may be beyond the client's effective control.

PROBLEMS OF SOCIAL TRANSITION. In this category the individual is experiencing difficulty in moving from one social position, role, or situation to another. Examples include discharge from hospital, becoming a parent, getting a divorce, moving to a new city. Dislocation and abrupt, often unwanted change are the common theme, and the client is frequently bewildered and anxious about how to cope.

PROBLEMS WITH FORMAL ORGANIZATIONS. A type of conflict between the client and an antagonist that is an organization rather than a person. Like interpersonal conflict, this is a situation where the client cannot simply ignore the other because a relationship of some meaningful dimension must continue.

INADEQUATE RESOURCES. In these instances the client lacks specific and tangible resources such as money, food, employment, social activities, and so on. Selecting this category of problem in living as the focus of intervention implies that the client and helper are going to work together in a systematic way to attain the needed resources.

Problem Identification in Practice

Reid and Epstein's categories are helpful in directing the helper toward the major areas of personal, interpersonal, or social dysfunction that may be affecting the client's life. Although not inclusive, they are sufficiently comprehensive to subsume the majority of client requests under one or another category. In addition, a given category may tentatively point toward a particular interventive strategy. For example, interpersonal conflict often requires a couple or family intervention, dissatisfactions with social relations suggest the possibility of social skill enhancement, reactive emotional distress (particularly depression or anxiety) may call for a cognitive-behavioral or interpersonal approach, and so on. Thus, as a problem in living is identified, the brief therapist, in his or her role as an expert problem solver, calls upon one or another of an eclectic range of interventive strategies that has empirical substantiation in resolving the given difficulty.

This emphasis on categorizing problems in living, however, should not be regarded as a quasi-diagnostic device so much as a systematized reminder to the practitioner that human difficulties are identifiable, concrete clusters of events occuring in the lives of our clients—and are readily identifiable by the clients themselves. The problem, then, is not that an individual "lacks ego strength," or "needs to develop explicit reinforcers," or that "generational boundaries are blurred," but that some meaningful aspect of life has become disrupted: a married couple quarrel frequently or can't enjoy sex together; parents are overwhelmed by their parental responsibilities or manage them ineffectively; an individual is overcome by the accumulation of everyday stress. The true test of the effectivess of any psychotherapy lies in its ability to respond to such common difficulties.

This is not to say that the therapist does not develop certain notions about the nature of the client's difficulties, based on a particular theoretical framework, or that he or she does not rely on this framework (and relevant research) to formulate a possible interventive approach. Thoughtful activity of this sort is a very necessary part of the therapeutic role. There is no doubt that therapists need some way of orienting themselves and organizing their thoughts, especially in the peculiarly stressful and intense moments of the first session. As Hansell (1973) has remarked, a theoretical framework can be remarkably comforting at such times. Such theoretical constructs, however, especially in the highly consumer-oriented context of brief therapy, are justifiable only if they are directly related to problem resolution and, in any case, must never be confused with the actual problem.

A Case Illustration

None of this discussion should be taken as suggesting that there are not times when there may be a need to define or redefine the problem in a way that makes it more workable or more specific. On the other hand, the clinician should not regard the client's problem identification as, by definition, superficial or irrelevant; such common mental health terms as *presenting problem, complaint,* or *symptom* all convey this demeaning notion. Reid and Epstein (1972) cogently warn against the dangers of "double-agenda" helping that this outlook can encourage—where practitioners apparently accept the client's stated problem but covertly decide that some other facet of the client's life (usually theoretically conjectured) is the "real" problem and bide their time until the client realizes this. Short-term treatment, in contrast, is usually a straightforward attempt to deal with the most immediately distressing life problem, since this is directly negotiated and contracted with the client. A case illustration drawn from an article by Weinberger (1971) will illustrate this philosophy in action:

> Mrs. B., a mother in her early twenties, felt both helpless and frustrated in coping with the temper tantrums of her four-year-old daughter. After an initial interview in which the specific dimensions of the difficulty were explored, the therapist initiated a six-session series of interviews. During the intervention period, Mrs. B. was, first, given information on the essential normalcy of her own and her child's reactions and, second, provided with instructions and encouragement in firmer handling of the troublesome behavior.

Many of the difficulties that clinicians encounter at later stages of the interventive process can be seen as related to weaknesses in problem identification in the initial interview. The difficulties that were most meaningful to the client were identified only vaguely at this point, sometimes because the client was reluctant or mistrustful, but just as often because the helper became intrigued with peripheral concerns—what Bloom (1992) characterizes as "attractive detours"—or simply didn't press for greater specificity.

ESTABLISHING A CONTRACT

Toward the end of the initial interview, as the client's major problems in living become apparent, the therapist will initiate discussion about the possibility of an explicit agreement to work on one or two of these areas. This should be done in as simple and open a manner as possible, as an excerpt from an interview transcript in Mann and Goldman (1982) illustrates:

DOCTOR: As I understand it, you have had a very difficult struggle and here you are . . . you're fifty-four years old and feeling very lonely and very hurt.

MRS. R. I guess that's it.

DOCTOR: Would you like to work on that problem to see if you can't find some way to handle it so you'll feel better about yourself?

MRS. R. I sure would. (p. 134)

Where the client does not initially respond to the contract offer, the therapist must pursue this vital issue, as an excerpt from my own practice illustrates:

THERAPIST: From what we've discussed I notice that you keep putting a lot of stress on how dissatisfied you are with your ability to make friends. Would you be willing to work with me on this difficulty?

CLIENT: I don't know, it's hard to say—sometimes I just don't think it's any use even trying. Do you think I could find out what keeps me from getting anywhere with people?

THERAPIST: I'm pretty certain that people can make some important changes in their lives, though sometimes it takes some real effort and you can feel awfully discouraged about trying it out. Are you interested in us working on this together?

CLIENT: I guess so. (Pause) I don't know if it's any use, but I haven't got much to lose.

THE THERAPIST'S LANGUAGE. It should be noted, particularly in the second of these dialogues, how the therapist persistently and personally phrases the offer of therapy. There is an emphasis on "working with me" and on "us working together," which, in very plain language, suggests that the therapeutic process is a mutual endeavor of two concerned people. Conveying this sense of a collaborative venture is characteristic of the engagement activities of brief psychotherapists across disciplines and theoretical frameworks (Wells, 1993). In both illustrations the therapist's choice of the verb "work" to characterize the helping process is also not accidental, but is a deliberate attempt to suggest that activity on the part of both therapist and client will be expected. Beyond this, the concept of work as a valued and understandable human activity carries the implication that the process of change will not be mystical or exotic but simple and ordinary, perhaps even a little sweaty. Finally, the therapist does not hesitate to convey optimism about the possibility of change, though this is clearly framed within the context of activity and effort.

It is easy to overemphasize the impact of such phrasing or the choice of particular words. A therapist would be naive to believe that every careful distinction, every subtle nuance of tone or gesture, has an immediate and direct effect on the client. All too often clients are caught up in such stress that only the gross dimensions of the therapist's responses are readily apparent to them. Despite these reservations, I believe that attention must be paid to the practitioner's words and nonverbal communication, which, in their totality, contribute to an atmosphere and ambience that must be continued and accumulated with a careful persistence before their effects will prevail.

DEALING WITH CLIENT RELUCTANCE. Similarly, the therapist cannot expect that the client will wholeheartedly grasp the offer of help. As the second excerpt indicates, the client's agreement may be tentative and clouded with discouragement and uncertainty. The essential point, however, is that the offer is clearly made and clearly accepted, no matter how weak the acceptance may be. Therapists must always wait for an answer to this question and never assume that silence is consent. If the client is unable to make even an ambivalent acceptance, then therapy, in its usual form, cannot proceed. At this juncture the therapist must fall back upon a secondary position, perhaps offering a further interview to consider the possibility of therapy. When the client's reluctance is obviously stronger—or if he or she clearly conveys disinterest—the therapist may only be able to suggest that the client think about the notion of help and resume contact at some later time.

VALIDATING THE CONTRACT. Psychotherapy, if it is to be meaningful, is a highly cooperative venture, and despite the sometimes impelling pressures of outside parties—authoritative judges and demanding bosses, irrate spouses and distraught parents—the therapist must be sure that a valid contract has been made. This careful attention to the interpersonal dimensions of the contract can be seen in Turner's (1992) first session with a depressed seventeen-year-old, Cathy, who had made an unsuccessful suicide attempt. Midway through this initial meeting Turner poses a key question:

> THERAPIST: How do you feel about being here today? Do you want to work on the issues you brought up? I know you were not too interested in being here in the beginning.
>
> CATHY: I did want to be here. I just wasn't sure anybody could understand me, or would want to take the time to understand me. It feels good to just talk. I needed someone to talk to.
>
> THERAPIST: Do you feel okay working with me? The reason I ask is that our comfortableness in working together makes a big difference in whether we get anywhere or not. That is the most important thing: to get you to where you are feeling stronger and solving your problems.
>
> CATHY: Yeah, I like talking to you. Besides, coming to see you is out of my choice, not my mother's. (p. 145)

DEFINING GOALS. Finally, it is usually appropriate to follow up on the contract with some brief goal definition concerning the identified problem or problems. This can be stimulated by the therapist asking, "What would you be doing if you no longer had this problem?" or "What would your life be like if the difficulty was resolved?" and similar attempts to identify what constitutes a reasonable level of change for this particular client. I don't believe that the goal statement has to be specified in as precise detail as the behavior therapy literature sometimes suggests, and in the context of conducting an initial interview in an hour's time, this is often unattainable.

The brief therapist should also remember that early task assignments are usually helpful in collaboratively defining both problem dimensions and goal expectations. In addition, knowing that initial tasks can be used to gather more detail in key areas of interpersonal and emotional functioning relieves the therapist of the pressure of trying to gather all of this information during the limited time span of the first session.

SETTING A TIME LIMIT AND ASSIGNING A TASK

After the client and clinician have reached a clear agreement, however tentative, to work together on a selected problem, two further steps remain that are especially important in initiating the process of planned short-term treatment: The first involves setting a time limit governing the duration of treatment (Hoyt, 1990); the second entails assigning some activity to the client that can be carried out prior to the next therapy session (Levy & Shelton, 1990). The time limit, of course, epitomizes the planned brevity of the brief therapy process, while the task emphasizes the active, practical nature of change.

Setting Time Limits

In this model of brief therapy, the time limit is always explicitly conveyed to the client, usually at the end of the initial interview. In some instances, as in single-session psychotherapy (Bloom, 1981; Talmon, 1990), the first session is the only contact but, more commonly, anywhere from one to about fifteen further sessions are selected for the interventive period. The therapist takes on the responsibility to select a suitable time limit and informs the client of this. Choosing a time limit may be negotiated with the client in a few cases but is most often formulated by the clinician as a function of his or her professional judgment.

Certain issues concerning the selection and employment of time limits will be considered later, but three major points will be emphasized here:

IMPACT OF TIME LIMITS. There is no doubt that the explicit use of a time limit places pressures on helper and client alike and that these pressures affect both the scope and the pace of the helping process. Once a time limit has been defined—eight sessions, let us say—the therapist understands that she or he must strive to define the contracted problem in even more specific terms and, most critically, choose and utilize a change strategy that will have definite impact. Most clients appear to be positively affected by the time limit, frequently finding the notion of a foreseeable end encouraging and hopeful and, as the study by Sledge and his colleagues (1990) substantiated, becoming less likely to terminate prematurely.

THERAPIST RESISTANCE. It is often difficult for therapists who are inexperienced in brief psychotherapy to conceive of significant change taking place within a relatively limited period of time (Hoyt, 1985, 1987). Many therapists have been educated to place a higher value on lengthy and ambitious therapeutic ventures. Beginning helpers may have a sketchier notion of the therapeutic process yet may still share the bias common among the educated middle class that treatment should somehow be wide ranging and long lasting. Clients from lower-middle-class, working-class, or low socioeconomic backgrounds do not necessarily share this viewpoint, and indeed there have been times when I have found myself hard put to convince such a client that even three or four sessions did not constitute an unreasonably long period of intervention. In other words, it is well for therapists to keep in mind that belief in the primacy of lengthy therapeutic ventures—quite aside from the empirical evidence challenging their effectiveness—is a predominantly middle-class bias that is not shared by large groups of potential clients.

RECONTRACTING. Although an explicit time limit is established at the beginning of treatment and the practitioner makes every effort to structure treatment within this time limitation, there is no doubt that a certain number of cases take longer (Gibbons, 1979; Parad & Parad, 1968). It is possible, in other words, to reach the predicted time limit and to see the desired goals still unattained. In such instances, therapist and client may negotiate a further series of sessions so as to continue the helping process toward its proper conclusions.

The brief therapist, then, is well aware that the predicted time limit with any given client is not inviolable—more or less time may be required—but this should not be a temptation to omit or needlessly qualify the time limit in short-term treatment. If the helping process is to derive useful impact from the pressures of time, the time limit should be presented in a positive manner, neither hedged nor needlessly overemphasized, and the change strategies employed should be shaped so as to fit reasonably within the predicted number of sessions.

Assigning an Initial Task

Homework tasks are frequently employed in brief therapy and serve at least two major functions:

1. They help to emphasize the active nature of the process of change and to engage the client in the purposeful dimensions of this process.

2. The assignment of tasks, which characteristically are carried out between therapy sessions, symbolizes the need for change to take place in real life and thus tends to reduce client dependence on the therapist or the therapeutic setting.

IDENTIFYING A FIRST TASK. As the initial interview moves to its conclusion, the therapist is concerned to prescribe an assignment that will impart to the client that active participation will be expected. It is often difficult to devise a task at this early point because the clinician has only limited knowledge about the client and the salient aspects of the client's major life problems. These very difficulties, however, suggest the direction that the initial task can take. That is to say, the therapist will ask the client to carry out a task that will add such needed information—a task, in other words, that will further explore a selected aspect of the contracted problem.

For instance, parents concerned about their child may be asked to keep daily notes on the circumstances in which the problem behaviors occur. A troubled marital couple can be asked to work out a list of the areas in their relationship that each would like to see changed—or, more positively, the aspects of the relationship that each partner values. It is critical at this beginning point, not that the most pertinent and focused task be selected, but that participation by individual, couple, or family be stimulated in a simple and direct manner.

EXPLAINING THE TASK. It is often helpful to offer clients an explanation of the general purpose of the task. This too can be done in a straightforward way, and indeed, it is best if the helper is as open and concrete as possible in any explanations that are given. If, for example, one is instructing parents to record the behavior of their child as an initial task, the explanation might take the following form:

> THERAPIST: As we've talked here, it seems that the major difficulty we are going to have to work on is how to help Tommy make more friends and become more confident in how he gets along with other children. To get us started on this, I'd like to ask you to keep a daily record over the next week of every instance where you see him involved with another child. Keep a record of who he is with,

what they do together, and anything else you might think is important. This will give us a much clearer idea, as we continue working together, of exactly how things go for Tommy in this area, what things he is managing all right, and exactly where he is having most difficulty.

The instructions would of course vary if the target problem involved aggressive behavior with other children or if the parent's were concerned about the child's study habits. The essential focus would be similar, however, in that it would involve the attempt to define a very clear-cut task for the parents to undertake, a brief connection of this task to the problem-solving work that lies ahead, and the suggestion of an active approach to coping with difficulties.

TASKS VERSUS ADVICE. Implicit in the use of tasks is the pervading belief of the brief psychotherapist that most change takes place outside the therapeutic session (Bolter et al., 1990; Budman & Gurman, 1983) and, moreover, is most effective and meaningful where clients are encouraged to take an active role in their lives. In contrast to the commonsense tactic of giving advice, assigning tasks in brief psychotherapy can be quite varied and subtle. One key difference, for example, lies in the manner in which the task is presented. Seldom if ever does the helper suggest that a particular task in itself is the solution to the problem. Rather, she or he explains that it represents a step along a pathway to resolution. Similarly, tasks can be conceptualized and presented as miniature learning experiences—offering opportunity for observation, experimentation, and challenge—and the therapist is careful to avoid presenting a task as involving anything so definitive as success or failure. The issue is not the outcome of a particular task, but the task's contribution, however small, to an ongoing process of change.

WHAT IS THE "REAL" PROBLEM?

The purpose of short-term treatment is to help people to cope successfully with the problems in living that they are experiencing. The major goals of the initial interview discussed in this chapter further emphasize that the clinician must pay close and serious attention to the client's expression of these difficulties, and that detailed exploration should be limited to the one or two problems the client views as most pressing.

This concentrated focus on the current, immediate problems in living, relying in large part on the client's identification of such problems, brings up an issue that is sometimes troublesome to clinicians. This is most often expressed as doubt about whether the client, in the rapid engagement process typical of time-limited therapy, is actually revealing the "real" problem. For some practitioners this is more than doubt; they believe that clients can reveal their symptoms or voice their complaints, but that these are only superficial aspects of a "real" problem of which the client may have literally no awareness. This issue has philosophical, theoretical, and practical implications that are worth examining.

A CONSUMER-ORIENTATION. Philosophically, of course, there is no doubt that the brief therapist is committed to the view that solving the immediate problems in living that impel people to seek professional help is the major purpose of time-limited therapeutic intervention (Bolter et al., 1990; Budman & Gurman, 1983). Furthermore, the brief therapist regards the client as the primary source of such problem identification. Epstein (1980) states this position unequivocally:

> Clients know what their target problems are. They may need help in stating them and understanding them. Some clients may understand them perfectly. Often the client's target problem seems to be at odds with the problem identified by a referral source or with a professional view of what the problem ought to be . . . (p. 49)

From this point of view, no matter how the practitioner may conceptualize the client's difficulties in relation to their etiology or current maintenance, the therapeutic obligation, if intervention is undertaken, is to enable the client to achieve a reasonable resolution of the real life problems that she or he has identified. William Reid (1985) takes a similar position:

> Related to the level of abstraction in problem formulation is the question of what is the "real" problem. A simple answer to the question is that all problems are "real" to someone. It is usually

impossible, and fruitless, to search for one problem that has some quintessential reality that others lack. . . . If any problems have a special degree of reality, they are those that clients say are causing them discomfort. (p. 31)

THEORY AND PRACTICE. Practitioners tend to translate client problem statements almost automatically into theoretically based formulations, yet we all too easily forget that no theoretical framework in the therapeutic arena, with the single exception of social learning theory (Bandura, 1977b, 1986), is supported by any substantial body of empirical research. Most theories—from Freud to Rogers, Berne, Satir, Glasser, Haley, and innumerable others—are simply explanatory schemas reflectively developed by especially clever and articulate practitioners as a way of explaining the development of human problems and justifying a particular method of therapeutic intervention.

At the theoretical level, practitioners may disagree about the meaning of a particular problem, or the most efficient way of treating it, with differing theories tending to emphasize selected aspects of the behavioral, affective, and cognitive components of the human experience. The eclectic framework presented in this book is an attempt to recognize the place of all three of these elements in promoting dysfunction and in facilitating change. Yet the philosophical or value stance remains the same: clients have a right to have the problems they identify taken seriously, and intervention must be directed toward these chosen goals of the client.

Therefore, since most of our theoretical frameworks lack great predictive power, my preference is to begin work on a client-identified problem unless there is palpable evidence that other difficulties will interfere. For example, I don't assume that the parents of a troublesome child must be experiencing (but denying) marital difficulties unless they are quarrelsome and antagonistic with each other right before my eyes. A trial of brief family therapy focused on the parent-child issues, with appropriate tasks calling for parental communication and cooperation, is much more likely to reveal interfering marital problems than a priori theoretical speculations.

CONTRACTING DILEMMAS. It must be recognized, however, that practical difficulties can arise in the process of identifying problems. As

Reid and Epstein (1972) point out, some clients may initially identify less important or less embarrassing difficulties in the beginning moments of their first encounter with a comparative stranger. This is a natural human reaction in such a situation, but it does not mean that the clinician should routinely treat the client's initial descriptions as unimportant or superficial. Many clients, in my experience, will reveal quite serious difficulties early in the first session, and those who reveal lesser concerns need to have these difficulties considered with empathy and respect. Otherwise they will have little realistic basis for trusting the clinician and, consequently, revealing concerns that cut closer to the bone.

Some of this difficulty in problem identification may also be a function of practitioner attitude. For instance, as I have gained personal comfort and confidence in working in the area of brief sexual therapy, my ability to inquire directly about my clients' sexual problems has significantly increased, but I still hear practitioners speaking of clients who are "not ready," even after many sessions, to talk about sexual difficulties. Yet I can see no difference between their clients and the clients with whom I have discussed sexual problems in the first interview. The question of *who* is "not ready" may be asked, particularly in relation to talking openly about life areas that are highly emotional or subject to social taboo.

RESOLVING THE DILEMMA. There is always the possibility that a particular client may consciously withhold the revelation of a serious difficulty because of shame, anxiety, or distrust. In some cases this could create an obvious gap in the client's problem presentation, and at an appropriate phase of the initial interview, the therapist might directly ask about this missing information or related area of difficulty. A parent might, for example, concentrate on difficulties with a child and at the same time neglect to mention (or even deny) a discernible marital conflict. Yet even direct inquiries may not bring about acknowledgment of the problem.

When clients take such a stance, in my opinion they are making a choice that, in the final analysis, only they are entitled to make. They have decided not to deal with a particular difficulty or refuse to recognize that it is a problem in their lives. The clinician, in turn, is confronted with a number of possible choices:

1. Are the problems the client *has* revealed sufficiently trouble-some to her or him that it is worthwhile expending professional (and client) effort in working on them? If so, therapy should proceed.

2. Are there such *obvious* (not theoretically conjectured) difficul-ties in other life areas that problem work on the difficulties the client has shared would be patently useless? In such cases it is the thera-pist's responsibility to clearly point out such an impasse. If the client does not agree to work on the obvious difficulties, a helping contract may not be possible.

3. Helper and client may initiate treatment around the revealed difficulties only to have the "hidden" problem thwart efforts at prob-lem solving. Again, confrontation around the impasse is called for, and if the client agrees to change focus, a new contract may be nego-tiated.

4. Finally, therapist and client may work relatively successfully on a lesser problem and reach a suitable termination and evaluation point. At this time the client may reveal the unacknowledged prob-lem and a further contract may be negotiated. In other instances the client may now be ready to work on an important problem that she or he acknowledged earlier but did not want to tackle.

Even if neither of these possibilities transpires, the therapist has provided the client with a legitimate helping experience in the prob-lem area where the client chose to struggle. In any case, the practition-er's therapeutic ambitions should not interfere with the client's right to effective helping, even if this is in a relatively minor area of life.

5

The Initial Interview: Process

> If the therapist fails to participate actively in the treat-
> ment, events will pass him by, ambiguity as to both
> process and goals will intervene, and what began as time-
> limited psychotherapy will become diffuse, indefinite,
> long-term psychotherapy.
>
> —James Mann, *Time-Limited Psychotherapy*

Practitioners of brief psychotherapy are beginning to pay more
attention to the specific techniques that are needed to encourage
clients to become involved participants in the therapeutic process
(Budman et al., 1992). The pervading theme has become one of an
engagement into therapy—the encouragement of a process in which
clinician and client mutually negotiate their expectations and roles.
It has become clearer that the therapist, too, must play an active part
in the engagement process if the client is to achieve the greatest benefits from whatever time-limited period of intervention is to follow.

This chapter begins by examining the directive role that the therapist must often take in structuring the initial interview, and is followed by descriptions and illustrations of the specific techniques
useful in supporting the relationship-building, educational, and management functions of the interview. Finally, these techniques and
strategies are related to a series of identifiable stages that characterize the first session and facilitate its effective implementation.

THE DIRECTIVE STANCE IN THERAPY

These two chapters on the initial interview collectively identify a
cluster of goals and related techniques and strategies toward which

the brief therapist deliberately and purposely directs much of his or her activity during the initial interview. This is the beginning of the often active and participant role that the clinician must assume in order to function effectively within the time constraints of short-term treatment. Such an approach to the therapeutic role may create certain philosophical or value dilemmas for some practitioners, or at least a sense of cognitive dissonance with the therapeutic stance conventionally taught.

Directive and Action Approaches

Twenty years ago Jerome Frank (1974) suggested that psychotherapeutic approaches, broadly considered, adopted either an evocative or a directive stance in relation to therapist-client interaction and therapeutic goals. Much of his discussion is still valid today. He pointed out that evocative therapies have dominated North American approaches and are characterized by a number of common features:

> Evocative therapies, often inaccurately termed "permissive," try to create a situation that will evoke the full gamut of the patient's difficulties and capabilities, thereby enabling him not only to work out better solutions for the problems bringing him to treatment but also to gain greater maturity, spontanaeity, and inner freedom, so that he becomes better equipped to deal with future stresses as well as current ones. . . . (p. 148)

The less fashionable directive approaches emphasize different facets of the therapeutic experience:

> [Directive] approaches try directly to bring about changes in the patient's behavior which, it is believed will overcome his symptoms or resolve the difficulties for which he sought treatment. . . . [They] focus on the patient's current adjustment problems and review his past only sufficiently to enable the therapist to reach an understanding of his present difficulties. . . . In keeping with differences in their goals and approaches, directive therapies tend to be briefer than evocative approaches. (p. 148)

An even more recent analysis by London (1986) has made a similar distinction between what he calls the *insight* and the *action* modes of psychotherapy. The insight approaches emphasize clients gaining greater awareness or understanding of themselves, with the therapist largely playing a nondirective or guiding role in this process. The action therapies, in contrast, are problem oriented, focus on changes in the here-and-now of the client's current life, and expect the therapist to play an active, even directive role in the intervention.

Following these definitions, there is no doubt that brief psychotherapy, in almost all of its varieties, is an action approach and takes a directive stance toward the management of helping. This will be evident not only in the initial interview but throughout the course of intervention. The very notion that helping should be "managed" implies an active and planned participation on the part of the helper.

Directiveness versus Nondirectiveness

Whether it is possible to be completely nondirective—as some therapies claim—is disputable. Haley (1976) argues that it is not. For example, if the therapist makes *any* decision about how she will conduct herself in relation to the client and attempts to carry this out in the interview, she will have some effect on the client and at least to this extent is directive. The silent therapist, who might appear to represent the height of nondirectiveness, can have a considerable effect on the client, particularly if the client expected that the therapist would be more active. Similarly, the therapist who directly or indirectly expresses the view that it is entirely up to the client to make decisions and choices (perhaps a more realistic version of the nondirective stance) is exerting a major pressure on the client who had hoped that the therapist would take some (or even all) of this responsibility.

However, it is just as difficult to be totally directive. If the therapist is at all influenced by the client, then to that extent he or she is not directive. As the practitioner must gain some inkling of the kind of difficulty the client is experiencing, control must be relinquished in order to gain this information. To the extent that the helper allows clients to explicate their situation and is affected by that description, to that extent the helper is moving away from a radically directive stance.

It is thus apparent that the notions of "directiveness" and "nondirectiveness" are stereotypes rather than accurate pictures of therapeutic activity. The needs and expectations of the client influence the role of the helper in a variety of ways and cannot be separated from the activities of therapy. What might appear to be a relatively unstructured role with one client will appear highly directive in relation to another. In addition, just as it appears to be impossible to be completely nondirective—that is, to have no direct impact on the client—it is as unlikely that one can be completely directive and achieve complete control.

Despite these general distinctions, however, I believe that the practitioner of brief psychotherapy does take a more directive role within the helping relationship than therapists have generally been taught to do.

1. The therapist takes considerable responsibility for guiding the course of therapy—from the first contact on—by such devices as asking questions to elicit needed information, limiting discussion in areas that do not appear to be immediately relevant, moving into areas of inquiry that do appear to be pertinent, and, in general, playing an assertive role in the immediate relationship.

2. Furthermore, the therapist takes responsibility for devising a plan of action that he or she believes will enable the client to resolve the problems being experienced. This strategy for change is explicitly discussed with the client so that he or she will become aware of its nature and the demands it will exert, but developing the therapeutic plan is seen as the sole prerogative of the therapist.

3. Finally, the therapist assumes that the purpose of the helping encounter is to bring about beneficial and tangible change in the client, in line with the goals that have been mutually contracted. Unless there is clear reason to negate this contract, the practitioner uses the full range of the therapeutic skills at her or his command toward achieving these goals.

Directionality

Thus, underlying the directive approach to helping is the belief that therapy should have directionality; that is, it should be purposeful and goal-oriented. Verbalized or not, it will often be apparent from the outset that the brief therapist is taking such a stance. However, there may also be times in the treatment process when it is both useful and necessary to make this clear. It may occur at an early stage with a client who, for example, has had one or more previously unsuccessful experiences with therapy. On the other hand, the assumption of directionality may need to be explicated at a midpoint in treatment to a client who has become bogged down in the very process of change. This latter instance represents the very essence of the technique of confrontation—facing the client with the therapist's expectation that progress is not only necessary but mandatory if the therapeutic relationship is to have any viable reason to continue.*

It will also be apparent that the initial interview in short-term practice is the first (and perhaps most significant) instance of the planned use of time. The practitioner must be acutely aware, as the first session begins, that a number of tasks need to be accomplished within a limited period of time. This awareness should serve to place a constructive pressure upon the therapist to pace the interview around these goals rather than to permit the process to be governed by whatever intriguing "dynamics" may be apparent in the client or in the very process itself.

The purpose of facilitating progress toward these goals should take precedence over anything except the most compelling concerns and happenings. Thus, the helper must be exquisitely aware of the passage of time during the initial interview and, where needed, must control her or his own range of exploration in relation to this limitation. Similarly, the therapist will take the responsibility of placing controls upon client activity in order to achieve the goals of the first session in as economical a manner as possible.

Ethical Concerns

Practitioners may hesitate to assume a directive stance on the grounds that this approach may seriously limit the client's right to determine the nature and course of her or his life. Social workers, perhaps more than any other of the helping professions, have stressed the principle of self-determination, and have often worked

---

* See Hammond et al., (1977) and Hepworth and Larsen (1990) for lucid discussions of the employment of confrontation techniques in clinical practice.

with groups of people, such as the poor and the various ethnic and racial minorities, whose lives have already been considerably limited by the restrictions of society. This heritage has made it more difficult for social workers to comfortably adopt a stance that may seem to place limitations on individual freedom. Several points need to be emphasized, however, in relation to this apparent conflict between therapist directiveness and client self-determination.

1. As short-term treatment begins, it should be readily apparent that the major goals of the initial interview postulated earlier can hardly be viewed as seriously limiting the client's freedom and opportunity. To the contrary, the emphasis on arousing hope, responding to troublesome emotions, and identifying major life problems is much more likely to *increase* the client's ability to act. By doing these things, the tendency of such a direct approach to helping will be to serve as a stimulus toward freedom.

2. The very process of defining a problem in specific and concrete terms makes the possibility of deciding whether to deal with this problem much clearer. The contract between helper and client can then be openly negotiated, and both participants will be in a better position to knowledgeably consent to its demands. The essence of contracting, of course, is the mutual consent of the individuals involved. The client is always at some degree of disadvantage in any process of contracting because it is the client who suffers from the effects of whatever the problem might be. To the extent that the client experiences such pressures, his or her choice cannot be regarded as completely free. However, even where freedom is limited by such factors, it is still better to have the choice of acting or not acting clearly posed, and there may well be times, at the beginning of treatment or later, when the client will decide that the status quo is preferable to the uncertainties of any movement or change. At such a moment the helper has no choice but to accept and, indeed, to respect the client's judgment.

3. This emphasis on directionality should not be taken to suggest that the therapist, in order to manage the pertinent therapeutic tasks, will deliberately ignore the need of an extremely anguished client to talk about his or her pain. The goals and procedures of any therapeutic method must be set aside in the face of an emotional crisis of significant proportion. However, what is more often the case in

unplanned or unproductive initial interviews is that the client simply rambles on in a disorganized way, offering detailed descriptions of this or that problem ("so then he said, . . . and then I said, . . ."), in the belief that this is what the helper wants to hear. The clinician, for lack of a better plan, either allows this to happen or, worse still—through misplaced courtesy—encourages it by supportive comments and interjections.

4. Just as it is possible for therapist activity to be abused and for the practitioner to usurp the client's prerogatives, so is it possible for an overly permissive role to be detrimental. The confused and anxious client, for example, may suffer if the therapist does not exercise a needed and legitimate expertise in helping to identify problems and goals. The overriding consideration in either instance is the helping professional's ethical concern for the client's welfare and benefit. This, of course, is neither theory nor technology and ultimately can be governed by neither.

A SURVEY OF ENGAGEMENT TECHNIQUES

William Schwartz, in his foreword to Schulman's *The Skills of Helping* (1979), points out that there has been a marked reluctance on the part of the helping professions to identify specific therapeutic techniques and, in contrast, an almost inordinate emphasis on the more general principles of diagnosis and treatment. He succinctly poses the resulting dilemma:

> The neglect of means has produced a professional literature that is extremely thin in its description of practice. It is largely concerned with diagnosis, conceptual analysis, philosophy and abstract discussion. (p. vii)

There is apparently a belief that clinicians must be encouraged to think in broad, inclusive terms, and along with this, a fear that to stress techniques will lead to narrowness and rigidity in practice. I believe that there is much to be said for a concentration on the minutiae of technique. Instead of fostering rigidity or narrowness, the careful development of a range of technical skills can expand the clinician's capacity for flexibility and diversity of response.

With such an objective in mind, this section will examine a number of specific techniques that the therapist can employ, as needed, within the engagement process that is being attempted in the first interview. These techniques derive from research studies of the therapy process, the published case studies, transcripts, audiotapes, and videotapes of experienced therapists, and my own direct practice experience.* They will be categorized into three groups:

1. Relationship or influence-building strategies
2. Educational or informational strategies
3. Management or survival strategies

I will briefly survey a number of engagement techniques under each of these headings and, in later sections of this chapter, illustrate their employment throughout the major phases of the first session.

Relationship or Influence-Building Strategies

Brief therapy is particularly dependent on the ability of the therapist to quickly establish an atmosphere in which the client not only feels understood but has enough trust and confidence in the clinician that the interventive strategies to be employed at a later phase will have sufficient impact. In contrast to conventional clinical practice, the emphasis in short-term treatment is on the rapid development of a significant relationship within the areas of pressing concern to the client. Of the techniques employed to expedite movement toward this goal, five predominate:

SOCIALIZING. This is a technique employed during the first few minutes of the initial interview where the therapist very briefly interacts with the client at a social level (Haley, 1976; Minuchin, 1974). It is used as a transition from the social level of the preliminary contact into the more serious therapeutic conversation that will follow. Some of the nuances of this seemingly innocuous engagement strategy will be discussed later in the section on the inception phase of the first interview.

---

* Certain aspects of this discussion will be based upon previous writing (Wells, 1980) in which I examined engagement techniques and strategies from the perspective of family and couple therapy.

FACILITATING. Almost every therapeutic approach emphasizes the empathic ability of the clinician, the ability to respond immediately and accurately to the emotional state of the client, whether such feelings are expressed directly or indirectly.

As the preceding chapter stressed, empathic response should be seen as a very literal process in which the therapist (1) reflects back the emotions the client has openly expressed; (2) explicitly labels major feelings that are expressed through the client's nonverbal behavior; or (3) identifies important feelings that are simply a part of the human context of the problem situation being described, as, for example, sadness from a loss or frustration when thwarted. In most instances, the most common and ordinary terms are employed. Words such as "worried," "angry," "sad," "relieved," "disappointed," "happy," "scared," and "concerned," should permeate the dialogue between helper and client as the problem situation and its emotional repercussions are explored.

JOINING OR ACCOMMODATING. In this important engagement technique the helper attempts to convey to the client that there are similarities or parallels at an intellectual, social, or emotional level between practitioner and client. Although most obviously useful in family or couple interviewing (Minuchin & Silverman, 1981), where the therapist is often confronted with the task of engaging a hostile or tightly defended family group, the use of joining techniques is as applicable in one-to-one intervention. Joining may involve minor bits of self-disclosure or the use of humor and words and phrases particularly attuned to the personal and cultural style of the client (Bandler & Grinder, 1976). Self-disclosure by the therapist was highly rated as a relationship-building skill in Schulman's (1981) large-scale study of client reactions to the therapeutic process. The technique is intended to foster identification between therapist and client and to expedite the clinician's assumption of a meaningful (though temporary) role within the client's social network.

MIMICKING. This refers to a number of *nonverbal* ways in which the practitioner indicates human similarities between himself and the client. The technique serves the same purposes as joining, but differs in its employment of the nonverbal level of interchange. Minuchin

(1974) calls this "mimesis" and suggests that such nonverbal responses are a natural human reaction in a close relationship. He offers some typical therapeutic examples:

> Experienced therapists perform mimetic operations without even realizing it. Mr. Smith takes off his coat and lights a cigarette. The therapist, who asks him for a cigarette, is aware of performing this as a mimetic operation. But he is unaware of taking off his own coat. As he talks with Mr. Smith, he also scratches his head in a puzzled, fumbling way, which robs him of authority and increases his kinship with the puzzled, fumbling patient. (pp. 128–129)

REFRAMING OR RELABELING. At a number of critical points in the initial interview the clinician may need to restate a remark by the client in such a manner that the words employed are less stigmatizing or blaming or, on the other hand, more hopeful. The therapist's restatement may also suggest that there are different attitudes, emotions, or motivations underlying the client's behavior. For example, a client's manifest anxiety about a problem might be characterized as a more laudable "concern" to do something about it or as an understandable indication of its importance in his or her life. In either case, the purpose of the techniques is to reduce dysfunctional emotional arousal and to begin to induce hope and understanding through the cognitive change effected by the relabeling or reframing. The technique also has educational implications (discussed in the following section) as it begins to convey the more optimistic, problem-solving framework from which the short-term therapist typically operates.

Using slightly different terms, almost all of the relationship-building techniques discussed here are vividly illustrated by David Treadway (1985) as he describes his initial approach to a troubled marital couple:

> At the same time I attempt to join each member of the couple. I use *empathy* ([to him]: "Nobody else really knows what a struggle the alcoholic goes through"); *matching* (he pounds his fist for emphasis, and I slap my knee when making a point); *self-disclosure* ([to her]: "I'm not much of a fighter myself"); and *positive connotation*: ("It seems that in some way these episodes allow the two of you to redis-

cover how important you are to each other and how committed you are"). (p. 161, italics in original)

Educational or Informational Strategies

During the initial interview, information necessarily flows two ways—from client to therapist and from therapist to client. Yet perhaps too often the therapist ends up with a good deal of information about the potential client, while the client has gained only the most indirect information about the therapist or the process of therapeutic intervention. There is a tendency for inexperienced therapists to assume that their clients are quite familiar with the expectations and demands of the helping process. Most helping professionals are middle class and expect that their clients share their own attitudes and values toward therapy. However, if the client has only a hazy notion of what therapy will be like, it is quite possible that many of the behaviors that appear to reflect "resistance" or "poor motivation" are merely uninformed attempts to respond to a new (and often puzzling) experience. Jerome Frank (1978) suggests that premature termination of therapy may be related to this issue of disparate expectations:

> Those who work with therapists-in-training in a clinic setting share the impression that a major reason why patients drop out of treatment is that they do not know what is supposed to be going on or how it can help them. Because they are in awe of the therapist, they politely answer his questions and he thinks everything is going well; meanwhile the patients are wondering what it is all about, until suddenly they quit without warning. (p. 22)

At the same time, the therapist also needs information about the client, and certain of the techniques in this category offer a means of managing this aspect of the initial interview. The therapist's mastery of a series of techniques for gaining precise information about the client's current functioning and major areas of difficulty is, of course, essential to the rapid engagement process of short-term treatment. Five main techniques serve in facilitating these related purposes of information gathering and client education:

STRUCTURING. The techniques that fall under this general heading refer to ways in which the clinician directly or indirectly conveys information about the process of treatment. Structuring may describe to the client what the therapist believes to be the most useful approach: "The main thing we will be doing together initially is trying to clearly identify the areas of your life that are causing you most stress" or "I'll be helping you to learn some specific ways in which you can better stand up to people." Lennard and Bernstein's (1960) content analysis of therapeutic interviews found that experienced therapists devoted significant portions of their input in early interviews to such activity.

On the other hand, structuring may emphasize what the client should *not* do, and in such instances it becomes an explicit control device. In brief therapy—especially in the initial interview—this type of structuring is characteristically employed to place restraints on the exploration and description of content areas judged to be irrelevant to the immediate goals of engagement. Thus, once a major problem or two has been identified, the clinician may limit discussion to examination of only these areas. Along with focusing the client in this direct way, therapists must also discipline themselves and assiduously avoid what Bloom (1992) calls "attractive detours."

TRACKING. In its most general sense, this term refers to comments and responses from the clinician that serve to encourage the client in conveying needed information (Minuchin, 1974). Additionally, tracking responses help to shape this information into the more specific and focused form required for short-term treatment. The client may be able to express her or his difficulties only in a confused and vague manner and thus may need considerable assistance from the practitioner in order to arrive at workable treatment goals. Tracking techniques offer a means of accomplishing this important task.

At its simplest level, tracking consists of nothing more or less than brief nods, attentive posture and gaze, or subvocal interjections such as "Mmmm-hmmm," which indicate the therapist's interest in whatever the client is describing. In short-term treatment, however, tracking often involves a more active participation on the part of the helper in order to expedite the identification and exploration of problem areas suitable for intervention. The therapist will then use such devices as close-ended questions, queries about "critical incidents," or the written formulation of target problems.

An excerpt from a case study by Hoyt (1993) vividly illustrates the active employment of tracking techniques in an initial interview. In this case Sue, a thirty-eight-year-old woman and a former alcohol abuser, had been brought into a managed-care setting by her parents on a walk-in crisis basis. Sue and her husband had been quarreling for many months. He had left her, taking their two young children with him, and she had resumed drinking. Hoyt was called in to assist in evaluating the possible necessity of short-term psychiatric hospitalization.

> Entering my colleague's office, I saw a timid, somewhat beaten-down looking woman. The psychologist began to "present" the "case" to me, but I quickly interrupted him and asked the patient why she was there. She hesitated—and I had to ask the other psychologist not to talk for her—and then somewhat haltingly at first, but with increasing fluency, she told her story with some prompting. "I can't do anything right, at least that's what Jim says, and he took the kids," she cried. With lots of active questioning and supportive listening, we soon learned the she felt "stupid," that she had been working as a clerk, and that she desperately wanted to see her kids (ages 8 and 2). Careful questioning revealed no psychotic thinking and no suicidal ideas, impulses, or history. (pp. 242–243)

SUMMARIZING. This technique can be seen as a heightened form of tracking and, as the term indicates, involves the therapist's attempts to pull together important aspects of the client's difficulties or to test out the accuracy of the therapist's understanding of these problems. In the preceding excerpt from Hoyt's (1993) case study, he concludes his active tracking with a summary in which he reframes Sue's situation from that of a potential psychiatric inpatient to that of a spouse in acute marital conflict, and probes the possibility of couple therapy:

> I told her I didn't know yet what would happen with her and the kids but "A first step will involve you and you husband. Obviously, you've been having lots of trouble—maybe we can help you there. Has he said anything about counseling?" She responded: "He said he was leaving until I get help. He said he doesn't want a divorce, but he's

had it with all the hassling and the kids running all over me and me being so upset." (p. 243)

Summaries should be employed frequently throughout the initial interview in order to help maintain a focus and additionally as a way of concretely demonstrating to the client the therapist's interest and effort to comprehend. An active use of summaries can have the very beneficial effect of changing the climate of the initial interview from that of a monologue by the client, supported by brief reinforcements from the clinician ("Uh-huh," "Go on"), to an active dialogue between two concerned people. Reframing and relabeling techniques can be built into summaries—they do not have to be confined to literal feedback on client content—or, as the Hoyt excerpt also illustrates, a summary can serve as a base for making a critical transition.

NORMALIZING. Through the use of normalizing techniques, the practitioner conveys to the prospective client that the difficulties he or she is experiencing, or the emotional reactions that are troublesome, are understandable human responses or, in other instances, are not uncharacteristic of the client's environmental situation or life stage. Some degree of depression, for example, is common following the loss of a loved one, or in the aftermath of divorce (Klerman et al., 1984); marital couples frequently find their relationship has become distant and unrewarding a few years into the parenting phase of the family life cycle (Haley, 1973). However, it is important to remember that normalizing should not become simple reassurance. The underlying (or even explicit) message of the normalizing response is not "Don't worry, everyone experiences this," but rather, "I'm not surprised (or shocked) that you have these problems, and they can be painful."

It must be stressed, moreover, that normalizing is not simply a clever tactic through which the clinician talks away the client's difficulties. The effective brief therapist must have sufficient experience with the human condition to know that most, if not all, of the problems people bring to helping professionals are simply heightened versions of the difficulties that any of us may encounter. This is the essence of Sullivan's (1953) one-genus postulate: "We are all much more simply human than otherwise, be we happy and successful, contented and detached, miserable and mentally disordered or whatever." (p. xviii)

DIRECT EDUCATION. There are times in the initial interview when the therapist must provide corrective information to the client in any of a number of key life areas. In a recent analysis of a series of brief therapy cases (Wells, 1993), I found that this direct provision of information was especially prominent in instances where the client was contending with marked anxiety or depression. In these cases the clinician moved rapidly to provide accurate, factual information about the nature of the troublesome emotion, as well as concise descriptions of treatment methodology.

The needed information may be provided verbally by the practitioner, often incorporated into explanations of the potential theraputic procedures. In other instances, there may not be sufficient time in the first session to impart important information. In brief sexual therapy, for example, where increasing client knowledge is an essential aspect of intervention, Beck (1990) describes the use of reading assignments:

> In cases where strong negative attitudes exist concerning sexuality, the introduction of self-help texts can assist the therapist in presenting sexual activity in a more positive light. Zilbergeld's book entitled *Male Sexuality* and Barbach's volume, *For Yourself*, are excellent examples of the kind of reading that can serve as therapeutic adjuncts. (p. 476)

The preceding examples highlight the importance of information giving in such highly emotional areas as depression or sexuality. Therapists should keep in mind, however, that clients often lack accurate information in much more mundane areas—child-rearing practices, or job-finding strategies, for example—where education is less dramatic but just as vital.

Management or Survival Strategies

Quite aside from the techniques intended to establish a relationship or educate the client in the ways of the therapeutic encounter, there are a number of techniques that help the therapist to contend with the difficult moments that can arise in the beginning phase of any close relationship. I commented on this issue in relation to family and couple therapy in an earlier work (Wells, 1980):

> Beginning therapists can slide, almost unwittingly, into major difficulties in an initial interview and often find themselves experiencing painful stress during (and after) a session. Overly idealistic therapists struggle with conflicts between the apparent polarities of "manipulation versus genuineness" or "spontanaeity versus structure" and consequently have great difficulty in achieving a workable style. Many seasoned therapists, however, come to realize that the personal and emotional survival of the therapist is paramount—not at the expense of the family, to be sure, but in order to offer effective help. Thus, such therapists, bit by bit, gain skill in using a series of techniques that help in this essential task of avoiding difficulties or, at the least, not making a bad situation any worse. (pp. 86–87)

The relationship and educational techniques suggested earlier should be seen as the predominant techniques of the initial interview. Yet the management techniques represent highly useful ways for the practitioner to navigate the sometimes difficult waters of the engagement process and, to my knowledge, are seldom openly discussed in the clinical literature. Judiciously employed—with the overall interests of the client clearly in mind—these strategies can avoid otherwise disastrous moments or, in some instances, the complete breakdown of the interview.

DELAYING. There are occasions in the therapeutic process when the helper, for any number of reasons, does not wish to make a direct reply to the client or believes that the pace of the encounter needs to be slowed down. Delaying responses serve an extremely useful purpose at these points. Such techniques are usually very simple and may consist of the repetition of the question a client has asked ("You're wondering about . . .?"), a request for amplification or clarification ("Tell me more about . . ."), or any plausible phrase or gesture that gives the practitioner a few seconds to consider a reply or to deflect the client's immediate concern. Similarly, in an interview that has assumed too fast a tempo, therapists may wish to deliberately slow down their own verbal cadence as a way of reducing the client's pace.

BLURRING. Sometimes the therapist may believe that it will better serve the immediate purposes of engagement if a reply to a client's query is broadly and generally phrased; hence the employment of deliberately generalized or blurred responses. Often there are times when, in the clinician's judgment, the emotional intensity of the moment has reached a height that is detrimental, and a blurred response can be helpful in reducing this emotional arousal. Any reader looking for an example of this technique need only observe a typical interview with a politician—or passages from any of the perennial presidential debates—to appreciate that even the most specific question can be given a vague yet plausible reply. As therapists we like to believe that our purposes and motivations are loftier than those of politicians, but the intent of blurring techniques is the same: to avoid potential entanglements through a carefully generalized response.

DEFERRING. This technique consists of *agreeing with*, rather than challenging, client statements and is usually employed where there is clear indication that the potential client is reluctant or ambivalent about professional intervention or where there is a need to avoid direct confrontation at an early stage of the initial interview. Thus, the therapist's comments are intended to implicitly convey the message that the client's independence or freedom of opinion and choice will be respected (Brehm, 1976). For example, an individual might present his or her difficulties as minor, and rather than disputing this viewpoint, the clinician might strategically defer to the client by openly agreeing that this could be true.

Thus, in an initial interview, a thirty-year-old Vietnam veteran told how his family had insisted that he seek treatment because of depression. However, he vehemently declared that he was "no more depressed than anyone else." The therapist accepted this position without dispute—even though there were many clinical indicators of depression evident in the man's presentation and demeanour—and asked him to describe "this everyday depression you're going through." Deferred to rather than challenged, the client readily entered into an exposition of a number of stressful life problems, including an understandable degree of depression.

In the multiperson contexts of family and couple therapy, deferring is an especially vital skill. A couple, for instance, may have radically different views about their problems, and the therapist can be considerably challenged to respond to each of them in an evenhanded manner.

> Mr. and Mrs. L., a lower-middle-class couple in their early thirties, presented highly contrasting versions of the status of their marriage as the first interview began. Mrs. L. was anguished about what she saw as great distance between them and deteriorating communication; she wept from time to time as she described these difficulties. Mr. L., on the other hand, stolidly maintained there were no problems and showed little reaction to his spouse's distress. In response to therapist inquiries about his opinion, he reiterated such phrases as "There's nothing wrong," and "I don't see any problems."
>
> Recognizing Mr. L.'s defensiveness, the therapist did not press him but began to use deferring phrasing when requesting input from him. Thus, as Mrs. L. continued to expand on her dissatisfactions, the therapist would solicit her husband's participation by saying, "I realize you don't think this is that much of a problem, but could you tell me . . ." or, "From your point of view this isn't really pressing, but give me your ideas about . . ." Consistently deferred to in this manner, Mr. L. gradually relaxed, and by the end of the initial session, both spouses had agreed about a problem or two of moderate degree, which formed the basis for further therapy.

EMBEDDING. In working with troubled people, there are moments when the clinician believes that it would be helpful to suggest a different outlook to the client, but anticipates that the client is likely to discount or challenge this position. For example, optimistic reframing of aspects of the client's difficulties, or normalizing statements with positive implications, if directly delivered, can be strongly disputed or deprecated by a pessimistic client. At other times the therapist may want to create a positive atmosphere within the session without appearing obviously reassuring to the client. The technique of embedding (Bandler et al., 1976) is especially useful for such strategic purposes.

Embedding consists of placing a key statement within the context of one or more statements of a less significant nature. The technique is frequently used in hypnotic inductions, where the therapist will embed suggestions for relaxation or calmness within a monotonous or irrelevant patter. Thus, a female client with difficulties in coping with a job described her discouragement with this situation, but at the same time contended that her problems were largely the result of unfair demands by her supervisor. The therapist wished to challenge this fixed idea but, at an engagement stage, was concerned about alienating the client. This was managed by an embedded response:

> THERAPIST: You must get awfully worn down and angry as you go through these pressures, day after day. That feeling of being unfairly treated can really get at you, and I guess that you almost have to fight at times to keep from looking at everything that way. The frustration can get so strong when you're caught in a real trap like this.

The therapist's summary is predominantly empathic, but embedded within it is a suggestion—"You must almost have to fight at times to keep from looking at everything that way"—which was intended to convey the possibility that the client's current belief system was playing a part in her difficulties. Like many of the engagement techniques described, embedding is intended not to evoke immediate change, but through cumulative repetition to create a climate in which varied possibilities can be considered. The objective, of course, is to offer a more functional alternative to the narrow or fixed beliefs and behaviors that have proved unworkable for the troubled client.

STAGES OF THE INITIAL INTERVIEW

A major aid in attaining facility with the action role of the therapist within the first interview is to develop a cognitive map—a structure in the mind—of the typical process or stages of this vital session. Short-term treatment is highly dependent on such heuristic schemas, and these occur and reccur at many different levels during the interventive process. The better the clinician is able to visualize a systematic sequence for any aspect of the helping process— whether concerned with management of the initial contact, ways of quickly building an influential relationship, or implementation of interventive strategies—the more effectively will the self-imposed time constraints of brief therapy be utilized.

It is obvious that the use of schemas of this sort often involves a deliberate simplification of seemingly complex situations. The practitioner must be willing to accept the risk this entails, tempered by the conviction that more often than not, the path of simplification achieves as good an outcome as more complex (and consequently lengthier) approaches. Because of the consistent research findings that with similar problem and client groups brief treatment is generally as effective as a lengthier approach, such a stance is justified.

Harry Stack Sullivan discusses many of the nuances of the initial interview in his book *The Psychiatric Interview* (1954). This neglected classic of the therapeutic art can be profitably read and reread by the practicing clinician of any discipline or theoretical persuasion. Although he ostensibly is addressing himself to the psychiatrist, Sullivan is careful to point out that his examination of the interpersonal process of interviewing has broad applications. He notes:

> In referring to the interviewee or client, I shall sometimes speak of him as the patient, but I imply no restriction of the relevance of what I say to the medical field, believing that, for the most part, it will apply equally well to the fields of social work or personnel management, for example. (p. 4)

Sullivan identifies four stages within the therapeutic interview, and I believe these form a useful framework for examining the process of the first session. However, within the context of brief therapy, I will place a somewhat different emphasis on certain aspects of each of these phases than did Sullivan. In contrast to the objectives outlined in the previous chapter, this delineation of stages within the initial interview is intended to give the practitioner a sense of the ongoing and interrelated process of this first meeting. Four stages are suggested:

1. Inception
2. Reconnaissance
3. Detailed inquiry
4. Interruption or termination

In the succeeding sections of this chapter, each stage will be briefly defined and its major characteristics discussed in some detail. Many of the engagement techniques presented earlier—as well as the five major goals of the initial interview—are related to particular phases of this process.

THE INCEPTION STAGE

This refers, of course, to the first few moments of the interview and, as Sullivan (1954) notes, "includes the formal reception of the person who comes to be interviewed and an inquiry about, or a reference to, the circumstances of his coming" (p. 37). The inception phase should also incorporate some reference to whatever information the therapist has been given about the potential client and should establish a reasonable purpose for the session. These beginning moments are often awkward and uncomfortable for both therapist and client. Perhaps because of this discomfort, the inception stage, despite its great importance, has been particularly neglected in the clinical literature.

INITIAL EXPECTATIONS. Prior to the literal moment when client and therapist first meet, both are, obviously, unrelated individuals, one of whom is experiencing some sort of difficulty in life, while the other is presumed to possess a special knowledge and skill in dealing with such problems. The beginning of therapy, then, brings together two human beings whose immediate characteristics may (or may not) result in their continuing to meet. If they continue their relationship, for whatever length of time, both client and clinician hope that these encounters will be beneficial to the client. Furthermore, the practitioner expects that the relationship will offer a gratifying opportunity to use the expertise that he or she has acquired in a chosen profession.

The outcome of any initial interview is at best a chancy matter. In a case example in the first chapter of this book, I described a pregnant young woman whose boyfriend was in jail and whose immediate family members were caught up in their own concerns. Unable to find assistance within her natural social networks, she felt concerned about how to cope with a number of financial, emotional, and practical issues over the next few months of her life. A medical social worker, at the suggestion of another professional, interviewed the young woman to offer help. Despite this juxtaposition of a person in need of help and a practitioner able to offer assistance, one might still question whether a viable relationship will occur. Will this young woman appear for further interviews, if these are planned? Or will she, like many other potential clients, drop from sight and never receive the benefits counseling might have offered?

REDUCING DROPOUTS. All of these statements may sound mundane and hardly worth discussion, yet it is well to remember that the *potential* relationship of helper and client, described above, does not usually continue for more than a short time. The findings on premature termination or early dropout (Garfield, 1986) tell us bleakly that only one of three clients will be seen after the initial interview, and that scarcely one of five will continue for more than a few sessions.

In other words, the critical problem of the initial interview is one of engagement—the clinician has about an hour to reverse the strong probability that the person being seen is not going to return or will do so for only a few sessions. As there is no reason to believe that the clients who drop out are different, in type or degreee of difficulty, from those who continue (Baekland et al., 1975; Garfield, 1980, 1986), there is good reason to carefully examine these early moments of the helping relationship. It is here that the clinician has an opportunity to influence the relationship in such a way as to increase the probability of the client's returning and benefiting from professional help. Indeed, because the data indicate that time is extremely limited, it is apparent that the therapist must utilize it fully if an effective relationship is to be established.*

SOCIAL VERSUS THERAPEUTIC CONVERSATIONS. In considering these beginning moments, it is useful to remember the many differences between a social relationship and a therapeutic relationship and, in particular, the differing conventions governing the conversation that takes place in each of these contexts. There are any number of rules,

---

* None of the foregoing discussion is intended to convey that every person who asks for help must become a client or that there are not a number of people who benefit from very brief contact (Talmon, 1990). However, careful attention to the management of the initial interview will enable those individuals who decide against continuing therapy, to make this choice under the best of circumstances. Further, those who need only a brief period of help will similarly benefit from a skillful handling of the first (and perhaps only) contact.

mainly unwritten, that govern the conduct of social conversations between comparative strangers. From the social perspective, for example, one does not ask questions of a highly personal nature, such as "How are you and your wife getting along sexually?" or make such plainspoken statements as "There must be times when you wish he wasn't even your child," which challenge the other's motivations. If a person becomes emotionally upset during a social conversation, it would be considered tactless to respond in such a way as to highlight or increase an individual's distress. All of these conventions, and more, will soon be broken in the therapeutic conversation.

SOCIAL BEGINNINGS. In order to make the transition from the social to the therapeutic context in the least jarring manner, it is often helpful if the therapist deliberately encourages a few moments of social conversation at the beginning of the initial meeting. This does not have to be a particularly scintillating exchange, and indeed it is often of a quite pedestrian nature. For instance, the helper may inquire about the weather or ask the client if parking was easily available. Hoyt (1993) describes the social interchange as he assists an elderly patient in a wheelchair toward his office:

> As I pushed him around the corner and down the corridor, we talked baseball. "What did you think of the Hawkin's trade?" and "How'd they do today?" got us talking and connected. He made a few remarks that showed a good knowledge of the game, and I asked intelligent questions. (p. 238)

This social exchange also gives the therapist an opportunity to greet clients by name and shake hands, indicate where they can hang up their coats and where they should sit, and carry out any other small amenities that may be useful to the client at this potentially anxious moment.

Moreover, the social aspects of the conversation, however stilted, serve several other valuable purposes. It must be remembered that the client is entering alien territory and, at a minimum, deserves some small chance to orient himself. In the unfamiliar confines of the clinician's office it can be not only a courtesy but a minor relief to be told, for instance, where to sit. Similar inquiries about whether the client wishes to smoke and, if so, furnishing an ashtray add to the sense of being welcomed and made comfortable. These familiar gestures are part of the social ritual of greeting and, by their familiar ring, can ease at least a portion of the client's uneasiness about what may lay ahead. In other words, the social aspects of the inception phase serve as a transition into the therapeutic relation and, like all transitions, attempt to make a change from one state to another less perceptible or jarring.

Such family therapy advocates as Haley (1976) and Minuchin (1974, 1981) have written about the socializing techniques of the first interview. Minuchin characterizes the therapist as "host" during these moments, making conventional but reassuring gestures of welcome, while Haley speaks of this phase as an opportunity for both practitioner and client to observe each other.

This latter aspect of the social interlude can be particularly useful. The client is as unknown to me as I am to him, and even a few moments of observation, cloaked by the social conventions, can frequently give me a beginning sense of the individual I am meeting. What does he look like? How is he dressed? How is this potential client handling herself at this very moment? A frown, for example, can indicate discomfort or suspicion, a trembling hand may suggest a person in acute distress, and so on. All of these clues are extremely tentative, of course, and usually require no immediate comment, but they can be helpful in orienting the clinician to what may lie ahead.

MOVING TO THE THERAPEUTIC. As these few moments of social conversation draw to a close, the need for a more distinct transition into the therapeutic conversation appears, and the burden of making this shift falls upon the therapist. Unless the client has literally walked in off the street, the therapist usually has a general notion of the problem that he or she is experiencing. This knowledge can be used as a part of the bridge needed to lead into the therapeutic discourse that will occupy the remainder of the initial session. Such a transitional statement by the therapist can take the following form:

THERAPIST: From what I understood when we talked on the telephone, you're quite concerned with some problems you're encountering having to do with anxiety and stress in your life and finding these hard to deal with. I realize that you may be feeling uncomfortable and edgey right now in talking to me, because I'm very much a stranger to you and I know it isn't easy to talk about personal problems. See if you can give me a better idea of what's concerning you, and let's spend this next hour that we have trying to decide if the kind of counseling I can offer would be helpful to you. Just start wherever you want, and if there are things I don't follow I'll ask some questions.

A very similar emphasis on this sort of transitional statement of practitioner understanding and purpose is discussed in Ewing's (1978, 1990) writings on crisis intervention as psychotherapy and in Schulman's (1979) brilliant examination of helping skills. Schulman suggests that the clinician "must attempt to clarify the purpose of the meeting by a simple, nonjargonized, and direct statement" (p. 29). He sees such openness as closely related to (and clearly anticipating) the contracting about purpose and goals that must take place between therapist and client later in the initial interview.

EMBEDDED UNDERTONES. At the same time it must be emphasized that the therapist's statement presented above is also a conscious attempt to influence certain aspects of the ensuing process in a way that will make engagement and the initiation of brief therapy more likely. Embedded within it are a number of suggestions that I believe play some part in the continuing process of engagement and deserve further comment.

At the very beginning of the statement, for example, the clinician is attempting to give the potential client a succinct version of what she knows about the client's difficulties. If the locus of the problem is more specifically known, this could be stated: "I understand you're very concerned about your marriage." In any case, the therapist keeps this part of the statement brief and in effect regards it as a starting point, subject to further amplification and correction, from which the client can proceed. I try to capture some aspect of emotional disturbance in this capsule statement of the problem because I want to suggest from the very beginning of the helping process that I am interested in emotions and will be frequently responding to this dimension of the client's life.

A similar emphasis on emotions appears in the next sentence as the clinician suggests that the client may be uncomfortable at this very moment. This is, once again, an effort to highlight the emotional dimension and to convey the therapist's willingness to address this issue directly. One might characterize this as "easy empathy" in the sense that almost anyone in the situation of being a potential client in a mental health or social service setting is likely to be experiencing some degree of discomfort whether they display this emotion or not. Thus, the practitioner is able to demonstrate, with minimal effort, a degree of understanding that can begin to accumulate toward this major goal of the engagement process.

The time limits of the initial session are spelled out through the therapist's comment on "this next hour," and it is suggested that some agreement about further counseling may be possible by the end of this time. My preference is to state this possibility in a tentative (yet positive) manner, since at this point I have little idea whether the prospective client is eagerly seeking help or has come only under the utmost duress. This is not to say that the therapist's conviction that therapy is highly useful to people has to be concealed; it simply recognizes that not everyone is immediately ready to grasp at this opportunity. Deferring to the client's possible reluctance in advance can save the helper from some difficult moments.

Finally, it will be noted that there is a frequent use of the personal pronoun "I" throughout the therapist's transitional statement. This, again, is a deliberate emphasis. The therapist expects that the client will talk personally and openly during the ensuing interview, and although actual therapist self-disclosure may not be appropriate at this time, the least the clinician can do is suggest her own involvement through such a choice of phrasing. This offers the client a minimal model of disclosure and is one of many attempts on the part of the clinician to increase the probability of more favorable outcomes.

The Reconnaissance Stage

Sullivan (1954) suggests that within this second stage of the initial interview, the clinician is "concerned with trying to get some notion of the person's identity—who he is and how he happens to be the person who has come to the office" (pp. 37-38). Sullivan speaks of the objective of this phase in terms of obtaining "a rough outline of the social and personal history of the patient" (p. 37). In brief psychotherapy—where historical data are usually de-emphasized—I believe that the reconnaissance is most usefully visualized as a time when the client is actively encouraged to describe how he or she views the current difficulties that have led to this initial meeting. The therapist does not gather any formal history, concentrating instead on responding to the client's immediate statements. But throughout this description there will be a number of places where the clinician may ask pertinent questions in order to clarify aspects of the client's life that are not obvious from his or her statements.

LIMITING THE FOCUS. Care should be exercised to avoid questions that are not essential to the concentrated focus of short-term treatment. For example, as Mr. Faber (see Chapter 3) described his difficulties in relationships with women and indicated that his parents had been moralistic and inhibiting about sexuality, it was not necessary to ask for many details of this early history; doing so would have involved taking one of the "attractive detours" that Bloom (1992) warns against. The issue of *how* his family had this effect upon him was not important, although the need for sexual reeducation in an accepting atmosphere became an immediate hypothesis for possible intervention.

As I pointed out in discussing the inception stage of the therapeutic encounter, the movement into the reconnaissance stage is stimulated by the practitioner's summary statement of the immediate objectives of the initial session. A few clients may query or challenge this statement, particularly if it runs counter to their expectations, and the therapist must respond to these objections. Where the client's negative feelings about being under duress or pressure to enter therapy are strong, discussing them adequately can require some time, and the therapist may need to schedule another interview to complete the tasks of the engagement process.

TYPICAL BEGINNINGS. Most clients, however, simply launch into an exposition of the difficulties in life that are currently troubling them. The manner and content of this beginning description vary, of course, from one person to another, along any number of dimensions. The series of initial interviews presented in Davenloo's (1978) *Short-Term Dynamic Psychotherapy* run the gamut of these differing presentations of self. These and other examples drawn from practice will offer illustrations.

Some people immediately begin to talk about themselves and the particularly bothersome emotions they are experiencing:

"Well the last few months I've been very depressed and I started to have tantrums because I felt so burdened mentally." (p. 201)*

Others speak of impelling actions:

"I just want to run away from everything, just leave the city, and go by myself." (p. 100)

The beginning focus may be terse and factual:

"The only thing that bothers me is that I've always got headaches and pains in my head." (pp. 277–278)

Some individuals are vague and apparently unfocused:

"I feel lost; I feel like I don't have a center. I feel out of touch with myself." (p. 247)

Or the client's initial expression of difficulty may touch on an important aspect of social functioning:

"I've been having this fear of being out on the street, and then it developed into being afraid of being at work—not all the time, just some days." (p. 225)

Hoyt's client, Sue—described earlier in this chapter—expresses both anguish and self-deprecation:

"I can't do anything right, at least that's what Jim says, and he took the kids . . ." (Hoyt, 1993, p. 242)

Some prospective clients I have seen in my own practice place their entire emphasis on the actions of other people:

"My husband's drinking himself to death and he won't do a damn thing about it."

In other instances there may be little the individual seemingly wants for himself as he grudgingly approaches counseling:

---

* With the exception of the illustration taken from Hoyt (1993), the page numbers after client statements refer to quotations from the Davenloo (1978) interview transcripts. The last two examples are drawn from my own clinical practice.

"They said I had to come here or I was going to get fired from my job."

Whatever direction the client's beginning thrust into problem expression may take, the practitioner's concern during this early phase largely centers on the question, "Who is this person and what is troublesome at present in his or her life?" Three major therapist activities predominate and intermingle throughout the reconnaissance.

EMPATHIC RESPONSE. First, the therapist must look for every opportunity to respond empathically to the prospective client's immediate emotions. As I have previously noted, this should be done in the plainest of language, avoiding technical terms and attempting to respond to the full intensity of the feelings that the client directly or indirectly is expressing.

Practitioners sometimes hesitate to recognize the depth of emotion the client is experiencing and consequently detract from this powerful relationship bond. Such hesitation is often rationalized on the grounds that some clients are "not ready" to have their emotions explicitly recognized, or that a forthright acknowledgment of turmoil or despair could somehow worsen their situation. Empathic response, as I noted earlier, attempts to recognize the emotions clients are plainly expressing or that are clearly part of the experience they are undergoing. There is unlikely to be any harm in directly acknowledging, for example, that the client who is directly expressing anger is angry, or in suggesting that someone who is undergoing a serious illness or a divorce may be anxious and frightened. Empathic response is not an attempt to probe into the client or to *interpret* his or her emotions, but, most fundamentally, a persistent attempt to establish a human connection with the client's pain or dissatisfaction with life.

ENCOURAGING PROBLEM IDENTIFICATION. Second, the process of problem identification has begun in a significant way in this early phase of contact, and the helper must carefully attend to the client's perspective on this central issue. The essential question is very simple: What major problems in living is this person experiencing at this moment?

As the client tells his or her story, the aspects of life that are most dissatisfying will begin to unfold. With many people this expression of difficulty does not suggest an individual ready to take an active and perceptive role in the process of change. Feelings of helplessness or doubt, projection onto others or self-blame may permeate the client's account. The clinician, however, makes little effort at this point to explore any problem in depth or to challenge the client's perceptions. In large part the clinician's concern is to encourage clients to range across their current life in an effort to describe its most troubling aspects.

Although the therapist is not inactive at this stage of the interview, most of his or her participation consists of supportive interjections and empathic responses, combined with the occasional clarifying question or summary. This phase is critical for relationship building through attentiveness and empathic response, and the therapist must eschew the temptation to take over and ask a series of orienting questions about the specifics of the client's emerging problems; these details can always be ascertained later.

It can be helpful, during the reconnaissance, for the therapist to make a brief written list of the major areas of concern as the client describes them. This should simply summarize each problem ("You're concerned about your child's bedwetting" or "You and your husband have a lot of difficulty in agreeing about how to discipline your children"), and the list, as it is composed, should be frequently shared with the client for revision and amplification. Paramount throughout this process is the brief therapist's firm belief that clients are well able to identify their real problems in life, however vague, scattered, or confused they may be in expressing them (Budman & Gurman, 1988).

AROUSING HOPE. Finally, the therapist must consciously make some beginning efforts to build hope in order to provide some foundation for the problem negotiation and contracting that will take place in later stages of the first session. During the reconnaissance, only the most tentative ventures can be made in this vital area, but they must be attempted, even while the major tasks in this stage still remain those of problem identification and relationship building.

The arousal of hope was discussed in the preceding chapter as one of the primary goals of the inital interview. Few clinicians would disagree with this emphasis, but some perplexing questions arise. How can one make what is said in an effort to elicit hope during the engagement process sound like more than a pious desire or an empty piece of rhetoric? What specific activities on the part of the therapist can be employed to build the sort of positive expectation in the client that will enhance engagement and, further, form a beginning basis for change?

A number of strategies and techniques designed to elicit hopefulness, either at this stage of the session or later, were suggested earlier in this chapter. Thus, redefinitions are utilized to suggest a more positive outlook toward perceived difficulties, or normalizing strategies are employed to convey to clients that a particular problem is not uncommon or unique to them. At the same time, the clinician does not try to promote an unrealistically positive atmosphere. Some edge of anxiety or dissatisfaction can be a useful motivation for seeking change.

Perhaps the single most helpful technique I have used during the reconnaissance stage entails the clinician listening carefully for any indication on the client's part that the difficulties being described are not what she or he wants from life. Whatever the intensity of negative emotion or negative belief being expressed, is the client conveying something about attempts, however feeble or misdirected, to cope with these forces? Such tentative practitioner efforts at enhancing hope can often be combined with empathic response—"You sound terribly discouraged about managing these problems with your daughter, but I get the idea that you don't want your life together to go on like this." In effect, the therapist's intervention is directed toward mobilizing the client's sense of self-efficacy (Bandura, 1986) through these preliminary suggestions that the immediate dilemma has a solution other than resignation or despair.

THE DETAILED INQUIRY

In many initial interviews, the movement from the reconnaissance phase into the detailed inquiry may be almost imperceptible. Its overall goal is to increase the amount of information available to both clinician and client. At this point in the interview, therefore, the clinician makes a deliberate effort to expand upon the nature and degree of the difficulties in living that the client has described. As Sullivan

(1954) points out, much of the detailed inquiry "is a matter of improving upon earlier approximations of understanding" (p. 90) and at times may involve a radical change in the impressions the clinician initially obtained. The helper may also inquire about important relationships or potential problem areas that the client's previous description has not covered.

In initiating short-term treatment, it is toward the end of this stage that the therapist begins the important process of negotiation that will determine the prospective focus and goals of treatment. During this part of the detailed inquiry, the client learns more specifically about the potential nature of the helping process. In some instances, clients may have proven so vague in description, or their expressed problems may be so complicated, that the movement into the detailed inquiry represents a turning point, where the therapist will need to decide whether to work toward a second "initial" interview, in order to complete all necessary engagement tasks.

A DUAL FOCUS. In essence, then, the two essential tasks for client and helper during the detailed inquiry are *clarification* and *negotiation*. The problems the client has identified during the preceding conversation need to be examined in greater detail, and client and therapist must engage in negotiating whether they will work together on one or two of these problems in an ongoing therapeutic relationship.

The helper should not feel compelled to examine each of the client's problems in their complete complexity, but must *selectively* explore. Once again, a deliberate process of simplification is apparent. The objective of the detailed inquiry stage is to fill in gaps and clarify aspects of the client's earlier presentation that have puzzled the clinician and that are most relevant to forming an ongoing working relationship.

HERE-AND-NOW EMPHASIS. Most of this exploration is sharply focused on the client's current relationships and living situation. Historical material is seldom gathered in depth unless it has an immediate relevance to the problems in living being discussed. Thus, with Mr. Jurecko and Mrs. Lorenson (see Chapter 3), practically all of the initial exploration concentrated on their current life and their problems of major concern. Limiting exploration so drastically may require a leap of faith for the therapist inexperienced in brief treatment, since conventional training has tended to emphasize a detailed exploration of almost every facet of the potential client's past and current life. Indeed, there was an era when all practitioners were taught to spend six to eight interviews in assessment and relationship-building activities—a period of time equivalent to the totality of many brief therapy encounters (to say nothing of its equivalence to the length of time the typical client remains in therapy [Garfield, 1989]).

The therapist may find it useful to follow a formal schedule of inquiry during this phase, asking the client about such areas as job, education, financial circumstances, social relationships, family, and marriage. Aspects of each of these dimensions of living may have been touched on earlier but may still require clarification. Others may not have been mentioned, and in these instances the practitioner will conduct a brief probe in order to elicit needed information. The tendency of the short-term therapist is to inquire directly about such possibly relevant connections, but to accept the client's assessment concerning whether a given area is problematic or nonproblematic. An extensive exploration is not attempted unless the therapist has urgent reason to believe this is necessary.

PRIORITIZING PROBLEMS. Perhaps even more important than the selective expansion on life difficulties is the question of problem priority. If a client is contending with four or five problems, which is the most meaningful? Which problem does the client most wish to solve? Therapists can place different values on living than their clients, and it is best to ask the client specifically for such an assessment.

> In a case I supervised, for example, the clinician was surprised to find that a young adult woman placed greater emphasis on working out some moderately distressing difficulties in her immediate social relationships than on grappling with a troublesome relationship with her mother. Since the two areas were only peripherally connected (theoretical views to the contrary), progress on the first area was quite feasible even while the other conflict remained unchanged.

In general, the practitioner in brief treatment is well advised to respect the client's wishes in matters of problem priority unless there is a strongly compelling reason to suggest shifting to another focus. The predictive powers of most of our available theoretical frameworks are not sufficient to justify this sort of shift except in a minority of cases.

The actual mechanics of prioritizing problems can be managed fairly easily if the helper has been tracking the client's difficulties by formulating a written list. I often ask the client to read through this list, reflect on the impact of each problem area, and numerically rate the problems from most to least pressing. This is usually an appropriate time to offer some explanatory structuring to the effect that the best problem solving takes place when one selects a single, important problem and concentrates on its resolution.

CLIENT REQUESTS. However, whatever the clinician may be thinking about the problems the client is experiencing or the potential help that therapeutic intervention might offer, it is necessary to elicit the client's views. The work of Arnold Lazare and his colleagues (1972; Lazare, Eisenthal, & Wasserman, 1975; Lazare, Eisenthal, Wasserman, & Harford, 1975) offers a number of empirically grounded guidelines for managing this important aspect of the initial interview. They point out that the concept of the patient or client's *request* has been confused with the related but different notion of *expectation*:

> Expectations ... represent the *anticipation* of roles, techniques, duration of treatment, and outcome. These expectations may be based on wishes, fears, or even stories from friends. Requests, on the other hand, represent hopes or desires. (Lazare et al., 1972, p. 873, italics in original)

Thus, in contrast to his or her expectation of what counseling will be like or how the therapist will act, the request represents what the client wants to gain from therapy. For example, a prospective client may *expect* that her difficulties will be met with scepticism or even blame from the unknown practitioner whom she is about to meet. On the other hand, her *request* (or hope) might be that she be given some useful advice on how to deal with her problems or an opportunity to release the pent-up feelings they have engendered.

Expectation and request may coincide or may be dramatically different. Where the request is not specifically elicited from the client, there is danger that the goals and process of treatment, if selected entirely by the therapist, will lead to a lack of cooperation from the client, or even premature dropout. The Lazare group's work has substantiated the prevalence of misunderstanding and confusion between clinician and client when the request is not directly obtained, and in relation to this task the group has identified fourteen specific categories into which client requests commonly fall (Lazare et al., 1972). These can be grouped into four major areas:

1. *Be a supportive person.* The requests here are for control, reality contact, succorance, institutional support, confession, ventilation, and advice. The researchers carefully differentiate each of these requests and offer some cogent clinical guidelines on the quality and quantity of therapist activity each requires.

2. *Be a psychotherapist.* Within this overall category, the individual may be requesting clarification about pressing internal conflicts or, more specifically, help with immediate personal and interpersonal change. Further research on client requests (Burgoyne et al., 1979) has found that low socioeconomic clients often make such requests but frequently combine them with requests in other categories. It also found that because of the prevailing mythology that people in the low socioeconomic group desire only concrete services or direct advice, clinicians have real difficulty in distinguishing their more therapeutic requests and responding appropriately.

3. *Be an authority figure.* Here the potential client is hoping to enlist the organizational, administrative, or social intervention powers of the helping person in relation to the problems being experienced. The client may believe, quite legitimately, that some specific service at the helper's command can offer relief. For example, the individual may envisage the clinician as a potential advocate in dealing with another agency or institution, or may wish to obtain a concrete resource that the practitioner controls. Helpers of all disciplines should be careful not to neglect or deprecate such intervention.

4. *Miscellaneous requests.* These are usually concerned with direction or referral to a more appropriate helping source (Lazare calls this "community triage"). For a small but significant group, literally *nothing* is desired; individuals in this group usually have been pressured or compelled to ask for help.

SOLICITING THE REQUEST. Lazare, Eisenthal, and Wasserman (1975) suggest that the request be elicited about midway through the initial interview. This allows enough time for rapport to develop, yet leaves sufficient leeway for client and therapist to negotiate, if the request is innappropriate. They offer some specific guidelines:

> We have been most successful in eliciting the patient request by asking, "How do you hope (or wish) I (or the clinic) can help?" The questions "What do you want?" or "What do you expect?" should be avoided as they are likely to be perceived as confrontation. The words "wish" or "hope," in contrast, give the patient permission to state requests he does not necessarily expect will be granted.... When the request has finally been stated and elaborated, it is important that the clinician acknowledge that he has heard and understood the request. Otherwise, the patient may wonder whether the clinician heard the request, was offended by it, or didn't believe it worthy of a response. (p. 554)

REACHING A CONTRACT. Understanding the client's request plays an important role in the process of contracting. The goal of contracting is for the client and therapist to arrive at an open decision whether to work together, in a clearly understood way, on a particular client problem. The contracting process, in this third stage of the initial interview, becomes a matter of reconciling client request and therapist judgment in relation to how to work on the problem area that has been selected for attention. If client request and clinical judgment are reasonably close, arriving at a contract is relatively straightforward. If there are discrepancies, however, negotiation must take place. It is then up to the therapist to explain, for example, how it might be more beneficial to the client to learn how to be assertive than merely to ventilate the feelings aroused by humiliating social relationships.

A clear agreement to work together on a specific problem is one of the hallmarks of professional helping and is an essential legitimization of the change strategies the therapist may employ at later stages of the helping process. Asking clients to disclose intimate aspects of their life, requesting task performance, confronting discrepancies between client verbalization and behavior, and so on, are only justifiable in the context of such an agreement.

EXTENDING THE ENGAGEMENT PROCESS. A final issue deserves some consideration. As the detailed inquiry begins, the therapist is faced with the decision about whether the goals of the initial interview can be met within a single session. Two major factors may necessitate extending the engagement process for another interview or two:

1. Certain clients, for a variety of reasons, have great difficulty in moving beyond vague, general statements of their life problems. Others, like Mr. Faber (described in Chapter 3), supply a wealth of often extraneous detail about their life circumstances. In either of these broad categories, so much time is consumed in the first session around problem identification that a further session is needed to properly manage the important considerations relating to the contract and, of course, time-limits and task assignment.

2. A number of our potential clients enter the first session under a greater or lesser degree of duress. These are not just those ordered into psychotherapy by the legal system, but many are individuals whose spouses, parents, teachers, or bosses have placed pressure on them to seek help. Additional time may be required within the engagement process to assist such clients in expressing their ambivalent feelings about entering therapy in this way and, most important, identifying the problems the *client* wants to work on, which may be quite different from those stipulated by the referring source.

In such instances the clinician may decide to devote the remainder of the interview to problem exploration or to attempts to enhance the relationship, contracting for a further session to conclude the usual goals of the first interview.*

INTERRUPTION OR TERMINATION

In the final stage of the initial interview, the therapist plays an active role in bringing the interview to a conclusion. This may represent an actual end of contact between helper and client or an interruption in

---

* Some clinicians contract for four to six interviews to explore the client's difficulties or ambivalent motivation. My preference is to avoid the vagueness or indecision this can sometimes foster by contracting for only a single further session. This strategy is an attempt to maintain the pressures of an explicit time limit and, in addition, to continue a concentrated focus on specific problem identification.

a process that will resume again. In either case, there are certain actions that the therapist can take that will either consolidate the termination or enhance the probability of the client's return if further contact is planned.

If the participants have arrived at a problem focus and have contracted to work together, the therapist must set a time limit and define an initial task (along with any other unsettled matters such as next appointment time or fee). Where a further interview has been negotiated in order to complete the engagment process, these tasks can usually be deferred to the next session. On the other hand, the initial interview may represent a termination of contact with the client since it may not have been possible to negotiate a viable helping contract or even a further session. The nuances of terminating, where the therapist has been deliberately working within the framework of single-session psychotherapy (Bloom, 1992; Talmon, 1990), will be discussed in the final chapter of this volume.

LIMITING TIME. Setting time limits merits further discussion. Practitioners unfamiliar with short-term intervention seem to have the notion that the setting of time limits is an exact science. Experienced brief therapists, on the other hand, are exasperatingly casual about this process and sometimes almost inarticulate about why, for instance, ten sessions were stipulated with a certain client rather than eight or twelve. Some aspects of the concept of time limits are quite clear, however. The basic position of most brief therapists is that time limits should be of a foreseeable length and should be clearly and confidently explained to the client during the one or two interviews of the engagement process (Sledge et al., 1990).

Many of the nuances of time management are examined in Michael Hoyt's (1990) perceptive essay, "On Time in Brief Therapy," a work that the serious student of brief psychotherapy will find highly instructive. Suffice it to say, in this discussion, that in clinical practice the determination of time limits can arise from many considerations. In some cases a research project (Fisher, 1980, 1984; Reid & Shyne, 1969) or simply an accustomed way of working (Mann, 1973) determines that every case will be offered a set number of interviews. Other therapists follow an agency policy that predetermines the number of sessions (Jacobson, 1965: Leventhal & Weinberger, 1975). Certain highly structured change procedures—

sexual therapy (Masters & Johnson, 1970) or interpersonal psychotherapy for depression (Cornes, 1990), for example—stipulate an expected number of interviews.

What all these disparate time durations suggest is that the exact length of time that is prescribed is less important than the therapist's willingness to set explicit time limits and confidence in working within them. In my own clinical practice, I am comfortable in contracting for six to eight sessions with the majority of the individual and couple problems that I see. This is done with the awareness that I can recontract for further sessions if such an extension becomes necessary. There is seldom any difficulty in managing the recontracting. In cases where serious depression is evident, or in couple therapy with sexual dysfunction, I will contract for twelve to fourteen sessions, since this is the optimum duration suggested by the clinical research for these problem areas.

Brief therapists are usually quite direct and matter-of-fact in stipulating time limits to their clients and often use this as a means of embedding a hopeful message: "I think that we should work together for no longer than ten sessions, and this should be enough to help you feel much more capable in handling your children." Another important dynamic, as I noted in the previous chapter, is the fact that the therapist does not negotiate the length of the contract with the client, but assumes this responsibility as a function of her or his professional role. Negotiating the time limit could suggest that the therapist is simply being solicitous about not inconveniencing the client. Such inappropriate deferral could tend to weaken the hope and confidence that firm time setting can potentially inspire.

ASSIGNING A TASK. Similarly, task assignment appears to be a highly subjective matter in many respects: therapists inexperienced in brief therapy seek exact guidelines, and seasoned practitioners tend to be rather casual. Like time limits, moreover, task assignment appears to be greatly influenced by such therapist factors as firmness, confidence, and the need to present the client with a plausible rationale for action. Most early tasks are attempts to gain additional information about the nature and degree of the client's problems or, in a very minor way, serve as a stimulus toward activity. There is no reason that either of these rationales cannot be explained to the client, and this is usually sufficient structuring to promote client cooperation in early task performance. Despite reports in the clinical literature in which the therapist immediately devises an ingenious task sufficient to almost magically propel the client into adequate functioning, the bulk of tasks in actual practice are quite pedestrian.

TERMINATION ISSUES. Finally as Sullivan (1954) notes, the initial interview may represent a termination of contact with the client. For some, a referral to a more appropriate helping source may be needed. With others, it may not have been possible to work out a feasible contract. In either case, the practitioner has an obligation, I believe, to try to pull together the conclusions that have been reached in the session.

Reviewing with the client the reasons that referral elsewhere has been suggested, and the benefits the client may gain from this, can significantly enhance the possibility of follow-through. Weisman (1976) outlines an even more active technology for referral, which he calls "linkage," on the grounds that data from empirical studies (Ryan, 1969) indicate that barely one out of four referred clients actually reaches the other helping source.

A similar review can be carried out where the therapist and client have decided not to continue further interviews. This is often in the form of a summary of the practitioner's understanding of the client's difficulties and, where appropriate, a frank recognition of the reasons the client does not want (or need) continued professional help.

6

Behavior Enactment Methods

> The thing is recovered from familiarity by means of an
> exercise in familiarity.
>
> —Walker Percy, *The Message in the Bottle*

Although seemingly dissimilar in theoretical orientation and therapeutic goals, behavior therapy and psychodrama have both made frequent use of deliberate enactments of real-life events—past, present,
and future—as a vehicle for learning and change. Whether we call
such dramatized vignettes "simulations," "role-plays," or "behavior
rehearsal," their essential commonality, I believe, is the attempt to
change the therapeutic situation from a conversation of a peculiar
sort, an interview, into a miniature replication of a fragment of the
client's life.

Behavior enactment and rehearsal methods offer the clinician a
powerful medium for change, with the potentiality to move beyond
exclusively verbal efforts to describe problematic or conflicted life situations into a visual or physical dimension. The attempt to portray the
client's actual or anticipated behavior in any troublesome encounter
can stimulate a novel awareness of inhibiting attitudes or beliefs
(Naar, 1990). Even though the simulation itself has certain limitations,
it can reveal the arousal of dysfunctional emotion or display deficits in
life skills more vividly than verbal discussion alone can. In effect,
enactments serve as a vehicle to bring reality into the therapy session,
just as tasks (which I will consider in the following chapter) serve as a
means of returning therapeutic learnings into the client's life.

Clinical writers from the most diverse theoretical backgrounds have contributed to this viewpoint. Thus, such family therapists as Minuchin and his colleagues (1974, 1978, 1981) have contended that it is futile even to attempt to understand the patterned, often ritualized dance of the family through verbal descriptions, which, at best, are secondhand. From an entirely different theoretical orientation, gestalt therapists (Fodor, 1987; Hatcher & Himelstein, 1976) have devised any number of ingenious therapeutic permutations (the "empty-chair" technique, or enactive awareness exercises, for example) intended to transport the individual beyond the boundaries of ordinary experience into realms where the unexpected may emerge or where hidden aspects of the self can be viewed.

Behavioral therapists (Bandura, 1977b, 1986) have become almost contemptuous, at times, of the efficacy of "talk therapy" to influence the course of human thoughts, behavior, and emotions and have strongly advocated the employment of direct observation and performance methods. Finally, J. L. Moreno's (1959) pioneering development of the enactive techniques of psychodrama has contributed a therapeutic methodology that, as Naar (1990) demonstrates, has a ready application in brief psychotherapy.

Paul Wachtel (1977), in his integrative work on therapeutic practice, *Psychoanalysis and Behavior Therapy*, points out the need for methods of enabling the client to transfer the learnings of therapy into the outside world:

> Without explicit efforts to bridge the gap between the nurturant therapy relationship and the more demanding world outside, there is a good chance that the patient will learn to discriminate and act one way with the therapist and another with everyone else. The therapist then has the conviction—correct as far as his (in-session) direct experience of the patient is concerned—that the patient has become freer, more open, more healthy and genuine; yet in the patient's day-to-day living, change is far less extensive. (p. 232)

Wachtel suggests that for many clients, change can take place more rapidly if there is an opportunity, through enactments of various kinds, to build new relationship patterns. The very difficulties of the troubled or inhibited person may have "limited the possibility of his observing and assimilating how people behave in various situations" (p. 233). Even though the individual, in a broad sense, "knows" what to do, this knowledge may not be particularly usable under the real demands of living. As Wachtel comments, "The patient may be able to describe what is called for, but not to put it into practice" (p. 233).

In his discussion of role-playing and rehearsal methods, Wachtel emphasizes their utility, not only in building social and interpersonal skills but as an integral part of the assessment process:

> Role-playing procedures are also of value in giving the therapist a picture of the patient's style in a way which no amount of description of the "So then I said that I didn't like what he was doing" variety can convey. . . . One discovers something in seeing the patient actually play out just what he said and how he said it that is masked in the patient's reporting of the event. (p. 234)

Some of the reluctance of clients to role-play comes from this very fear of exposing themselves to a scrutiny that might have been easily avoided by a purely descriptive statement. Although he cautions the helper against absolutely insisting on the client's role playing, Wachtel also points out how the client, though initially hesitant, may benefit from an enhanced understanding of self in real-life interaction, even from a feared enactment. He also stresses that the role reversal that takes place in some types of simulation can frequently build client awareness of the other person's feelings or of the client's own impact on his interpersonal world. Wachtel comments:

> When the therapist models the way the patient *has* acted, the patient can be helped to understand his impact on the other person; when the therapist models how the patient *might* act, the patient may gain some insight into himself, into what he is on the verge of feeling inclined to do. (p. 237, italics in original)

Corsini's (1966) discussion of role-playing techniques in psychotherapy is one of the most complete accounts of this medium of change. He points our that role-playing methods are "generally based on the inductive principle; one learns complex matters best from unit behaviors which lead to generalization" (p. 33).

Three major theoretical constructs support the utilization of role playing or (in the terminology employed in this book) behavior enactment:

1. *Simultaneity*. In Corsini's view the greatest theoretical advantage of role playing is its capacity to elicit the full range of cognitive, affective, and behavioral elements contained in a problematic situation. Not only can significant aspects of thinking, feeling, and acting be concurrently exhibited and experienced in the enactment, but, as Corsini points out, "due to the summating effects of each on the other, they tend to be heightened—exaggerated—forced to fuller limits" (p. 13).

2. *Spontaneity*. Corsini defines spontaneity as "natural, rapid, unforced, self-generated behavior in new situations" (p. 13) and suggests that enactment methods can tap this potential reservoir within the individual. He acknowledges that although it would undoubtedly be better if the client could simply attempt new behaviors in real life, this is often unlikely. Behavior rehearsal offers a protected opportunity for unexpected capacities to emerge. At the same time, the client's self-protective tendencies, so often exhibited through censored or prevaricating verbal description, are less likely to be operative.

3. *Veridicality*. Corsini compares role-playing experiences to the simulated training apparatuses employed in airplane pilot instruction. Although the participant knows that the apparatus, or the enactment, is not real, it can assume a subjective or psychological reality. Much of this depends on the attitude of the clinician, who must convey a sense of confidence that, within understandable limits, behavior rehearsal can capture many of the nuances of real life. At the same time, the helper should be careful not to oversell the method, but should clearly recognize its boundaries.

BEHAVIOR ENACTMENT IN ACTION

In clinical practice it is not at all uncommon for the therapeutic process to become bogged down, particularly as clients attempt to grapple with highly emotional aspects of their lives. In short-term treatment, where the pressures of time are continually present, therapist and client need ways of surmounting such barriers, and enactment can offer such a tool.

Following the break-up of her marriage, a forty-year-old woman sought help with a pervasive and lingering depression. Conventional exploration of feelings and task assignments aimed at restoring social contact and functioning were only minimally helpful.

Since the helping process seemed at an impasse, she was asked to visualize herself in an imaginary dialogue with her ex-husband in which she could talk to him in any manner that might be helpful to her.

In a faltering, hesitant voice, she began to speak to him of her anger and hurt about the divorce but stopped, after a few phrases, visibly trembling. Several repetitions of this scene clearly demonstrated, to both her and the therapist, the intensity of her feelings of loss and, most importantly, how frightened she was to express these feelings, even in an imagined encounter.

The powerful, self-directed emotion dislodged even in an apparent simulation became a central theme in subsequent working through of her grief.

There are many helping situations in which behavioral enactment can give both therapist and client an opportunity to discover the presence of behavioral or skill deficits. Such gaps in social facility can be easily obscured in purely verbal description, which frequently emphasizes the client's emotional reaction to life events instead of accurately portraying the literal interaction.

For example, a nineteen-year-old part-time college student described a series of failures in obtaining dates with girls and saw much of his dissatisfaction with himself as related to these difficulties. Enactments of his approach to beginning a casual conversation with a young woman—far short, of course, of his goal of dating—revealed extreme difficulty with such basic behaviors as eye contact and initial small talk, and the need for intensive social skill training became apparent.

In other instances it may be that the client's facility with language is simply not sufficient to capture the subleties of tone, gesture, or stance that can significantly qualify social relationships. Enactment allows the client to demonstrate aspects of self that words alone could not convey.

Similarly, behavior that has become repetitive or habitual may be omitted from any verbal description, not as the result of a deliberate act of censorship, but because of its very everydayness—its practiced familiarity. In such cases the behavior enactment, in a deliberate act of simplification, seeks to reveal the importance of the mundane.

In a like vein, the therapist can utilize a behavioral demonstration to portray alternative approaches to an apparent dilemma or to illustrate elements of selected social skills, with an economy and impact far superior to ordinary suggestion and advice. The client then can imitate such demonstrations, receiving necessary guidance and encouragement in an immediate way that pushes beyond the confines of language.

Both therapist and client may be reluctant to use this unfamiliar dimension of change. We are most comfortable with conversation, and there is no doubt that the acquisition of language, the ability to express oneself through words, represents one of the most distinctive milestones of human development. Yet Hamlet, in a bright moment of candor disguised as madness, denounced it all as "words, words, words," and from time to time therapists also have become disenchanted with this medium of human interchange. Behavior enactments, in their varied forms, offer an alternative.

PHASES OF BEHAVIORAL ENACTMENT

Behavior enactment and rehearsal methods constitute a readily available means of bridging the gap between words and action, yet involve an approach that can be adapted to a wide range of therapeutic orientations and styles without radically altering their character. The major requirement in utilizing this approach is that the helper must be comfortable in entering a visual and physical dimension and, further, must be able to prepare the client for this same transition.

The process of behavior enactment can be conceptualized as containing three potential phases, and the therapist may employ one or all of these phases. In the first phase, the *enactment* proper, the client is asked to portray how a specific problematic situation is presently managed. In the second phase, *modeling*, the therapist demonstrates an alternative method of coping with the same situation. Finally, in the third phase, *practice* (or rehearsal), the client attempts the same situation again, but endeavors to incorporate aspects of the therapist's prior demonstration. After each phase the clinician and client discuss the impact of the enactment, and wherever the client has attempted new responses, the helper must offer consistent reinforcement, assessment, and feedback on these efforts. Similarly, the client must be encouraged to realistically evaluate her or his own level of performance.

In each of the phases, of course, the client and the therapist role-play, or simulate, the participants in the selected situation. Both therapist and client may find that moving into this new dimension can initially evoke considerable discomfort and awkwardness. There is also an implicit challenge in asking people to demonstrate their actions. "Show me" has a much more confrontational quality than "Tell me," and therapists often are wary of confrontation, even in minor forms. Similarly, troubled clients may prefer to create a fabric of words around their concerns rather than expose themselves to the uncertain risks of portrayal.

Goldfried and Davison (1976) discuss behavior rehearsal in their book *Clinical Behavior Therapy* and offer many useful suggestions on its application. They especially emphasize the need to prepare the client for behavioral rehearsal, and they identify three major therapeutic tasks during this transition:

1. *Client acceptance of the need to develop new behaviors.* Goldfried and Davison (1976) point out that "even though it may be fairly clear that the client's problems stem from a deficiency in certain social skills, the client himself may not be construing his difficulties along these lines" (p, 139). Clients, for example, may see the attitudes or behaviors of others as the sole cause of their difficulties or may ascribe their problems to bad luck or fate. In such extreme instances no therapeutic approach has much chance of success. Fortunately, many clients tend to be uneasily balanced between these unworkable polarities.

Meichenbaum (1975) has similarly stressed the need for client and helper to develop a "common conceptualization" of the goals of therapeutic intervention. In the active context of brief treatment, the therapist must be able to provide clients with a sufficiently hopeful rationale for even attempting to change themselves. Much of the engagement process during the initial interview is aimed at directly eliciting this sort of motivation and shared viewpoint.

2. *Explaining the relevance of behavior rehearsal.* Although clients may accept the position that new responses must be developed, they

may have little notion how this can be done. Goldfried and Davison (1976) suggest that the helper begin by explaining behavior rehearsal in rather general outline, providing more specific detail only when it is apparent that the client is interested in attempting the approach. They offer a transcript of a clinical interview (pp. 139–141) that merits close scrutiny because the practitioner, through careful redefinition of the client's initial viewpoint and clear explanation of rehearsal procedures, builds a persuasive case for using enactment. This does not mean that one has to be excessively cautious in introducing behavior rehearsal, but the tendency to oversell the approach should be avoided. The practitioner who advocates enactment at the first hint of a behavioral deficit is more likely to stir up client resistance than to elicit cooperation.

3. *Allaying client awkwardness about behavior enactment.* Finally, Goldfried and Davison (1976) note that "some clients react negatively to behavior rehearsal when it is described to them, partly because they feel this technique would not help them *really* change, and partly because they feel generally awkward about playacting" (p. 139). They suggest that the gradual introduction of enactment procedures helps to diminish this sense of apprehension. On the other hand, I have often found it helpful to manage the client's potential uneasiness by recognizing this uneasiness in the preliminary explanation. Rather than wait for the client to express uncertainty or discomfort, the therapist can incorporate this in his structuring—"You'll find some of this awkward and artificial as we begin, but that will improve as you become more comfortable with the process." In other words, the client's discomfort is redefined as normal and understandable even before it is mentioned, but the possibility of moving beyond this shaky beginning is confidently predicted.

There are many variations possible in employing behavior enactment. Issues in timing, combining, and managing each phase of it will be discussed and illustrated throughout this chapter. Like any helping intervention, behavior enactment must be applied with sensitivity to the unique characteristics and situation of each client. I will discuss each of the phases of behavior enactment in some detail, attempting to identify the essential characteristics of each. Clinical examples will be presented at a number of points to illustrate the way in which enactment can be introduced to the client, operationalized in different areas of a helping practice, and connected to the goal of positive therapeutic change.

The Enactment Phase

Therapists are all too familiar with the client who repeatedly describes difficult, even devastating encounters occurring in daily life but appears to have little notion of how to move beyond this level of discourse. Other clients are vague or inarticulate about the problems they are experiencing with family, friends, or associates beyond conveying that these relationships are dissatisfying or frustrating. In other instances, clients may appear to be highly perceptive about the beliefs or emotions that are impeding their response, yet this apparent awareness does little to affect change. Something vital is missing, and helper and client alike have become trapped within the limitations of language.

In each of these instances the helping process is effectively stalled. The therapist may have a number of hypotheses about what is affecting the client's ability to cope with the problematic issue, but any efforts to determine such factors will be blunted by the paucity of description offered and the inability of conversation, in its conventional verbal form, to convey the essential elements at play in human relationships. An example from practice will illustrate:

> Mrs. Franz saw herself as trapped, after more than twenty years of marriage, in a relationship with a husband whom she perceived as distant and unemotional. She saw him as consistently blocking all her attempts to improve the relationship and to deal with many concrete matters connected with the daily management of the household and the children. With considerable bitterness, she described how impossible it had been, over many years, to obtain his agreement to renovate and redecorate their living room, despite adequate financial ability to do so. The frustration and futility of any effort in this specific area symbolized to her the essential—and unchangeable—stinginess and lack of caring of her husband.

At a descriptive level the impasse was considerable: as long as Mrs. Franz perceived her husband in this light, there was little reason for her to believe that anything other than bitterness and frustration could transpire between them. This, of course, was further compounded by the refusal of Mr. Franz to involve himself in counseling, implicitly confirming his wife's view of his obstinate and ungiving nature. Practically speaking, this also deprived the therapist of any opportunity to directly observe and intervene in their relationship.

It is at a point such as this—a seemingly unsolvable dilemma—that a shift into behavior enactment can be particularly illuminating. Asking Mrs. Franz to demonstrate, within the confines of a simulated role-play with the therapist, how she might initiate a discussion with her husband about redecorating the living room transformed the situation from one of apparent hopelessness into a very different dimension. New possibilities quickly became evident.

> Like many clients, Mrs. Franz was reluctant and awkward about actually demonstrating her approach to her husband. After some mild insistence by the therapist and explanation of how the enactment might offer important clues, she attempted the vignette. Several repetitions of the scene were needed before Mrs. Franz could agree that she (and the therapist in the role of husband) were enacting a typical version of the situation.
>
> Almost immediately apparent in the enactment was the profoundly negative manner in which Mrs. Franz approached her husband. Her tone of voice, bodily posture, and gestures all conveyed that she expected refusal and indeed was anxious to get the matter over with, whatever the outcome, as quickly as possible. The verbal content of her request was also negatively phrased—"I don't suppose you want to do anything about the living room?"—and she gave up her effort almost immediately in response to the slightest indication of her husband's disinterest.
>
> Playing the part of the husband, the therapist was struck by the sense of power that he experienced in relation to Mrs. Franz as he noted how easy it was to fend her off, with hardly more than a shrug of indifference.

This brief example illustrates how the helping process must penetrate beyond the conventional in a meaningful way if movement is to occur. Human experience takes place in several dimensions, each of which, alone or in interaction, is capable of assuming prepotency in determining an individual's life choices. Beliefs can become fixed or, as Albert Ellis (1962) has argued, can assume irrational proportions, effectively blocking action or arousing inhibiting affect. Emotions, however aroused, can also pervade our being, with crippling impact on many aspects of functioning. Finally, the behavioral repertoire itself may be limited, either through a lack of requisite learning or through the habituating effect of repeated interactions, and consequently may offer the individual little sense of self-efficacy (Bandura, 1977a, 1977b) or any realistic opportunity for mastery (Liberman, 1978).

In order to move into behavior enactment, an identifiable interpersonal situation must be isolated that is problematic in some way for the client. The difficulties may be idiosyncratic to a particular relationship. Mrs. Franz was adequately functional in other relationships, and enactments therefore concentrated on her difficulties in the marital system.

On the other hand, the identified problem may be representative of a wider class of situations in which the client experiences discomfort or conflict. An initial behavior enactment may be a prelude to the extensive employment of this process of therapeutic change, as in assertion or communication training (Lange & Jakubowski, 1976; Wells & Figurel, 1979).

With some clients, only the enactment phase will be used, and the observations that can be made from this sequence will be sufficient to stimulate awareness of facets of approach or response, within the target relationship, that need to be altered. Discussion of alternative approaches, followed by pertinent task assignment, can then take place.

It can sometimes be helpful to audiotape or videotape the enactment dialogue and replay it with the client in order to facilitate observation and discussion. I have seldom used such equipment in my own practice and find that if the dialogue is kept sufficiently short—two or three minutes is usually enough—accurate recall of the content and relevant cognitions and feelings is possible. Taped reviews of behavior enactments can become too complex, bogged down in detail, and thus risk losing the essential action emphasis of enactment.

Following an enactment, there is an opportunity to discuss the behaviors that have been demonstrated or to explore the particular reactions—affective or cognitive—that the client experienced during the vignette. Where the major objective of treatment is to enhance interpersonal or social skills, it is often useful for the therapist to begin the discussion by summarizing major aspects of the role-play. If the client has experienced considerable difficulty in the dialogue, or where the enactment is the first of a gradated series of rehearsals (as, for example, in assertion training), the summary should be carefully selective. It should initially emphasize some *positive* aspect of the client's behavior, however minor, and then point out a few aspects of the dialogue where specific difficulties were evident.

Lange and Jakuboski's (1976, pp. 155–165) discussion of behavioral rehearsal clearly illustrates the consistent use of this sequence of reinforcement and feedback. Following each enactment (in their case, in a group setting), the client is first given encouragement for competent responses and then provided with specific suggestions or modeling for improving skill. Additionally, the client is taught to realistically assess his or her own performance after each vignette. The pacing of learning is critical, and the helper must always be sensitive to the possibility that the enactment itself can become yet another instance of failure, with the client feeling humiliated by the all-too-obvious deficits portrayed.

The enactment by Mrs. Franz, described earlier, was a typical instance of an intial rehearsal where there was seemingly little of a truly positive nature for the therapist to identify. The helper was hard put to find some glimmer of hopefulness to recognize and, with a considerable effort, suggested to Mrs. Franz, "It must have taken some real courage to even try that situation again, you've been through it so often with such discouraging results." In work with clients attempting to develop social skills, where beginning efforts frequently show little or no real facility, the clinician has to make this same sort of supportive leap.

It is critical, I find, for the therapist to sharply distinguish between enactments that are a prelude to direct behavior change (usually some variant of social skill training) and enactments intended to arouse awareness of conflicted feelings or identify troublesome cognitions. In the latter situations, the helper may be much less supportive and indeed may allow the impact of emotion or the recognition of dismaying beliefs and attitudes to build, deliberately inducing stress in the helping encounter. Wachtel (1977), for example, describes enactments with clients experiencing difficulties in close relationships where the deliberate repetition of enactments was needed in order to force the client to face the blocked or evaded emotion.

If the therapist suspects that there are cognitive factors impeding the client's behavior in a particular relationship, it can be helpful to cue the client to look for these as the enactment takes place. "What do you say to yourself as you ask a girl for a date?" stimulated one young man to capture the catastrophic consequences—a slap in the face, or a stinging verbal rejection—that he inwardly anticipated. Despite its name, behavior rehearsal can never be completely behavioral. The skilled therapist maintains a careful balance between the performance aspects of the enactment and the important beliefs, attitudes, and emotions that may be interacting with client behavior. Yet behavior enactment, through bypassing the limitations of descriptive language, offers an opportunity for any (or all) of these elements to be brought into view.

THE MODELING PHASE

After the enactment phase has been discussed and its particular difficulties identified, it is often appropriate for the therapist to demonstrate, in a further simulation, a way in which the situation might be differently handled. In this sequence the helper will assume the part of the client and the client will, of course, play the significant other. Usually the preceding enactment has set the stage sufficiently that the therapist need only briefly describe the reversal of roles and the dialogue can then proceed. Occasionally a client may be reluctant or self-conscious about portraying the other person—whether spouse, employer, or friend—and the therapist will need to encourage the attempt. Acknowledging that the client may feel awkward or foolish in the assumed role is usually sufficient. Most clients are much more anxious about portraying themselves in the enactment phase. This is the far riskier exposure of self, and it is uncommon for any significant reluctance to develop at the modeling phase. Indeed, at times seemingly inhibited clients can play an aggressive spouse or employer with surprising flair and realism.

A critical facet of the modeling phase lies in the selection of exactly what new behaviors to demonstrate. The therapist has to be careful to choose only a very few aspects of new behavior for emphasis and to ensure that these are clearly and unambiguously demonstrated. Such a selection is based, in part, on the difficulties that were evidenced in the prior enactment and pinpointed in the discussion of that phase. In addition, the helper exercises judgment in choosing the elements of more functional behavior that are most likely to be successfully managed by the client in the subsequent rehearsal.

Among a variety of interpersonal problems confronting her, thirty-year-old Joyce B. had emphasized her continuing difficulty in approaching her employer about a potential promotion and salary raise. In an enactment of this dilemma, several features of her approach to the employer had stood out: her diffident and meek posture and voice; her reluctance to directly state her concern about the promotion; and finally, a futile reliance on indirect hints about the matter. All of these, in conjunction with a busy, rather insensitive employer, resulted in inevitable failure and further discouragement for Joyce.

In discussing the enactment, the most salient difficulties—her anxious manner and the indirect approach—had been readily identified as problematic, although Joyce, like many clients, was pessimistic about whether she could ever behave any differently.

In the first modeling phase, the therapist decided to simplify these difficulties even further: the demonstration concentrated on showing Joyce how some direct eye contact and the essential phrase "I'd like to talk to you about a promotion" could transform the situation. More subtle aspects of the skills needed to manage this anxiety-provoking interaction were disregarded and left for later modeling demonstrations and rehearsals. It was enough that the client be presented with a very few changes that she could fairly successfully imitate before attempting to grasp the totality of the assertive skills involved. As the previous discussion has emphasized, behavioral enactment is an occasion for learning and growth, not for more challenge and failure. The helper has to exercise judgment in estimating the boundaries within which the client can operate, even within the protected atmosphere of the helping session. The methodology of enactment can give the therapist a handy guideline for intervention, but as this example illustrates, such procedures have to be carefully guided by the judgment of the skilled helper.

Therapists need to gain facility in utilizing behavior enactment in much the same way as clients—by actually practicing the procedures and skills involved. Supervisors, moreover, should not assume that the inexperienced practitioner, no matter how familiar with the technical procedures of enactment, is able to clearly demonstrate social relationship skills. Clinicians planning to use behavior enactment need to literally practice these skills in training workshops, supervisory conferences, or with colleagues in order to gain confidence and facility. The more experienced practitioner may find it useful to enact particularly difficult situations with consultants or colleagues. As a valuable by-product of this practical emphasis on performance, I have found that my own comfort and facility with such vital human skills as assertiveness and intimate communication has increased, not only professionally but personally. There is no reason, of course, why therapists should not benefit from the same wisdom and practical learnings they impart to their clients.

THE PRACTICE PHASE

In this final phase of the enactment sequence, the elements demonstrated by the helper are attempted by the client, with an emphasis on behavioral mastery, and any troublesome cognitions or affects stirred up by this effort are elicited so as to be available for further examination. The importance or pertinence of these aspects of the practice phase will vary from one client to another, or even from time to time for the same client, and the therapist will again need to exercise careful judgment about where to place stress.

The attempt at behavioral mastery of the aspects of interpersonal skill that the helper's demonstration highlighted should not be underemphasized. No matter how adequate the client may appear to be in the context of the helping relationship or from descriptions of self in other encounters, the therapist must remember that a perplexing and troubled facet of the client's life is being isolated and examined. It should not be assumed that the helper's demonstration and the client's agreement that this represents a more functional or desirable coping with the situation are a sufficient examination of the dilemma; the behavior must be attempted by the client.

If the client is able to manage a reasonable facsimile of the elements of the modeling selected for emphasis, then the therapist can provide suitable encouragement and either discuss the sequence or move on to another demonstration. Even if the client's effort is labored and flawed, explicit praise of the attempt must be offered. In this latter situation it may well be necessary for the helper to move back to the modeling phase and repeatedly demonstrate the relevant aspects, with the client gradually gaining mastery.

Where the client is experiencing marked difficuly in managing the repetition, the therapist has to exercise considerable care in determining which aspects of the demonstration to emphasize. It is little use trying to teach someone the words to employ in firmly denying an unreasonable request if, for example, his ability to maintain eye contact is minimal or he can speak only in faint, frightened tones. Enactments would have to concentrate on these nonverbal dimensions of assertiveness, through whatever demonstration and practice is needed, before even attempting to work upon the actual verbal content.

It is equally important to identify any critical beliefs and attitudes that may be impeding the client—that one has no right to stand up for oneself, or that one must be liked by everyone—for these may also require change. Indeed, one of the most significant recent advances in assertion training, as well as in behavioral therapy in general, has been the increasing recognition of this cognitive element (Lange & Jakubowski, 1976). This has encouraged the development of package of intervention designed to influence both behavior and thought.

Chapter 9 will discuss the cognitive therapies in greater depth. At this point it will be sufficient to note that access to important cognitions may vary as behavior enactment progresses. I suggested earlier, in discussing the enactment phase, that the clinician should attempt to elicit the client's immediate thoughts as a vignette is attempted. At this beginning point, however, it is not unusual for little except overall discouragement or hesitancy to be forthcoming. In the practice phase, as the client attempts a more adequate response, a different situation may ensue. That is to say, the very attempt to be assertive, for example, may stimulate inhibiting cognitions in a way in which the previously inadequate responses did not. The therapist thus should not assume that client imitation of suggested responses and behaviors is a simple matter of practice and implementation. Higher levels of response, often completely novel to the client, can generate quite unexpected reactions.

The concept of the logical or emotional hierarchy, discussed in

Chapter 3, is also highly pertinent to this issue. The helper should be completely familiar with all of the component elements needed in such essential social skills as assertion, intimate communication, and problem solving, and be able to quickly identify those missing from the client's repertoire so as to accurately determine the point in the hierarchy where learning must begin. It must be remembered, moreover, that any hierarchy is simply a rough guideline for the practitioner and may require careful adjustment for a particular client. What may seem to the therapist to be an easy and logical transition from one step to the next may represent an awesome leap to the uneasy client.

Similarly, it may be necessary to gauge clients' emotional reaction to any given level of social interaction in order to scale the demands of enactment to their immediate capacity.

> Mr. Quinlan, a twenty-two-year-old auto mechanic, had never successfully held a job in his field. He either was fired or quit after a month or two in a position because of his difficulties in getting along with supervisors, fellow workers, and customers. With a wife and two young children to support, he had become increasingly desperate about his problems.
>
> As counseling began, he had just found a new job and was struggling to cope with its demands. He spoke of being bothered by customers who insisted on talking to him as he worked on their cars, and the therapist asked him to enact this situation. The therapist then demonstrated some polite but firm ways of handling customer inquiries, and Mr. Quinlan attempted to practice these. Midway through the rehearsal he became visibly upset and was unable to manage even a mildly assertive response. Recognizing his anxiety, the therapist moved to much simpler levels of social skill and additionally contracted to teach Mr. Quinlan ways of managing the pervading tensions he was experiencing on the job.

FUTHER CLINICAL APPLICATIONS

In the clinical setting perhaps the predominant use of behavior enactment and rehearsal methods has been to teach the client new ways of coping with specific life situations (Goldfried & Davison, 1976). Many therapists are familiar with the employment of behavioral rehearsal in such structured change procedures as social skill or assertion training. Indeed, the major area of documentation for its effectiveness as a teaching device has been in assertion training (McFall & Lilliesand, 1971; McFall & Twentyman, 1973). It would be a pity, however, if we were to limit usage of this powerful tool to only a narrow range of applications. Enactments can be utilized in many helping situations and adapted to a variety of therapeutic orientations and styles; their employment need be limited only by the imagination of the therapist and the unique life goals of the client.

Enactments are especially adaptable to very brief contacts where a specific difficulty, often of some urgency to the individual, needs to be dealt with in a focused way. For example, behavior enactment and rehearsal have been used in work in a hospital setting with patients who are experiencing anxiety around discussing their medical condition with their physician.* This problem can be aggravated in a large hospital by the impersonality of a busy medical staff, and the patient will often feel extremely frustrated and defeated after repeated but ineffectual attempts to gain information.

Since at least some of the difficulty experienced by such patients may arise from anxiety about their condition, it is usually helpful, prior to any enactment, to spend some time with the individual writing down a list of the questions he would like to ask the physician. This not only concretizes the goal of the intervention—obtaining specific medical information—but also has some effect in moderating the patient's anxiety about these questions as they assume a more tangible form. There is also opportunity during this phase to shape certain of the patient's beliefs—by statements such as "You have a right to this information," "You have to take responsibility to get it," or "You often have to teach your doctor how to talk to you"—so as to prepare for later steps in the intervention.

The therapist makes the transition to behavior enactment, once the basic concern is clearly established, by beginning to question the patient about the specifics of his or her previous encounters with the physician. The form of the questions—"How did you ask the doctor?" "What did you say then?" or "What did the doctor do?"—is designed to make the patient aware of the actual behaviors in the situation and to serve as a natural prelude to behavior enactment. It is

*I am indebted to Larry V. Pacoe, Ph.D., for this illustrative material.

best for the therapist to take the initial risk of enacting by explaining that it is still unclear from the verbal description what is going wrong and adding that it might be helpful for the therapist to play the part of the doctor so that the patient can convey his or her concerns more clearly. From this initial enactment it is an easy transition to further modeling or practice sequences that will enhance the patient's ability to cope with the encounter.

The essential step, it must be emphasized, is to give the patient some explicit practice in actually stating the specific questions to the physician. The written list that patient and therapist have already worked out is, of course, highly useful, but the actual experience, in enactment, of voicing these concerns cannot be omitted. During the rehearsal it is also possible to teach the patient some simple techniques that will be useful in managing some of the common difficulties that may arise. For example, lightly placing a hand on the physician's arm can stop him from walking away; simply saying "I don't understand" can be a response to unclear medical terminology. The intervention is concluded by instructing the patient to keep the prepared list of questions nearby and to actually use it in the session with the physician. Additionally, the therapist should make a note on the patient's chart to the effect that "the patient has a number of questions." Finally, the therapist should initiate a follow-up interview with the patient in which the meeting with the doctor will be reviewed, gaps in the information obtained will be discussed, and any new questions will be identified and rehearsed.

A more general clinical application can be seen in Lange and Jakubowski's (1976) volume on assertion training, which outlines a sequence for behavior rehearsal that is highly adaptable to many other problematic social and interpersonal situations. Their model emphasizes a series of successive enactments by the client in which the elements of adaptive response to a complex situation are gradually developed in a step-by-step fashion. During this phase of skill enhancement the role of the antagonist (boss, spouse, peer, etc.) is carefully controlled so as to avoid any reactions that might be unmanageable for the learner during the early stages of development. Each enactment in the series concentrates on a few clearly defined (or modeled) aspects of the desired behavior, and following each rehearsal the client is given immediate encouragement and feedback.

Only after the client has gained reasonable facility and confidence in coping with the situation are more difficult or conflictful elements introduced into the antagonist's role. Lange and Jakubowski (1976) describe this approach in relation to a young woman attempting to deal with a difficult employer:

> Judy then practiced several more interactions. At first the employer was encouraged to be cooperative and support the request. When Judy successfully completed the entire scene to her satisfaction, the trainer then asked her to practice the scene with the employer responding negatively (e.g., anger, threat, indifference, guilt, or whatever "hooks" her). The situation was then practiced until *Judy was satisfied* with how she assertively handled the employer's uncooperative response. (pp. 161–162)

In effect, this is yet another illustration of the learning hierarchy and can be seen as a combination of the logical (simple to complex) and the emotional (least anxious to most anxious) elements of this learning paradigm. In addition, this adaptation of the behavior enactment model draws upon an aspect of the approach that has considerable clinical significance—*behavior rehearsal is simultaneously real and unreal*. Although enactments are capable of arousing very tangible emotions or revealing significant skill deficits, they are *not* the real-life situation. The imaginative therapist can capitalize on this characteristic of enactment to protect the client, particularly during the early stages of change, and thus heighten the possibility of effective learning.

Finally, Lange and Jakubowski (1976) discuss the combination of relaxation training with behavior rehearsal procedures. No matter how much the clinician may simplify the rehearsal situation, there are some clients who become quite anxious at even elementary levels of enactment. Mr. Quinlan, the harried auto mechanic described earlier in this chapter, was an obvious example of this sort of person. Teaching the client some simple tension reduction methods—relaxing words, calming scenes, deep breathing—may be necessary in order to make participation possible. Even for those who do not appear to be unduly tense, the acquisition of stress management techniques can be a highly useful adjunct to the behavioral and cognitive changes induced through behavior rehearsal. Chapter 8 of this book will discuss stress management approaches in greater detail.

These few examples will convey some notion of the adaptability of enactment procedures to various situational contexts and diverse client characteristics. In subsequent chapters, further uses of behavior enactment methods will be considered. Their value will be especially evident as the development of social skills is reviewed. Modeling and rehearsal procedures are heavily utilized within the therapeutic interview to assist the individual in skill development. Similarly, cognitive changes in a number of key areas are often identified and induced through variations on enactment.

7

Tasks and Homework

One must put tasks in their way which they can accomplish and from the accomplishment of which they gain faith in themselves.

—Alfred Adler, *The Practice and Theory of Individual Psychology*

The concept of the task as a means of controlling and shaping one's destiny has played an integral part in human endeavor throughout history. Such heroes of mythology and folklore as Hercules were required to demonstrate their worthiness and courage through seemingly impossible task accomplishment. The miller's daughter in *Rumpelstiltskin*, to her utter dismay, found she had to prove her suitability for marriage to the king by weaving straw into gold. At an everyday level, we all know the satisfaction of completing a piece of work, obtaining an excellent grade, or mastering a new facet of a sport or hobby. Whether heroic or ordinary, the task confronts us with challenge from the environment and with the opportunity to demonstrate our capacity to cope with the demands of living.

The use of tasks has become particularly developed and refined in short-term treatment (Levy & Shelton, 1990), and this chapter reviews certain key aspects of such theory and practice. Initially, however, I will survey the history of task usage across all psychotherapeutic approaches. Liberman's (1978) discussion of the concept of

The assistance of two former students, Rosemary Armany and Barbara Lonardi, in gathering material on which parts of the original version of this chapter was based, is gratefully acknowledged.

159

mastery is used as a central theoretical construct underlying task assignment and performance, and a number of clinical considerations will be related to this core theme. A classification of tasks as observational, experiential, or incremental are suggested, and practice examples will be employed to illustrate these categories. Finally, methods of improving task performance, enhancing compliance, and dealing with common difficulties in clinical application will be discussed throughout the chapter.

TASKS IN CLINICAL PRACTICE: A BRIEF HISTORY

In one of the earliest extensive discussions of the employment of tasks and homework in therapeutic practice, Shelton and Ackerman (1974) define tasks as "assignments given to the client which are carried on outside the therapeutic hour" (p. 3). While many therapists may employ tasks on an irregular basis, a major characteristic of most contemporary brief psychotherapy is the use of homework in a consistent, systematic manner throughout the intervention. Levy and Shelton (1990) state this position forcefully:

> We do not see tasks as an adjunct, even a critical adjunct to brief psychotherapy. Rather, we see them as *the basis for action in brief psychotherapy*. If therapy is to be effective in a short period of time, the therapist *must* encourage the efficient conduct of the client's activities—both in and outside the therapy session. (p. 145, italics in original)

Precedent for the use of assignments to be completed outside the therapy hour is not difficult to find. Dunlap (1932), for example, contended that clients could learn to extinguish unwanted behaviors through the use of repeated homework assignments. An early work by Herzberg (1941) offered a similar rationale. Andrew Salter (1949)—one of the pioneer writers in behavior therapy—described patients with a wide range of difficulties utilizing self-instigation, as he termed it, to effect changes in their own behavior. From a psychodynamic perspective, Stevenson (1959) underscored the importance of homework in enhancing the development of assertive, affiliative, and communication skills.

A series of reviews by Shelton and his colleagues (Levy & Shelton,

1990; Shelton, 1979; Shelton & Ackerman, 1974) identify three major influences underlying the development of therapeutic homework. The first of these, as Chapter 3 noted, is the notion of instigative therapy, particularly as conceptualized by Kanfer (1979). In this view of the therapeutic process, the emphasis is on change taking place *outside* of the actual therapeutic session. The interview situation is seen as an opportunity to plan how such change will be initiated and to systematically review the client's attempts to achieve this. The instigative perspective is heavily dependent, of course, on a means to carry out such attempts, and the development of realistic and flexible task assignments becomes a necessary ingredient of the approach.

A second major influence, as Shelton points out, has been the direct sex therapy approaches pioneered by Masters and Johnson (1970), which were among the first to employ systematic homework assignments as an integral aspect of the therapy. Moreover, there is evidence that task compliance is essential to effective sex therapy. For example, Lansky and Davenport (1975) describe a relatively unsuccessful series of sexual therapy cases, but at the same time report that most of their clients did not carry out the prescribed homework. Lansky and Davenport point out an almost exact correspondence between those clients who carried out the exercises and those who benefited from the treatment.

More recent studies (Hawton, 1991; Whitehead & Mathews, 1986) have reinforced this finding in regard to sex therapy, while other investigations (Holtzworth-Monroe et al., in press; Whisman & Jacobson, 1987) have found a similar relationship between homework compliance and positive treatment outcome in brief marital therapy. In cognitive therapy, Layden and her colleagues (1993) review several research studies that support the position that "patients who invest time in therapy homework tend to make swifter progress, and to maintain their gains more readily in the years and months following the completion of treatment" (p. 78). All of these studies underscore both the firm empirical base and the clinical utility of tasks and homework.

Finally, Shelton's own work has been a factor in promoting the planned use of tasks and assignments, and his monograph on the utilization of homework in psychotherapy (Shelton & Ackerman, 1974) represents a signal contribution to the field. In addition, Shelton has been active in the empirical examination of the effects of task assignment, and in several studies (Chesney & Shelton, 1976; Shelton, 1973, 1975) has demonstrated its positive effects in enhancing change.

OTHER MAJOR INFLUENCES

Two additional sources of influence on task utilization need to be recognized. Within the social work field, the efforts of William Reid in the development of task-centered casework have been especially significant. In one of their earliest works, Reid and Epstein (1972) point out that the development of task-centered casework was stimulated by the notion of drawing upon the "natural task-setting and task-achieving of individuals in difficulty" (pp. 94–95). Reid and his colleagues not only pioneered an approach that places an explicit emphasis on task accomplishment but have also persistently gathered empirical data supporting various facets of the method. Reid's (1975) work on the task implementation sequence—a procedure for enhancing the probability that the client will undertake assigned homework—will be examined in greater detail later in this chapter.

Additionally, the employment of tasks and directives within the field of family therapy has many implications for brief psychotherapy generally. A number of family therapists who might not consider themselves short-term therapists have utilized tasks extensively, both in and out of the therapeutic session. Salvador Minuchin (1974; Minuchin et al., 1978), for instance, in some of his influential works on structural family therapy, offers many examples of this aspect of practice, which are worth examining in more detail. Two modes of task usage predominate:

IN-SESSION TASKS. First, there are instances where the structural family therapist will ask a family member to try out a new bit of behavior right in the therapeutic session. Thus, a husband may be instructed to help his wife talk to their teenage son about a troublesome topic. In another family the task might be for the father to do exactly the opposite—to allow his wife to talk to their son without in any way participating. In an initial interview in his volume on work with anorexia nervosa, Minuchin (Minuchin et al., 1978) asks for a shift in the family's seating arrangement in order to challenge their habitual patterns of interaction:

> MINUCHIN: Can you answer your mother, Loretta? Carlo, let Mama sit near Loretta. Loretta, talk with Mother, because she says that you are controlling the house. (p. 307)

In all of these examples the therapist is suggesting certain behaviors for the client, and the task is to try them out immediately. This use of tasks within the therapeutic session is obviously quite similar to the enactment or behavioral rehearsal methods.

BETWEEN-SESSION TASKS. Minuchin also discusses the use of tasks in a manner analogous to the instigative approach, that is, as activities to be carried out *between* therapeutic sessions. In the same initial interview cited above (Minuchin et al., 1978) he concludes the session by asking the father and daughter to spend at least half an hour twice during the following week talking together about themselves. His instructions are very explicit:

> MINUCHIN: For this week, before you return again, I want you, Loretta, to talk to your father twice for half an hour. Carlo, you will select two evenings to talk to your daughter. Today is what? Friday? Talk with him during the weekend one time, and talk with him next week, Loretta. If she doesn't do that, you make the time, Carlo, and you say, "I want you to know me," and you talk no more than half an hour.
>
> FATHER: Okay.
>
> MINUCHIN: No more than half an hour and twice during this week, Loretta. (p. 322)

Minuchin's approach to giving task assignments is exemplary, offering a clear model for what might be called the *language* of task-giving. The reader should note carefully, for example, how directly and succinctly the task is prescribed. There is no doubt about what Minuchin is asking of his clients, and his vocabulary is simple and entirely nontechnical. He describes when, where, and how the task is to be carried out and, furthermore, keeps its demands extremely limited. It is difficult for the family members to complain that talking together twice for half an hour each time is too burdensome an assignment.

TASKS AND MASTERY

Liberman (1978) suggests that successful task accomplishment promotes "a feeling of mastery, control over one's internal reactions and relevant external events" (p. 75) and consequently plays an indispensible role in maintaining individual self-esteem. His analysis of the role of mastery, both in daily living and as an effective ingredient in successful psychotherapy, is highly pertinent to the consideration of tasks that is the subject of this chapter. Much of the following discussion is heavily indebted to Liberman's review.

He points out that many different psychotherapies have emphasized the concept of mastery and directly or indirectly have used task performance in enhancing it. For some therapies task performance will take place within the actual therapeutic session and may consist, for example, of recalling dreams, exploring feelings, or actively participating in emotionally arousing experiences. For other therapies the emphasis is on task assignment outside of the session, and the client may be directed to visit with extended family members, practice relaxation exercises, read selected books and articles, and so on. The commonality of these many approaches to task performance may lie not in the physical location or the specific nature of the task activity, but in its requirement by the therapist as a socially sanctioned expert. Implicit in this requirement is the belief conveyed to the client that following such procedures will lead to relief from suffering (Frank, 1974).

Whether carrying out tasks will promote mastery, however, depends on the manner in which the client approaches and interprets his or her performance. Liberman reviews a series of research studies identifying five factors that can significantly influence this interpretation. In sum, these factors can be regarded as a cognitive framework within which the client is likely to view the assigned task:

BACKGROUND VARIABLES. There appear to be individuals whose personal background and current environment make them especially open to change efforts. Some of the research findings confirm the not surprising conclusion that, on average, such factors as middle-class background, college education, and white-collar occupation tend to support the impetus toward mastery. In contrast, people from working-class, low socioeconomic, and ghetto backgrounds are more likely to see their lives as externally controlled and, as Liberman suggests, "primarily a matter of luck, fate, chance, or some powerful outside agent" (p. 41). Hence, clients from these latter groups will more often request help with concrete aspects of their environment or immediate context of living.

Both empirically and clinically, however, the matter is not as simple as one of middle-class people necessarily being the most "desirable" clients. All therapists have had frustrating experiences with the intellectually inclined client who simply stays at this level, hesitating to put his or her verbalized awareness into any concrete form. On the other hand, Burgoyne and his colleagues (1979) found that lower socioeconomic clients often desire the more conventionally therapeutic forms of helping, but tend to *combine* this request with requests of a more tangible nature. Difficulties arise when the therapist, biased perhaps by common clinical beliefs about the low socioeconomic group, responds only to the concrete request. Tasks can serve as a middle ground between these two polarities, challenging the intellectualizing client to put insights into action or, with the more practically oriented client, providing a vehicle for developing greater cognitive or emotional awareness.

TASK RELEVANCE. As Liberman emphasizes, "a person's involvement and committment to a task are also dependent upon the relevance of the task to him" (p. 43). Whatever the tasks required by the psychotherapy, inside or outside the therapy session, it is essential that clients see these tasks as meaningfully related to solving the difficulties they are experiencing or achieving the goals they desire. Neither free association or interpretation in psychodynamically oriented therapy, or the relaxation procedures of systematic desensitization in behavior therapy, from this point of view, will have an optimal effect unless the client views them as pertinent to problem resolution. The same considerations apply to tasks carried out in the natural environment.

Two major implications for practice can be drawn from this construct:

1. Difficulty around task relevance can be avoided if the clinician utilizes homework assignments that are directly related to the goals of change desired by the client. This may appear to be an obvious consideration, yet many practitioners hesitate to work directly on the

client's difficulties in living. It may seem embarrassingly simplistic to suggest to the client that problems with close relationships, for example, can be improved through deliberately increasing one's personal contacts, or that leaving the parental home can involve little more than planning and carrying out the steps needed to make such a move. Too often our theories have suggested that the solutions to all problems must be complex and indirect, and consequently clinicians have lost the ability to be simple and immediate.

2. The client's understanding of the relevance of the task can be heightened by adequate explanation from the therapist, especially during the initial engagement process. Earlier research into what has been called the role-induction interview (Heitler, 1976; Orlinsky & Howard, 1986) found that providing clients with factual information about the nature of therapy and the expected client role increased participation and lowered premature dropout rates. This kind of structured information giving has been incorporated into a number of the brief approaches. In a recent analysis of a series of case studies of brief psychotherapy (Wells, 1993) the provision of information was especially apparent in the approaches dealing with such powerful emotions as depression and anxiety. Here the need was not only to increase client cooperation with tasks but to demystify and normalize these often bewildering emotions.

TASK DIFFICULTY. The experience of mastery gained from performing a task is also related to the perceived difficulty of the assignment. For instance, as Liberman points out, "tasks which are perceived as too easy or too difficult yield feelings neither of success nor of failure" (p. 45). On the other hand, though certain tasks may be so complex that the behaviors necessary for their performance are not within the client's existing repertoire, there are instances where even unsuccessfully performing a very difficult task can bolster the individual's ability to cope with less demanding tasks in the same problem area.

All of these considerations suggest that the clinician must exercise some care in task selection. The task must, in general, be one that the individual is able to carry out, yet demanding enough that its performance has meaning. Some clinicians suggest that the task should represent a distinctly higher level than the client's present functioning. In their discussion of tasks in rational-emotive therapy, Walen and her colleagues (1980) suggest that "large steps" be employed in order to challenge the client. This is reminiscent, of course, of the approach employed in the implosive or emotional flooding approaches (Stampfl & Levis, 1967) where the client, in imagery or *in vivo*, is confronted with the most demanding situations possible. Most clinicians, however, prefer to follow the principles of shaping (Bandura, 1969, 1986) and, except in unusual circumstances, choose initial task assignments at the simpler and less anxiety-provoking end of the client's subjective continuum. Certainly the employment of shaping principles has the firmest empirical substantiation and should be utilized in most cases. But the clinician should not be excessively cautious, and judgment must be exercised to ensure that the task is not too simple or nondemanding.

ATTITUDES OF SIGNIFICANT OTHERS. The manner in which important people in the client's life react to a task may affect the meaningfulness of the performance. Although the client may have some initial trepidations, many of the significant people in the immediate environment will be surprisingly supportive of change. In addition, despite the emphasis of some theories, we should not regard the natural environment (or the people that populate it) as necessarily malevolent or inherently unhelpful. To the contrary, there is more reason to see the natural remedial forces as at least as helpful as anything we can offer within the therapeutic arena, and as I have frequently emphasized, the effective therapist makes every effort to tap this resource. Maguire's (1991, 1993) work on using the client's social networks has expanded on the many clinical applications of this position.

At the same time, Liberman suggests that the therapist, during the course of treatment, often assumes the role of a significant other and can play an influential part in supporting task performance. He points out:

> The therapist can heighten the effects of success by praise or approval and can ameliorate the effects of failure by indicating that the poor performance has not diminished his regard for the patient. (p. 46)

Liberman also notes that a task may be carried out, at least in the early stages of treatment, in order to please the therapist, but like most brief therapists, he regards this as an acceptable motivation at a starting point. His emphasis on the importance of therapist attitude toward task performance also underscores the necessity of the therapist's following up on task assignment. If the therapist neglects to inquire about the client's performance on an assigned task, an attitude of depreciation is implicitly conveyed and the client will invest less in future tasks.

ATTRIBUTION OF PERFORMANCE. It is essential that the individual believe that performance on the task is the result of his own efforts and that success or failure can be ascribed to himself. If the client sees his efforts as due to luck or fate or the intervention of others, then his own role will be significantly diminished or, in some cases, entirely disqualified. The therapist must look for opportunities to influence the client's attribution processes so as to heighten the possibility of self-attribution. Liberman suggests certain tactics:

> The therapist can also play a role in the attribution process by convincing the patient that his gains are due to the patient's own efforts. . . . Conversely the therapist can reattribute failures so that the patient does not view them as presumed defects in character. (p. 46)

The importance of the clinician carefully monitoring client attribution as tasks are carried out cannot be overemphasized. It is deflating, to say the least, to discover, *after* a series of tasks have been performed, that the client has ascribed his success to pure luck or, worse still, entirely to the therapist's support and guidance. On the other hand, as difficult a situation can develop if the client has failed at a task and attributes this entirely to his own inadequacy or incompetence. Perhaps not surprisingly, clients seldom blame the practitioner for task failure ("If you hadn't told me to do it . . ."), although this is a common apprehension among beginning practitioners. I will discuss some further methods of redirecting attributions later in this chapter.

CLASSIFYING TASKS

Tasks have been categorized in a variety of ways. Reid (1975), for example, speaks of *unique* tasks, which require a one-time performance by the client ("Get information on the child care facilities in your immediate neighborhood"), and *repeated* tasks, which ask the client to act in a particular way in a series of situations ("Talk briefly to someone in your class every day this week"). Haley (1976) divides tasks into two distinct categories based upon the therapist's intent in task assignment:

(1) telling people what to do when the therapist wants them to do it, and (2) telling people what to do when the therapist does *not* want them to do it—because the therapist wants them to change by rebelling. (p. 52)

Tasks in Haley's second category, the so-called paradoxical task, have been a subject of considerable fascination for many clinicians. Actually, there is a paradoxical undertone to all task assignment— how else can one ask anxious or depressed clients to carry out the very behaviors they fear and avoid while, at the same time, conveying an attitude of caring and regard? The *explicitly* paradoxical task, however, will not be discussed in any detail in this book as there is little, if any, research evidence supporting the effectiveness of this approach. Instead, I will concentrate on the large number of tasks used in clinical practice that are relatively straightforward in their intent to pinpoint or stimulate change, since these have ample empirical support (Levy & Shelton, 1990). Within this overall category of tasks, three subcategories can be distinguished, based upon their function within the process of brief psychotherapy.

OBSERVATIONAL OR MONITORING TASKS. These are tasks whose main purpose is to gather more information on a selected aspect of the client's life or, in other instances, to increase the individual's awareness of significant behaviors, emotions, or beliefs in a given area of difficulty.

EXPERIENTAL OR CHALLENGING TASKS. There are times when a task is deliberately designed to arouse emotion in a client or to challenge beliefs or attitudes that are playing an integral part in maintaining the individual's problem. This type of task is particularly applicable where passivity or the repetitive use of ineffectual behaviors is maintaining or worsening the difficulties.

INCREMENTAL CHANGE TASKS. The tasks in this category are designed to stimulate change directly toward a desired goal, in a step-by-step manner. Incremental tasks are usually devised in an interrelated sequence and arranged along a logical or emotional hierarchy relevant to the client's personal style and particular area of difficulty.

Observational or Monitoring Tasks

In the beginning phases of brief therapy, the therapist frequently asks clients to keep a log or diary of some selected aspect of their lives. Parents concerned about a child's behavior can be instructed to keep a record of the child's activities with friends. An adult can be asked to keep track of every interpersonal contact over a given week. Another client may be requested to keep a log of the amount of food consumed each day and the circumstances in which eating occurs. The variety of possible observational assignments is limited only by the imagination of the helper and, of course, the specific needs of the client.

> In an initial interview with a young man, recently separated from his wife, it was apparent that he was almost deliberately isolating himself from social contacts. Although he verbalized his strong feelings of loneliness, he was narrowing his world to the few people he saw on his job. An early task was to ask him to begin recording, in simple diary form, any human contacts he experienced during his evenings and weekends. It was emphasized that this information would help in understanding who was available to him. Additionally, the therapist believed that his awareness of the manner in which crisis was constricting him would be dramatized.

This type of assignment is, obviously, borrowed from the behavioral therapists and serves some of the same purposes that they identify. It establishes a baseline of frequency for a problematic behavior and adds further specification to the problem definition already worked out with the client. If the client is concerned about drinking, for example, how often does this occur, and under what circumstances? Where the client wants to develop certain social skills, it is usually necessary to know something about his or her present level of skill. Like behavioral enactments, tasks add flesh to the verbal descriptions obtained within the interviews.

Tasks in which the client follows a particular aspect of life, recording its occurrence and observing its characteristics are especially useful as treatment begins. It is at this point that more detail is needed. One of the disadvantages of the relatively rapid process of engagement by which short-term treatment is initiated is the lack of such detail. Thus, for example, the therapist can concentrate on relationship development in the initial interview rather than elaborate problem exploration; knowing that such informative devices as behavior enactment and observational assignments are easily mobilized in the early stages of treatment allows such latitude.

This is not to say that the use of diaries and logs should be restricted to the early sessions. One of the major benefits of this type of homework assignment at later stages of treatment lies in the perspective it can offer the ongoing therapeutic work. Many therapists are familiar, I am sure, with the situation in which the client begins to describe a problem that came up during the preceding week. As the description continues, affect is aroused—discouragement or anxiety, let us say—and it becomes exceedingly difficult to untangle events and emotions. If the client has been assigned to keep a daily diary focused on interpersonal contacts, then a very different picture can be seen. From the diary it is possible to ascertain, for example, that one or perhaps two days were difficult, while others were not. This is very different from having to rely on the client's entirely selective recollection of the week and to find later, as so often happens, that these recollections are highly skewed. Even if the diary reveals that every day contained difficulties, at least this is a more concrete indication of the client's level of functioning than his or her unaided recollection.

Observational assignments can be shaped to fit the personal style of the particular client. Some individuals respond very well to a concrete and specific form of recording in which a chart with suitable headings is worked out and the behaviors of interest are noted. Others are less responsive or even antagonistic to this approach, viewing it as too mechanical or constricting. In such instances the client can be asked to keep a diary, with a much greater literary or poetic license allowed in the recording. The point of either assignment is that clients attempt to observe their life activities in a manner that is more systematic and self-conscious than their typical fashion.

In two of the cases described in Chapter 3, daily logs were kept. Both Mr. Jurecko, in his attempts to gain greater control of his anger, and Mr. Faber, whose concern was to develop increased confidence in relationship to women, kept such charts at some point in the treatment process. However, there were a few distinct differences in the purpose of each assignment that bear further discussion at this time.

Mr. Jurecko was instructed to record in his notebook any incident at work that was upsetting to him. He was simply asked to make a brief note of these so that he and the therapist could gain a better notion of the frequency and severity of episodes that were likely to increase his stress level or to provoke anger. The clinician's intent in this assignment was to heighten Mr. Jurecko's awareness of stress-producing incidents and, further, to obtain a somewhat more objective estimate of the effect of the tension reduction methods that Mr. Jurecko was beginning to learn.

The employment of a daily log came at a somewhat different point in intervention with Mr. Faber and consequently had a different purpose. He was not asked to keep a count, so to speak, of discrete episodes, but was to use a particular type of event as a signal for a closer examination of himself. Specifically, he was to try to become more aware of the thoughts and fantasies—positive or negative—that occurred when he was in close association with a woman. The recording of these observations was to take place at a convenient time after the event and was more in the nature of keeping a personal diary than doing a behavioral or numerical type of charting. The purpose, of course, was to stimulate and uncover any intruding cognitions that were interfering with his ability to manage these relationships.

In a similar vein, the cognitive-behavioral approaches to the treatment of depression and anxiety (Beck et al., 1979; Morretti et al., 1990) also employ observational tasks as an integral part of the therapeutic process. Burns and Beck (1978) describe a "Daily Diary of Dysfunctional Thoughts" that the client is trained to use:

> This is a form that patients fill out on a daily basis between therapy sessions and record their uncomfortable emotions (including sadness,

anger and anxiety) as well as negative thoughts. They are then to write down a rational response to the negative thought and monitor the degree of emotional relief they experience. (p. 128)

This task, it will be noted, goes somewhat beyond simple observation because the client not only tracks disturbing thoughts and emotions but attempts to counter the negative cognition through substituting a rational response.

There are many advantages in beginning a task at an observational level, even if the therapist is well aware that the task may implicitly involve elements of challenge and change. During the initial assignment of such a task, it is helpful to place the greatest emphasis on its monitoring aspects, that is, the information that carrying it out will provide. The attempt to alter negative cognitions or to attain emotional relief (as in the example above) should be pictured as strictly experimental and, at least initially, quite difficult to manage in any consistent way.

By downplaying the more active portion of the assignment at these early stages, the practitioner can reduce much of the pressure concerning success or failure that the client may feel about task performance. This is an especially important consideration with individuals who are already placing inordinate demands upon themselves and whose sense of demoralization is great. In effect, the therapist's effort is to present the task in such a way that it is practically impossible for the client not to achieve some measure of success.

Finally, one must also keep in mind that there is evidence (Orlinsky & Howard, 1986) that the very act of monitoring can induce change. This finding comes from the voluminous research literature on behavior therapy and suggests that desired behaviors tend to increase, and undesired behaviors to decrease, under observational conditions. These shifts are not necessarily great or longlasting, but their appearance can be utilized clinically to point out to the client that change is beginning to take place. This can arouse hope in dispirited clients and motivate them to a continued effort that will often serve to consolidate the less substantial initial gains. Frank Pittman (Haley & Hoffman, 1967; Pittman et al., 1990), in his work on family crisis therapy, calls this "making a small change look big," and regards it as an essential clinical maneuver in mobilizing client strengths.

Experiential or Challenging Tasks

When life difficulties arise that the individual cannot manage, a common human reaction is to wait for circumstances to change so that the problem will resolve itself in some spontaneous manner. Or the person will repeatedly attempt a previously successful solution in the hope that, sooner or later, the desired results will ensue. There is nothing inherently wrong or irrational in either of these common-sense tactics, but, at an extreme, either may act to compound or perpetuate existing difficulties. Thus, the need for action can be inhibited by either inaction or passivity; creative response can be blocked by the repetition of familiar but now unworkable responses.

Experiential tasks are designed to help the baffled client break through impasses of this sort. It is not at all surprising, of course, to find that people in difficulty have drastically limited their range of behavior and in many instances are repetitively enacting unworkable patterns of reaction and response. In much less stressful circumstances, parents scold and nag, children belligerently rebel, despondent individuals reduce their associations with others, and the more aggressive respond with overt hostility. Hansell (1973, 1975) sees these repetitive patterns as an integral, though potentially dysfunctional, part of the normal human response to accumulated stress or crisis. The experiental task is used to stimulate the individual to break out of this habitual pattern or to provide an experience that will challenge the patterns of negative thought and emotional arousal that maintain it.

Experiential tasks come in many forms. Haley (1976) describes a case in which an eight-year-old boy was seen because of his strong fear of dogs. The fear was having adverse effects on the child's emotional stability and social adjustment, and a year of insight-oriented therapy had done little to resolve it. The task-oriented therapist gave an early assignment to the boy and his parents: they were to purchase "a dog that was afraid," and, together, the boy and his family were to help the animal overcome its fears. Whatever else one may conjecture about this task, its experiential and challenging elements are clear.

Similarly, the homework tasks categorized by Walen et al. (1980) as *action assignments* have a significant experiential component. These authors combine such tasks with a rational-emotive approach (see Chapter 9) and subdivide them further into risk-taking and shame-attacking variants. In either case the underlying purpose is to challenge clients' fixed beliefs about themselves or the nature of their world.

Risk-taking assignments may call upon the client, for example, actually to have an experience with failure. Thus, Walen et al. (1980) describe a young man with dating anxiety who was instructed not to make three successful social contacts but to "go out and collect three *rejections* in the next week" (p. 225). Their use of shame-attacking assignments is even more dramatic: "Go up to a stranger and greet him or her warmly. Ask about his or her health. Be effusive," or "Yell out five successive stops on the subway or bus" (p. 226). As they point out, these assignments, aside from arousing strong emotion, are designed to "challenge the dire need for conventionality . . . and . . . help clients evaluate the accuracy of their predictions of how the world will react to them" (pp. 226–227).

Experiential tasks are especially applicable where the individual is struggling with immobilizing depression or anxiety. Indeed, the cognitive-behavioral approaches to these widely prevalent mood disorders (Beck et al., 1979; Morretti et al., 1990), in addition to restructuring the client's thinking processes, also place a heavy reliance on tasks designed to provide a new experience to the sufferer. Burns and Beck (1978) succinctly discuss the underlying assumptions of the approach:

> The thoughts, feelings and behaviors of the depressed or anxious individual typically interact in a predictable manner. Because the patient takes his cognitions seriously and places a high degree of belief in his thoughts, he tends to experience many adverse emotions. He then takes these emotions as confirmatory evidence that his beliefs are in fact correct. (p. 110)

Unless this self-perpetuating cycle is breached, there is little likelihood of the person's gaining control of the depressive or anxious reaction. Burns and Beck go on to describe a thirty-five-year-old salesman who had been caught up in a chronic depression since a divorce six years earlier. As the depression worsened, he found it more and more difficult to maintain his job and began to spend increasing amounts of time at home, ruminating on his difficulties and seriously considering suicide. The therapist directly confronted him with this cyclic pattern of inaction and emotion, and assigned him the twofold task of contacting his employer and visiting one customer. Like some experiential tasks, the immediate effects were salutory:

> The employer expressed support and empathy and assured him that his job was not in danger. When he called the customer, he did receive some ribbing about "being on vacation" for the past six weeks, but also landed a small order. He later reported with surprise that the discomfort of being teased was actually quite small in comparison with the intense depression he experienced every day at home avoiding work. (pp. 125–126)

Burns and Beck (1978) regard a series of such experiences as necessary to lessen the depressed client's pervasive conviction that he is worthless and inadequate. Moreover, they do not see tasks alone as sufficient and caution the clinician that "the tendency of some depressives to maintain such beliefs despite considerable evidence to the contrary is quite impressive" (p. 120). Indeed, it would be a mistake for the therapist to assume that an experiential task will automatically induce the desired changes, as the following vignette illustrates:

> During an initial interview with a depressed woman, she described how she and her husband had invited another couple over for dinner later in the week. She expressed considerable doubt and dismay about her ability to cope with this impending event saying "I'll never be able to manage it."
>
> The therapist carefully reviewed with her each of the practical steps she needed to take in planning for and carrying out the dinner, and made it clear that this was one of her tasks for the coming week. In the following session the client recounted how she had been able to mobilize herself and other family members in the necessary activities and had, indeed, carried out the social engagement successfully. However, she now reported that "nobody had enjoyed themselves."

Although some clinical writings suggest that a single experiential task is all that is necessary to bring about major change, such "Eureka!" reactions are relatively rare, and the client more often needs considerable help from the therapist to gain maximum benefits from tasks of any sort. The conceptual framework suggested by Liberman (1978) and reviewed earlier in this chapter can be utilized in this process of examining and potentiating task performance.

PROMOTING TASK RELEVANCE. Task relevance should not be viewed as a static client perception, but can be heightened by therapist activity and attitude toward prescribed homework. Relevance is underscored by careful follow-up and review, and a clinician is well advised to inquire about an assigned task at the beginning of the succeeding session with the client—"Let's begin by discussing the assignment you were to work on." Direct inquiry of this kind offers a more specific entry point into the interview than the ubiquitous "How did things go this week?" and additionally helps to promote the focused discussion needed in brief intervention.

INFLUENCING ATTRIBUTION. The issue of attribution of performance has already been emphasized as critical to enhancing task performance and particularly to the development of a sense of mastery. However, the clinician may need to approach this facet of client perception rather cautiously, in contrast to the directness employed in other areas of task management. As clients describe or discuss their task performance, the practitioner must listen carefully for indications of attribution and, as the client's viewpoint becomes apparent, consider how this might be handled. The object is to avoid precipitating the client's ascription of attribution prematurely, especially where this may prove problematic. Difficulties can arise in relation to either success or failure; the dispirited client may disclaim any credit for success or, conversely, may entirely embrace failure. The clinician's goal, of course, is to support positive attributions and to decrease or reframe negative attributions.

Reinforcement and reframing, direct or implicit, are the major tactics for influencing attribution. During the client's description of task performance, for example, the therapist looks for any opportunity to highlight aspects of the client's performance that suggest initiative, courage, determination, creativity, and the like. Sometimes I have had clients report that an assignment went well on one occasion but badly on another. I then suggest that we talk about the "failure" experience first, explaining to the client that one often learns more from adversity than success. Implicit in this reframing is the suggestion that the client has done well even while failing the task.

In any case, as tasks are performed and change (at whatever level) takes place, the practitioner should take great care to ascribe *all* of this success to the efforts of the client. The very direct manner in which this can be done is apparent in an interview transcript reported by Haley (1976). In the same case where the therapist had directed the parents and child to purchase "a dog that was afraid," the therapist later referred back to the successful accomplishment of this task:

THERAPIST: What I want to say is whatever progress Stuart has made has been basically because of you.

FATHER: I don't know.

THERAPIST: I think so, and I think it's not the time to be modest now.

FATHER: I'm not trying to be modest.

THERAPIST: You see, what I'm trying to point out to you, both of you, but basically you, is that there are a lot of things that are—there are a lot of things that you have done about Stuart's fears. (p. 128)

This is particularly important in termination interviews as the practitioner prepares the client for the time interval between this session and the follow-up interview. The helper's effort, of course, is to ensure that the progress that has taken place during intervention will continue (or at least stabilize) during the follow-up interval. Reinforcing the client's sense of mastery, through emphasizing task accomplishment, is a tangible contribution to this process. Quite aside from clinical conviction, there is some suggestive research evidence (Liberman, 1978) that the client's positive perception of task accomplishment during treatment tends to promote greater gains at follow-up.

Incremental Change Tasks

As I pointed out earlier, one of the hazards of natural problem-solving efforts is the tendency to attempt change too rapidly or in a global manner. The troubled individual is sorely tempted to attempt major change "at one blow," the New Year's resolution phenomenon, and the risks of failure, of course, are great. Tasks in the incremental change category, by contrast, are designed to bring about personal or environmental change in a systematic, step-by-step manner.

Such tasks usually follow a hierarchical arrangement, based on logical or emotional considerations, so as to capitalize on the principle of shaping. The series of tasks utilized with Mrs. Lorenson (see Chapter 3) as she sought to move out of her parental home is an example of this approach to task assignment. As Chapter 8, on social skill training, will explicate, these educational approaches typically involve such carefully arranged and individualized sequences and their supporting incremental change tasks. Many examples of such tasks will appear in that chapter, but a brief case vignette will illustrate here:

> Roger A., a young, college-educated man in his mid-twenties, was referred by another therapist, who was seeing him in long-term therapy, for the specific purpose of training in social skills. He had few friends and found social relationships both confusing and demanding. In the initial interview with the brief therapist, it was decided that training in affiliative skills, followed by further work on assertiveness would be helpful. The training was structured to take place over ten to twelve weekly sessions.

The sequence of tasks utilized with this young man in the affiliative area will suggest the process of incremental change:

1. Identify through reflection and observation potential friendships and possible social activities.
2. Attend selected social activities but only to observe how others interact and identify potential areas of discomfort.
3. After in-session role-plays, experiment with initiating brief factual conversations with others.
4. After in-session role-plays, experiment with expressing and responding to feelings in conversations.
5. After in-session role-plays, experiment with concluding conversations with others in a positive manner.

Incremental change tasks often follow what might be called a function-dysfunction or "matching to groups" paradigm. That is to say, where an individual is having difficulty in a particular area, the goal of intervention is to assist this person in becoming more like those who are considered functional in this same area—to match their performance. This requires that the practitioner have specific knowledge of the characteristics of adequate functioning so that, usually through a series of successive approximations, these characteristics can be replicated in the client. Clear instructions and appropriate models of the desired behaviors at each stage of the learning process are essential.

Identification and sequencing of tasks in sexual therapy have been greatly aided by knowledge of this very sort. Masters and Johnson (1966), in their landmark study of sexual behavior, empirically identified the characteristics of good sexual functioning prior to developing their remedial program for sexual dysfunction. Thus, instead of depending on purely theoretical speculation about sexual behavior—as had most earlier and unsuccessful therapeutic approaches—the change process could be clearly anchored to objective data. Similar considerations will be apparent in the following chapter, where such areas of skill development as assertion training and stress management are discussed. Incremental change assignments, following a carefully gradated sequence of tasks (both inside and outside of the therapeutic session), and firm links to empirically derived norms of performance are the sine qua non of these approaches.

IMPROVING TASK PERFORMANCE

The importance of task utilization—"the basis for action in brief psychotherapy," to reiterate Levy and Shelton's (1990) phrase—has been heavily emphasized throughout this chapter. In addition, I have noted the consistent research support linking task compliance and positive treatment outcome in brief therapy. Because of these factors, it has been a matter of concern to brief therapists to find ways of ensuring that clients actually complete their assigned tasks.

A frequent question from beginning therapists is, "What do you do when clients don't carry out their tasks?" But Whisman and Jacobson (1990) express the view prevalent among experienced therapists that it is better to deal with task noncompliance *before* it occurs. In their discussion of short-term marital therapy, they identify several strategies that are adaptable to all brief methods:

First, we use the term *between-session task* with couples to avoid resistance individuals may have with the phrase *homework assignment*. Second, the importance of the task is stressed to the couple. Third, the therapist elicits from each spouse a commitment to do each task. Fourth, the therapist asks the couple to anticipate anything that may interfere with completing the task, in an effort to eliminate potential excuses in advance. Finally, if the task is complicated the couple is asked to either write it down or repeat it back to the therapist to ensure that it is understood. In addition, completion of each task is reinforced by spending time at the beginning of each session debriefing the past week's assignment, with the therapist praising its completion. (pp. 339–340)

These and other strategies were included by William Reid (1975) in his earlier research into the effect of what he termed the task implementation sequence (TIS), a structured procedure for enhancing client task performance through therapist explanation and support. Reid found that with clients in mental health and public school settings, this procedure significantly increased the probability that tasks would be carried out. The five steps of the TIS are as follows:

1. *Enhancing commitment.* Following assignment of the task, the practitioner reviews with the client the potential benefits that could be gained by carrying it out. Thus, the task's potential role in supplying needed information, challenging detrimental beliefs and attitudes, or beginning a process of desired change should be clearly related to the client's anticipated goals.

2. *Planning task implementation.* The clinician must carefully define the specific details of the task, including what the client will do and when and where. Any sequence of steps the task might involve is spelled out. The therapist should avoid task assignments that are vague or general ("Try to talk to your wife") and, if several steps are involved, should consider whether a more limited task would be more likely to succeed.

3. *Analyzing obstacles.* Client participation is solicited to examine any potential problems that might arise in carrying out the task. For example, negative reactions from significant people in the client's environment should be realistically considered and, if necessary, methods of handling such reactions should be worked out.

4. *Practice through modeling and behavioral rehearsal.* Certain

tasks may need to be practiced within the interview, especially where such social skills as clear communication and assertiveness are called for. Feedback from client rehearsal can identify yet another possible point where the task assignment must be modified, especially if the client's facility in the needed skills proves to be low.

5. *Summarizing.* In the final step of the TIS, the clinician restates the assigned task and also the plan worked out with the client for its implementation. The therapist's expectation that the task will be performed can be underscored by writing it down on a sheet of paper or in the client's notebook (where observational tasks are being recorded) as a reminder.

In planning task implementation and identifying obstacles, some negotiation may need to be conducted with the client, especially if this is the first task assigned and the therapist wants to ensure success. Friedman's (Friedman & Fanger, 1991) description of his work with a shy young man who wanted to improve his social interactional skills is instructive is this regard:

> The task I first suggested to him was to arrange to have lunch with a co-worker. He found this much more than he could handle, and asking someone to have coffee with him was only slightly less daunting. We finally settled on his offering someone a stick of (sugarless) gum, a task he thought he could do. (p. 142)

An article by Hepworth (1979) offers some highly usefull discussion of the clinical application of the TIS. Hepworth considers the step of analyzing (and removing) obstacles to be particularly vital in stimulating effective task performance. He points out that, in eliciting potential barriers, the clinician should be alert to the nonverbal cues that could indicate client hesitancy or apprehension:

> Such cues include looking away from the worker, speaking diffidently or unenthuisiastically in discussing the task, changing the topic, fidgeting atypically, shifting the posture, and tightening facial or body muscles. If such reactions are detected, the worker is well advised to further explore the presence of undisclosed barriers and to work further on resolving obstacles already identified. (p. 319)

At the same time Hepworth notes that the therapist should not expect that the client who is ready to attempt a task will not feel some degree of apprehension:

Such readiness, however, should not be confused with feeling comfortable; it is neither realistic nor desirable for the worker to expect the client to feel comfortable with the task. A certain amount of tension and anxiety is to be expected and may positively motivate the client to risk the new behavior embodied in the task. (p. 319)

Finally, as noted earlier, carrying out tasks concerned with distressing behavior and emotions may, in some instances, assume a paradoxical quality as the clinician directs clients to observe or grapple with the very aspects of their lives that have been most troublesome. Burns and Beck (1978), for example, describe an intensely anxious woman who was referred for therapy but phoned to report that she was afraid to come in even for an initial interview. Her apprehension was that she would pass out on the train as she traveled to the clinic. The therapist discussed these fears with her during the telephone conversation and instructed her to "look for upsetting visual images and frightening thoughts and make notes about these on the train, including a numerical count of the number of such images as well as the content of the fantasies" (p. 127). They describe the immediate effect of the assignment:

> This paradoxical maneuver of instructing the patient to look for and write down these thoughts and fantasies undercut the patient's fear and avoidance of such anxiety reactions. She appeared in person at the next therapy session and reported that there had been no cognitive or emotional upset since the telephone call, although she had been diligently looking for one! (p. 127)

Despite the seemingly paradoxical quality of such tasks, I believe they are examples of client response to the demand characteristics or placebo effects implicit in entering a therapeutic relationship. That is the very act of seeking help usually stimulates powerful beliefs (and corresponding emotions), implying that relief from suffering will take place (Frank, 1978; Shapiro & Morris, 1978). This change in the client's belief system, toward a more hopeful point of view, elicits similar changes in behavior and affect. Shapiro and Morris (1978) offer extensive documentation of the effect of such factors in both physical and psychological therapies. Similarly, Bergin and Lambert's (1978) review of the impact of even minimal therapeutic contact suggests that the arousal of more hopeful attitudes is a potent force in personal change.

The therapist's assignment of a task concerned with the client's actual difficulties thus conveys the belief that the client can master these problems and that they need not be avoided. This is not to deprecate such responses as unreal or superficial. Creative brief therapists use initial placebo effects just as they employ the so-called reactive effects of monitoring noted earlier in this chapter—as a means of arousing client hope and encouraging further progress.

UTILIZING TASKS AND HOMEWORK IN PRACTICE

Directing clients to carry out tasks and homework is a core characteristic of time-limited intervention. It is through the performance of task assignments that much of the personal and behavioral change needed to achieve the goals of therapy is implemented or triggered. In addition, as the preceding chapter suggested, behavioral enactments carried out within the interview are intimately related to this same process. Enactments may suggest potential tasks or may be used to prepare the client for the implementation of an assignment between sessions. Several other underlying themes are implicit in the utilization of tasks:

THE INSTIGATIVE EMPHASIS. At a fundamental level the use of tasks typifies the interest of the brief therapist in bringing about change in the immediate problem the client is experiencing. Asking a client to carry out a task, however minor or peripheral it may appear, conveys to the client how serious the therapist is about the expected outcome of the helping process. The clinician assumes that the client has a similar concern about goal attainment, but has had to turn to a professional helping source because of difficulties in mobilizing personal resources or because of a lack of assistance from the people in his or her immediate environment. Requiring the client to behave differently through performing tasks not only suggests the active, goal-oriented nature of brief treatment but offers a direct test of the client's willingness to engage in change attempts.

REAL-LIFE CHANGES. At the same time, the fact that tasks take place outside the therapeutic session conveys an important message to the clinician as well as to the client. The concept of instigative therapy, as I have already noted, reduces the importance of the therapeutic session and, in its place, highlights the primacy of change in the natural environment. What really matters are the changes that take place in the client's actual life. From this perspective, therapist and therapeutic methods are only servants to this essential goal. Such a focus tends to reduce client dependency and promotes an important theme of self-management or personal coping.

TASKS VERSUS ADVICE. There are some distinct differences between the employment of tasks and the everyday tactic of advice giving that need to be examined at this point. Tasks are assigned within a context in which the practitioner, as the individual prescribing the task, has an explicit mandate—a contract with the client—to bring about some type of desired change. Advice giving, at least in its everyday manifestations, seldom has so clear-cut a sanction, so advice is commonly given with such introductory phrases as, "Why don't you try . . .?" or "Have you thought of . . .?" Task assignment, as the Minuchin transcript illustrates, is unabashedly direct. The therapist simply says, "For this week, I want you to . . ." and spells out the exact nature of the assignment. At times the therapist may employ what Bandler et al. (1976) have called the "polite command" ("What I would like you to do, if you would, is to . . ."), but even here the directive intent is clear.

In contrast to advice, then, it is quite apparent that the practitioner expects the task to be carried out. Furthermore, the clinician lets the client know that each assignment will be explicitly followed up and, in succeeding sessions, there will be salient discussion of the individual's performance, successful or otherwise. Advice, of course, is of a much more tentative nature and is seldom given with these expectations of performance and follow-up. Therapists therefore need to keep in mind the typically direct and directive language used in task assignment, for difficulties with client compliance can result from the therapist being too casual or indirect. When that happens, the client may not carry out a task simply because he or she didn't realize the therapist was assigning one.

TASK NONCOMPLIANCE. Finally, a nagging concern for clinicians is how to manage situations in which the client does not carry out the assigned task or, more commonly, only partially completes it. The sensitive and consistent use of the guidelines discussed earlier (particularly Reid's task implementation sequence) should reduce this possibility, but there is no doubt that it will occur from time to time in anyone's practice.

In such instances the first consideration that the therapist must address is the question of task difficulty: Was this an assignment that was beyond the existing capabilities of the client? If so, how can the task be scaled down to a level where satisfactory performance is possible? The partially completed task is less problematic because its successful elements can be reviewed (and reinforced) and the uncompleted portions can serve as a basis for further assignment. If necessary, the clinician and the client must discuss the relevance of the assignment to the goals of therapy as the *client* perceives them, and determine whether the failure to perform was related to some aspect of this issue.

Finally, if the client has been consistently neglecting task performance, it may be necessary to review the entire contract to ascertain whether therapist and client have the same objectives in working together. In some cases failure to perform tasks may be the only way clients have of indicating that they are reluctant about change or, because of outside pressures, have agreed to a contract they have no desire to keep. It is better to discover and face these important questions at a relatively early phase of the therapeutic process rather than continue an endeavor that has little realistic possibility of benefiting the client.

8

Teaching for Living: Enhancing Social Skills

Few things are impossible to diligence and skill.

—Samuel Johnson, *Rasselas*

Problems in living frequently involve relationships and interactions with other people that have become troubled or dissatisfying. Wives and husbands are unable to talk together without quarreling, children are bewildered by the demands of their peers, and for many others, young and old, making requests, developing new friendships, and coping with social pressures have become burdensome and stressful. It has become increasingly common in recent years to regard such difficulties as manifestations of social skill deficits rather than call upon more elaborate explanations (Curran & Monti, 1982; Rose, 1990; Wells, 1992). Troubled individuals are simply seen as never having had the opportunity to learn the requisite social skills required for effective living or as not having developed skills suitable for managing the life situation presently confronting them. The therapeutic task, then, is one of providing training in the particular skills that are missing from the client's repertoire or that have been only haphazardly developed.

Skill training approaches covering many facets of living have been developed (Hollin & Trower, 1986), but this chapter focuses on two major areas of skill development—assertion training and stress management—and considers how these two essential aspects of effective living can be adapted to short-term intervention with troubled individuals. Both of these skill areas will be described in some detail and illustrated through practice examples. It will be apparent that in some cases, skill training constituted the major focus of intervention.* In other instances, however, the training was very specifically focused and formed a part of a package of interventions.

ASSERTION TRAINING

Possibly the earliest distinct use of assertion training in clinical practice was described by Andrew Salter (1949) in his book *Conditioned Reflex Therapy*. Salter, one of the pioneers of behavior therapy, distinguished between "inhibitory" and "excitatory" behaviors, the latter term coinciding with what we now call assertiveness.

Following Salter's work, other behavior therapists continued the refinement of assertion training techniques. The writings of Wolpe (1990) and Lazarus (Wolpe & Lazarus, 1966) have been particularly influential. At the beginning of the 1970s there was a significant increase in public awareness and interest, and soon a remarkable number of self-help books appeared on the commercial market.† Around the same time, feminist writers and therapists recognized that assertive skills were a neglected aspect of female experience, and many women's groups began to incorporate such training (Jakubowski-Spector, 1973; Linehan & Egan, 1978).

Basic Components

Lange and Jakubowski (1976) provide a comprehensive description of assertion training, integrating both behavioral and cognitive con-

---

*This is consonant with Laura Epstein's (1980, 1992) position that providing skills is one of the two main procedures of short-term treatment. Epstein considers providing resources as the other major short-term intervention. I can agree with her position as long as one can view the provision of resources in its broadest sense, that is, as including not only tangible and concrete services but the more intangible resources of information and education.

†These included works by Alberti and Emmons (1990), Fensterheim and Baer (1975), and Smith (1975). Such books can serve as valuable reading assignments for clients during the early stages of training.

structs, and their work continues to be a highly useful guide for the clinician. They identify four major components in the training process:

(1) Teaching people the difference between assertion and aggression and between nonassertion and politeness; (2) helping people identify and accept both their own personal rights and the rights of others; (3) reducing cognitive and affective obstacles to acting assertively, e.g., irrational thinking, excessive anxiety, guilt, and anger; and (4) developing assertive skills through active practice methods. . . . (p. 2)

Initially, however, assertion training must be identified as a reasonable method of reaching the goals the client wishes to achieve or as a useful adjunct to dealing with a particular life difficulty. It is only occasionally that a client will specifically request assertion training. What is more often the case is that the client's identified problems involve noticeable difficulties in dealing with some (or all) of the people in his or her immediate environment.

Mr. Q., a thirty-five-year-old divorced man, sought counseling in an employee assistance unit because of dissatisfaction with his current job. He held a lower-level managerial position and had recently been passed over for promotion, a decision he regarded as unfair and arbitrary. He described the staff he supervised as unreliable and difficult to manage and frequently found himself caught between their discontents and the demands of upper management.

The client often will view these difficulties as due to the intractability or insensitivity of these significant others, and one of the therapist's initial tasks will be to explain how increased assertiveness on the part of the client could be pertinent to problem resolution. Other clients may be experiencing considerable discouragement or anxiety stemming from persistent problems in important interactions. Assertion training may serve as a viable means to the client's goal of gaining relief from this reactive emotional distress, as Becker and his colleagues (1987) demonstrated with their work on depression. In such cases, it must be noted, the brief therapist is not utilizing assertion training as an end in itself or as a substitute for the client's desired goal. Skill training is employed as a *procedure* specific to achieving the client's chosen goals.

Case Illustration: Coping with Harassment

The reader will recall Mr. Antonini (see Chapter 1), who was extremely anxious and depressed as a result of many months of verbal harassment by his fellow workers. This largely consisted of innuendoes about his masculinity and suggestions that he was homosexual. Mr. Antonini thought the difficulties began after an incident when, he believed, he had been overheard masturbating in the factory washroom.

INITIAL INTERVENTION. Therapy had begun with several sessions of sexual reeducation, since Mr. Antonini's reactions, in part, stemmed from sexual guilt and misinformation. He believed, for example, that anyone who masturbated was homosexual and that he somehow "deserved" this harassment. Direct sexual education for both Mr. Antonini and his wife involved reading assignments, discussion, and specific tasks—adapted from the sensate focus exercises of sexual therapy (Masters & Johnson, 1970)—designed to impart accurate information and, additionally, to enhance their satisfaction with their own sexual relationship. As Mr. Antonini's guilt and confusion about sexual matters diminished, he needed to acquire some direct means of coping with the daily gibes he was enduring, and training in assertive skills became appropriate.*

ASSESSING ASSERTIVENESS LEVEL. Initial exploration of his method of coping with the ridicule revealed that Mr. Antonini generally tended to ignore the remarks or tried to avoid the men who were most active in tormenting him. It was almost inconceivable to him that he could make any direct reply to their sallies. He had thought of physically attacking them, but although he was a relatively husky man, he was apprehensive about the consequences of such direct action and fearful he might lose his job.

---

*This interesting case took place long before the current public and professional concern about sexual harassment issues and, moreover, illustrates that in certain circumstances men, as well as women, can be sexually harassed. The treatment approach involved, first, altering certain of the victim's own beliefs that were impeding action and, second, enhancing the skills needed to take appropriate action.

The therapist explained the difference between aggression and assertion and used this explanation as an entry point into evaluating Mr. Antonini's general level of assertiveness. This was done through a series of hypothetical critical incidents—"What would you do if you bought a shirt at a department store and found it was slightly defective after you returned home?" "How would you go about telling your foreman that you think he's demanding too much work from you?" and so on. These suggested incidents were varied so as to cover a range of situations containing minor to major degrees of stress, and all, of course, were potentially applicable to Mr. Antonini's life context. As he described his typical reactions to these stressful situations, it became apparent that assertiveness was problematic for him. Although not as unassertive as some clients, he tended to handle even mild difficulties through inaction or indirect means.

AFFIRMING THE CONTRACT. As the clinician described the procedures and goals of assertion training, Mr. Antonini somewhat hesitantly agreed that developing this ability might be helpful to him. He clearly realized that he needed more effective ways of dealing with the harassment and at this point was ready to grasp at any straw. The practitioner was willing to accept this positive, though weak, level of motivation rather than struggle to attain a stronger one. As Hepworth (1979) points out in relation to task performance, *readiness* to attempt an assignment (or in this case, a change procedure) should not be confused with a lack of any uncertainty or ambivalence. Early stages in the helping process are often associated with considerable client reluctance.

CREATING A TRAINING HIERARCHY. From the preceding discussion and further brainstorming on existing social situations, a series of incidents were developed in which Mr. Antonini found assertiveness problematic. Wolpe's (1990) Subjective Units of Distress Scale (SUDS) was employed to arrange these into a hierarchy. Like most clients, Mr. Antonini was easily able to grasp the experiential continuum suggested by the SUDS and to rate incidents from 5 or 10 (minor tension) up to 90 or 100 (extreme anxiety). This resulted in the following training hierarchy:

SUDS Level	Social Situation
10	Correcting poor service in a restaurant
15	Reacting to someone cutting into line ahead of him
25	Asking his foreman for overtime
35	Stating a differing opinion to his wife
45	Disciplining his children firmly
50	Contradicting his mother's opinion
55	Purchasing condoms at a drugstore from a female clerk
60	Arguing with older men at work
75	Stating his own opinion with his father
100	Responding directly to harassing sexual remark

DEVELOPING SKILLS. These incidents formed the basis for a series of behavior rehearsals (and accompanying tasks) during the five sessions devoted to assertiveness training with Mr. Antonini. The role-plays began with the least demanding situations in his hierarchy and, session by session, progressed up this continuum. Since his wife attended most of the sessions, she was asked to play the part of various participants in the enactments; where only therapist and client are available, these roles must be shared. The behavior rehearsals typically followed the standard format of enactment-modeling-practice (see Chapter 6), and Salter's (1949) guidelines were employed to articulate the following principles of effective assertion:

1. *Nonverbal dimensions.* The client's initial task is to develop such physical aspects of assertiveness as a firm voice tone and suitable volume, reasonable eye contact, appropriate bodily stance, and, in general, a freer use of gesture. These are modeled by the therapist in early role-plays, which the client is encouraged to emulate. Although the clinician must present an adequate model of assertiveness throughout the training process, care should be exercised in the beginning stages not to overwhelm the client with too many aspects of the skill to imitate in a given rehearsal.

2. *Encouraging appropriate self-disclosure.* At a beginning level

trainees are encouraged to use the personal pronoun "I" in stating a request or denial, rather than the impersonal phrasings typically employed by the nonassertive person. More revealing levels of self-disclosure are introduced, as appropriate, as training progresses.

3. *Expression of feeling.* Rather than employ blaming or defensive responses, the client is taught to express the emotional reaction ("I was upset when you did that") aroused by the situation. At early stages of training the level of intensity expected must be carefully gauged in order to avoid alarming the trainee or, in a few instances, promoting aggressiveness.

4. *Improvisation.* Throughout the entire sequence of enactments the client is supported in developing a natural and spontaneous style of assertion. The clinician frequently emphasizes that there are no specific formulas for effective assertiveness, only general guidelines, but that through practice the client will gain facility in adapting these to a variety of situations. The fact that behavior rehearsals *must* be improvised helps to promote this valuable facet of assertive response.

5. *Expressing disagreement.* Unassertive people often need concentrated practice in expressing disagreement, even within the protective confines of an enactment. Manuel Smith's (1975) "broken record" exercise is highly useful in this area. Thus, during structured role-play the trainee is allowed to use only a single sentence of disagreement (e.g., "No, you cannot borrow my car") no matter what persuasive tactics the other individual in the enactment may employ. The single phrase must be repeated again and again without qualification or variation. The exercise, which may initially be enacted around hypothetical situations, can have a startling effect in desensitizing the trainee to expressing disagreement.

6. *Expressing (or responding to) positive feelings.* The client may need help in directly expressing the positive feelings that are appropriate to a situation, particularly where these must be combined with the assertive denial of a request. Expressing intimate feelings or accepting compliments (without disqualifying oneself) may also be problematic and require attention.

ASSIGNING TASKS. Whether broadly or narrowly focused, task assignments are given as training progresses. These are used to test out the level of skill achieved or to deal with a specific situation that has been rehearsed in the interview. It is not at all unusual for situations demanding assertiveness to appear almost spontaneously from session to session. This seems to be a matter of the client's having developed greater awareness and increased confidence so that previously avoided situations are now noticed. Trainees should be cautioned against undertaking an encounter that is too far above the hierarchy level practiced in the session, although, generally speaking, overreaching themselves is not a common characteristic of the unassertive. The more common problem is one of motivating task performance, but careful attention to the gradient of assignment usually circumvents this problem.

Observational tasks can be employed at early phases of training to augment its effects. Clients are instructed to observe and record in a notebook the assertive, nonassertive, and aggressive actions they encounter among their friends and associates. An assignment of this kind can help the fearful or pessimistic client to realize that assertiveness not only is possible but does not have dire consequences. Thoughtful observation and analysis of the style of assertive friends and acquaintances can also offer clients an important model, drawn from their own immediate milieu, for further study and emulation.

Similarly, situation comedies on contemporary television often use nonassertiveness as a plot device where, for example, a character's reluctance to say no to an overbearing or importuning friend will lead to further complications. Clients can be asked to identify such incidents and to formulate more assertive responses to each situation.

COGNITIVE RESTRUCTURING. Throughout the training process, attention must be paid to what Lange and Jakubowski (1976) characterize as "cognitive obstacles" to developing more assertive behavior. This begins, of course, with the important educational work done in the initial stages of training as the therapist assists the client in understanding the difference between aggression, assertion, and passivity (nonassertion). Many unassertive individuals genuinely believe that there are only two alternatives in any situation—to passively endure or to respond aggressively. Others are confused about the meaning of assertiveness and, when I used the term with one client, he immediately responded, "Yeah, we've got guys like that at work—they're always blowing up."

Along with making these distinctions clear to the client, the therapist should include explicit statements that we all have a legitimate right to assert ourselves, as long as we do not violate the rights of others (Alberti & Emmons, 1990). Practitioners must keep in mind that assertion training, like all psychotherapies, involves teaching the client a new set of values (Beutler, 1984). The difference is that assertion training does this directly and openly—"You have a right to stand up for yourself"—rather than indirectly or implicitly.

As the client carries out the tasks assigned at each level of training, other cognitive obstacles may become apparent. These can include negative self-talk ("I can't do it") or demanding expectations ("If I don't manage perfectly it's no good"), and many other variations of such self-defeating cognitions. Cognitive obstacles can be identified as the therapist uses the task implementation sequence (see Chapter 7) to prepare the client in carrying out an assignment, or will become apparent when reviewing incomplete or failed task assignments. A series of strategies for cognitive restructuring are fully discussed in the following chapter of this book.

MANAGING STRESS. Finally, the clinician should be watchful for situations in which an accumulation of stress is impeding task performance or affecting the client's use of already acquired skills. If stress levels are significant and pervasive, it may well be necessary to provide overall training in stress management, as the next section in this chapter describes. In a number of instances, however, the unassertive client needs only some brief training in a simple relaxation method, for example, in order to manage a particular task better.

FOLLOW-UP ASSESSMENT. Assertion training with Mr. Antonini concluded at the eighth session of the agreed-upon intervention. By that time he had not only worked through the less problematic situations on his hierarchy but had rehearsed several appropriately assertive responses to different versions of the harassment. He and his wife were seen in a follow-up interview five months later and reported that his work situation was quite satisfactory. Not only was he no longer being harassed but, it turned out, he had never had to make any direct response to his co-workers' ridicule, despite being prepared to do so. It appeared that his generally enhanced assertiveness, evident through his overall manner and physical bearing (and his no longer avoiding his antagonists), had been sufficient to dispel the difficulties, and the taunting had dwindled away.

Case Illustration: A Passive Husband

With some clients assertion may generally be adequate, but difficulties with a particular person may be evident. In such instances the training hierarchy must concentrate on a graduated series of demands within this troublesome relationship. For example, Mr. Howard, a middle-aged man, found any degree of assertion with his wife extremely difficult, and their relationship was strained by his apparent passivity. The following hierarchy was developed with him and served as a basis for assertion training:

SUDS Level	Relationship Situation
10	Speaking to wife about messing up the bathroom
15	Asking wife about any of her relatives
25	Speaking to wife about work she brings home from her job
30	Asking wife to go to a movie
50	Asking for help with household chores
60	Complaining to wife about household disorganization
70	Handling discussion when wife becomes angry
80	Discussing wife's medical problems
100	Responding to wife's threats to leave the marriage

This case illustrates how the development of an individualized hierarchy for each client guards against a common clinical error in working with the nonassertive. A practitioner who attempted to work with a client such as Mr. Howard on how to handle discussion with his wife when she was angry (a SUDS level of 70) would obviously be beginning assertive training far too high up the scale. Even if this were Mr. Howard's expressed problem, it could only be resolved by first training him in assertiveness in less demanding but still troublesome areas of interaction with his spouse.

STRESS MANAGEMENT METHODS

Like assertion training, the notion of stress management has received considerable public exposure, particularly in the self-help literature (Benson, 1975; Freudenberger & North, 1985). Despite their great usefulness, however, self-help manuals are often insufficient for many people, and a surprising number of them are not exposed to such material. The average client's knowledge of stress management or assertion training methods is likely to be scanty and limited to a vague notion that there are ways of dealing with such difficulties.

The Need for Stress Management Skills

As Cotton (1990) points out, major changes in basic societal values, along with the growing complexity of Western living, have made emotional stress an almost accepted aspect of life. As in other areas of skill training, the therapist attempts to develop a common conceptualization with the client during the initial interview regarding the need for skill training. Clinician and client need to reach a mutual understanding that stress reactions are playing a significant role in the client's difficulties and that learning more effective tension-reduction methods seems to be a reasonable approach to dealing with this problem. For example:

> Mrs. Loniero, age thirty-seven, returned for individual counseling two years after she and her husband had been seen in marital therapy. In the previous contact only slight improvement had occurred in their long-standing difficulties. Mrs. Loniero described a deteriorating situation in which her husband had resumed heavy drinking, refused further counseling, and she was now seriously considering divorce. At the same time, she spoke of her own anxiety and fear about making this decision and how she was finding herself becoming isolated from friends and experiencing many perturbing physical reactions. Her family physician had found no organic difficulties and had prescribed a tranquilizer. Mrs. Loniero and the therapist discussed the possibility that stress management training would be a necessary supplement to meeting her request for help in evaluating her decision to seek a divorce.

In other situations such needs will be evident when an individual, despite adequate facility in certain areas, repeatedly experiences difficulty or failure in managing important social interactions. Finally, behavioral signals such as tightened facial muscles, rigid body posture, fidgety movements, sighs, and pronounced expulsion of breath may be immediately apparent within the first interview and can lead the practitioner to query the presence of dysfunctional levels of stress.

Explanation from the therapist on the effect of stress on human functioning adds to this development of mutual understanding, and along with these more general explanations, the educationally oriented therapist usually provides the client with a clear but succinct description of the training process. In contrast to less specific methods of treatment, the social skill training approaches have the advantage of lending themselves to this sort of concise, nonmystical explanation.

Basic Components of Training

With this initial base established, training in stress management (Hollin & Trower, 1986; Vattanno, 1978) emphasizes three major phases: (1) developing awareness of stress signals, (2) gaining facility in relaxation procedures, and (3) practicing coping with actual stress situations.

IDENTIFYING STRESS SIGNALS. Some clients are able to identify when undue stress is affecting their lives, but others are seemingly unaware of it until it has reached overwhelming proportions. The client is taught that stress is cyclical and is most effectively managed when it can be interrupted or reduced in its beginning stages. Training typically begins with observational assignments in which the client tracks various life situations where tension is experienced, with a particular emphasis on identifying its earliest manifestations. These may be through specific physical reactions, repetitive worrisome thoughts and ruminations, or vague but powerful feelings of growing stress. Whatever their form, these reactions are pinpointed and reframed by the clinician, not as events to be dreaded, but as the necessary signals from the body and mind that stress management is required. Learning the early signals of growing stress offers individuals the opportunity to employ the coping strategies taught in the next stage of training.

DEVELOPING RELAXATION SKILLS. Relaxation training has been characterized by Cotton (1990) as "without doubt the cornerstone of any stress management program" (p. 128). Several approaches to tension reduction have been described in the literature and, singly or in combination, can be taught to the client during the second phase of stress management training. Although relaxation training has been presented in some instances as a lengthy procedure, Marks (1978) reviews several empirical studies suggesting that relatively abbreviated methods offer the client as much benefit as more extended versions. The therapist should regard each of these methods as *potential* entry points to relaxation and view the training process as one of assisting the individual client to discover which method (or combination of methods) works best for him or her.

1. *Words and images.* It is best to begin training with the simplest approaches, teaching the client to use various cognitive cues to induce relaxation. These include the repetition of key words ("relax," "calm," "gentle") or visual images of pleasant scenes (a sunny day or an idyllic beach). I usually verbally guide the client through a five- or ten-minute induction process in which a variety of these cues are interwoven to determine which are most appropriate. From discussion of this experience, and further home practice, clients identify the cues that are most useful to them in reducing tension. They may report that other cue words (e.g., "floating," "slow," "mellow") occurred spontaneously during the relaxation process, and these should be incorporated into the induction as what Smith (1990) has called "deepening suggestions." The advantage in beginning with these verbal and visual cues is that, in contrast to the more elaborate muscular relaxation exercises (discussed below), they can be employed by the client in an unobtrusive way in many public situations.

The clinician should practice the induction process privately before beginning to utilize it with clients and should tape-record these initial attempts. This will provide useful feedback for developing convincing voice tone, cadence, and verbal fluency and also—as a self-relaxation experience—provide the practitioner with a beneficial appreciation of the immediate effects of the process.

2. *Breathing and meditation.* Additionally, a simple meditative method emphasizing breathing awareness can be taught to the client and, as in other procedures, greater facility can be gained through daily practice. Benson (1974) has popularized an effective version of this approach:

In a quiet environment, sit in a comfortable position.

Close your eyes.

Deeply relax all your muscles, beginning at your feet and progressing up to your face—feet, calves, thighs, lower torso, chest, shoulders, neck, head. Allow them to remain deeply relaxed.

Breathe through your nose. Become aware of your breathing. As you breathe out, say the word "one" silently to yourself. Thus: breathe in . . . breathe out, with "one." In . . . out, with "one."

Continue this practice for 20 minutes. You may open your eyes to check the time, but do not use an alarm. When you finish, sit quietly for several minutes, at first with your eyes closed and later with your eyes open. (p. 74)

Frequently clients will spontaneously report enhanced awareness of their breathing during the cue-word and visualization exercises described earlier. In such instances, this mode of relaxation should immediately be incorporated into the induction routine. Indeed, following what Milton Erickson (1967) has characterized as the *utilization principle*, therapists should incorporate into the induction any client response that supports the achievement of increased relaxation.

3. *Muscular relaxation.* Finally, based upon Jacobson's (1929) seminal work on the physiology of muscular tension, a series of exercises has been developed for inducing relaxation in each of the many muscle groups throughout the body. This procedure is most useful in instances where the client has gained a degree of facility with relaxation induction through cue words or breathing awareness, but continues to experience tension in a particular muscle group. Cotton (1990) summarizes the process:

The basic procedure involves asking the client to tense the identified muscle for five to ten seconds, during which time the therapist aids in keeping attention focused by making statements which point out to the client what is happening. The client is then instructed to relax the muscle for 30–40 seconds while the therapist continues to discuss the developing feelings, and the contrast between tension and relaxation. (p. 144)

The therapist verbally guides the client through this procedure within the session and then assigns similar exercises as daily homework. Goldfried and Davison (1976) discuss this approach in detail and offer several versions of such an induction process.

Throughout this stage of stress management training the necessity of systematic practice is consistently emphasized with the client. Daily practice is needed in order to develop a beginning sense of mastery and, equally important, to identify the aspects of the tension reduction procedure that most reliably induce relaxation for the individual client. Some individuals find cue words most beneficial, others respond best to meditative or visual signals, and so on. The clinician points out that this is an individual matter that can only be determined through consistent practice.

COPING WITH STRESS. As clients gain facility in inducing relaxation in the practice situation, they are encouraged to begin testing out this facility in real-life encounters. The emphasis is on *unobtrusive* means of reducing stress, so the client's ability to employ cue words or breathing devices becomes especially relevant. However, the clinician should point out that complete control of stress is neither necessary nor desirable, since the client's own stress reactions of worry or various physical manifestations must be used as signals for the employment of stress management. In this sense, a certain level of stress is needed in order to trigger the appropriate coping mechanisms. Indeed, the theme of coping more successfully should be highlighted at various stages of the training, as this constitutes the most realistic goal of the training.

The observational assignments employed earlier to pinpoint stress signals can now be used to help identify situations where the newly acquired skills in relaxation can be employed. Monitoring should now include any self-defeating cognitions ("This is going to be awful," "I'm going to fail, I know") that are increasing anxiety, and the client is assisted in devising realistic counters to these cognitions, or in substituting more positive statements. Such cognitive restructuring can be an essential component of effective stress management and is discussed more fully in Chapter 9.

Practice Applications

As clients experience success in better stress management across the relevant areas of their life, it will often become apparent that difficulties once regarded as fixed or insoluable can now be approached in a problem-solving manner. Physical and emotional energies that were previously dissipated by stress can now be turned toward better time management, renewed recreational outlets, improved sexual functioning, and so on. Similarly, as overall stress is reduced, the individual can more rationally consider important goals and make simplifying choices that will assist in the continuing process of eliminating self-induced tensions, as well as avoiding or decreasing environmental pressures.

Stress management training, like other skill enhancement approaches, can constitute the major intervention with some clients, whereas with others it may be employed to augment other change strategies. For example, an adaptation of stress management training was the core intervention in helping Mr. Jurecko to control his anger outbursts (see Chapter 3). However, with Mr. Faber and Mr. Toman, it will be recalled, relaxation exercises were highly useful but peripheral to other interventions. Another vignette illustrates this potentiating effect:

> Mr. and Mrs. Thompson, a lower-middle-class couple in their early thirties, were seen for short-term sexual counseling. The major sexual dysfunction was Mrs. Thompson's inability to achieve orgasm. They were initially quite responsive to the structured sensate focus exercises in the sexual therapy regime. However, it soon became evident that Mrs. Thompson was experiencing considerable stress in her daily work as a beautician and that the relaxation components implicit in the sensate focus exercises were not sufficient to reduce this factor. Portions of two sessions were then devoted to individual training for her in stress management. Following some practice, this additional intervention was successful in diminishing the extraneous pressures that had been interfering with sexual function.

It should be noted that this additional change strategy had effects in areas other than the problem area directly contracted with the couple; Mrs. Thompson became much more comfortable and functional in her work, as well as sexually. Thus, although the focused nature of short-term treatment calls for a deliberate restriction in intervention, there is no reason that, from time to time, change strategies introduced to achieve a desired effect will not convey benefits elsewhere. The brief therapist, however, does not indulge in such excursions for their own sake but only if, as with this couple, they are manifestly required to attain the contracted goal.

Further Applications in Practice

Social skill training has the reputation among some practitioners as being mundane and unexciting and, moreover, applicable only to highly dysfunctional individuals, such as formerly institutionalized mental patients. In some ways this reputation is deserved. Compared to the excitement and mystery evoked by intrapsychic exploration or the feeling of power experienced in devising and applying paradoxical interventions, skill training follows a very routine and orderly course. There is no denying the profound simplicity of its procedures and goals. Helping someone to deal with a prying neighbor or an overbearing employer, or to manage the everyday strains of living is very ordinary stuff. Yet this very direct relevance of social skill training to frequent problems in living constitutes its power and makes selected aspects of training an often essential component of brief treatment.

AREAS OF TRAINING. Over the past three decades, many kinds of social skills have been identified; a sampling of the skills discussed in the two volumes of Hollin and Trower's *Handbook of Social Skills Training* (1986) includes the following:

- Parenting skills
- Heterosocial (dating) skills
- Problem-solving skills
- Friendship/conversational skills
- Sexual skills

- Job-finding skills
- Interview skills
- Couple communication skills
- Negotiation skills

CLIENT POPULATIONS. As in assertion training or stress management, similar procedures have been identified—based largely on the shaping, modeling, and positive reinforcement principles of social learning theory (Bandura, 1969, 1986)—for developing client facility in one or more of these skill areas. Training has been carried out with adults, adolescents, conflicted marital couples, school children, former mental patients, divorced persons, dating couples, juvenile delinquents, and so on. Most practitioners have some familiarity with assertion training (Alberti & Emmons, 1990), and in family and couple therapy, Guerney's (1977, 1988) relationship enhancement method is receiving increased recognition. Less well known is the employment of skill training as a critical interventive component in such major areas of mental health concern as depression (Becker et al., 1987; Nezu, 1989), child abuse (Scott et al., 1984), and relapse prevention in schizophrenics (Goldstein et al., 1978).

COMBINING SKILL TRAINING.

The imaginative therapist will find any number of uses for skill training, especially when combined with other interventive methods. In many instances, for example, the client may not need complete assertion training but just enough help to be distinctly assertive in an identifiably difficult situation.

Mrs. Anton, a twenty-three-year-old college student, was striving to emancipate herself from a highly dependent yet conflictful relationship with her widowed mother. Many issues concerning her father's death, her mother's recurrent illnesses, and her own values and attitudes as a daughter were related to this struggle.

Careful exploration and reflective discussion of her reactions and responses within the immediate relationship with her mother formed the major intervention and proved helpful. As this aspect of treatment progressed, however, Mrs. Anton felt helpless in contending with her mother's frequent late-night telephone calls and the lengthy and exhausting conversations that ensued. Assertion training was initiated, focused entirely on how to firmly terminate such calls, and was behaviorally rehearsed over a session or two. This was sufficient to manage this particularly frustrating aspect of the relationship while work on the other areas continued.

In another case, stress management training was used as part of a four-session intervention with a woman who was involved in a series of medical tests to determine the extent of a potentially serious physical condition. The training enabled her to cope with her immediate anxiety and freed her to put energy into such tasks as obtaining full information from her physician and evaluating the treatment options available. In a women's health center, yet another creative practitioner used an extremely brief form of the stress management approach to ease the tensions of mentally retarded women about to undergo a gynecological examination. This intervention was all the more remarkable for being implemented in the only time available—during the fifteen or twenty minutes of a preexamination screening interview.

GROUP TRAINING. It should be noted, however briefly, that many of the forms of skill training are easily adapted to group therapy (Garvin, 1990; Rose, 1977, 1990). Indeed, assertion training is probably more frequently conducted in groups than in one-on-one intervention. Many other variations are possible:

As part of a community mental health center's outreach service to an inner-city area, teachers in a junior high school were asked to identify preadolescent boys who were difficult to manage in the classroom or the playground. Ten boys, twelve to thirteen years in age, were recruited and, with the permission of their families, assigned to two short-term skill training groups.

Training concentrated on the development of assertion and communication skills (Gittellman, 1965) in a variety of social situations, using modeling and role-play procedures. These included how to ask for directions in a strange neighborhood, telling a storekeeper you had received the wrong change for a purchase, requesting help from a teacher with a homework problem, responding to criticism from a peer and from an adult, and so on. The group members themselves were helpful in generating many of these items.

The boys participated enthusiastically in this very specific, care-

fully structured approach, and teacher evaluations (using a standard-
ized rating form) indicated significantly better school adjustment at
the conclusion of the training. Such children have often been treated
in loosely structured groups in which it is believed that verbal discussion, recreational activities, and, in general, identification with
the group leaders will promote beneficial changes in social adjustment. The skill training approach, by contrast, is an attempt to focus
directly on imparting the desired behaviors and skills rather than
hope they will arise through less direct means.

9

Cognitive Restructuring Methods

And thus the native hue of resolution
Is sicklied o'er with the pale cast of thought.

—Shakespeare, *Hamlet*

Human experience can be conceptualized along three major dimensions—behavior, emotion, and cognition—and the mainstream practice theories have each tended to accentuate one of these factors to the neglect of the others. Yet there is ample evidence that each of these facets of the human experience, alone or in interaction, is important. This chapter, however, will deliberately isolate a single element, reviewing the important developments over the last two decades in the cognitive approaches to psychotherapy and the clinical applications of these intriguing theoretical and technical advances.

Four major theoretical constructs used in the cognitive therapies are discussed, and the supporting references for each of these suggest further readings for the interested practitioner. I first examine the social learning theory concept of self-efficacy, regarding this construct as the central factor in both cognitive and behavioral change. Succeeding sections review the cognitive theory and practice related to irrational beliefs, faulty thinking processes, and inhibiting or facilitating self-dialogues, as well as change strategies related to each of these areas. In the concluding sections, some additional cognitive change techniques are described and illustrated, and alternate approaches to the treatment of depression are examined.

EVOLUTION OF THE COGNITIVE METHODS

The notion that cognitions—our thoughts, beliefs, attitudes, and values—can affect our emotions and actions is scarcely new. Both common knowledge and a variety of psychological theories have stressed this relationship. Although widely espoused, however, these viewpoints have been rather general, and at a therapeutic level it has been difficult to identify *which* cognitions need to be changed and *how* such change can be most effectively and efficiently accomplished. In addition, there has been insufficient recognition of the immediate and ubiquitous process of cognitive mediation in affecting our judgments and arousing often undesirable emotion. The development of a number of cognitively oriented therapies over the past decade has materially altered this picture.

In recent years the behavior therapists have been particularly active in devising techniques specifically aimed at cognitive change and, interestingly, it is difficult nowadays to find a therapeutic approach in this area that can be regarded as exclusively "behavioral." This trend has also led to a degree of rapprochement between the behavioral and psychodynamic methods (Wachtel, 1977) and a vigorous movement toward eclecticism (Norcross, 1986). In contrast to previous approaches, Mahoney and Arkoff (1978) contend, the emerging cognitive and cognitive-behavioral therapies have been marked by several distinctive features:

1. An emphasis on the specific identification of intruding or detrimental cognitive *processes* as current factors in the person's functioning;
2. The development of discrete techniques for inducing change in these factors;
3. A general emphasis on cognitive change as a *procedure*, rather than an end in itself. (p. 689, italics in original)

This last feature is especially consonant with the emphasis in short-term therapy on the primacy of change efforts aimed at the client's selected problem in living. Although cognitive changes should not be sought for their own sake, they can be utilized, alone or in combination with other strategies, toward the contracted goals of the intervention. The issue for the brief therapist, therefore, is whether achieving change in a target problem such as a conflicted relationship or reactive emotional distress can be most efficiently and effectively attained through a cognitively oriented intervention or through some other strategy.

The practitioner interested in cognitive change procedures will soon become aware that, as in almost any area of psychotherapeutic endeavor, there are a number of cognitive approaches available. In the eclectic spirit emphasized in this book, these differences will be regarded as complementary rather than competitive, and the usefulness of these various strategies to the immediate purposes of brief intervention will be evaluated.

SELF-EFFICACY: THEORY AND PRACTICE

In outlining the immediate goals of the initial interview, I suggested that arousing hope was the primary objective of the early engagement process, referring to Bandura's (1977b) discussion of efficacy assumptions and suggesting that the individual's belief in his or her own competence to act was an essential ingredient of hope. Bandura (1986) has continued to examine both theoretical and empirical aspects of this central construct and, indeed, has produced persuasive evidence that changes in self-efficacy are closely related to all forms of personal and behavioral change. From this standpoint the effectiveness of *any* therapeutic procedure is governed by its ability to heighten the troubled individual's sense of competence.

THEORETICAL BASE. Bandura (1977a) differentiates between two types of expectancy belief. He defines an *outcome expectancy* as "a person's estimate that a given behavior will lead to certain outcomes" (p. 193). For example, as a faculty member at a school of social work, I consider it most likely that I will receive a raise in salary if I directly request this of my dean. On the other hand, an *efficacy assumption* is "the conviction that one can successfuly execute the behavior required to produce the outcomes" (p. 193). In relation to my previous example, I may have only a low level of belief in my actual ability to approach the dean with such a direct request. Bandura (1977a) points out a number of consequences that can follow from the individual's perceived level of self-efficacy:

The strength of people's convictions in their own effectiveness is likely to affect whether they will even try to cope with given situations. . . . People fear and tend to avoid threatening situations they believe exceed their coping skills, whereas they get involved in activities and behave assuredly when they judge themselves capable of handling situations that would otherwise be intimidating. (pp. 193–194)

As a central mediator between information and action, self-efficacy is also seen as influencing coping efforts once they are under way. Higher levels of perceived self-efficacy will tend to promote greater persistence and strength in the individual's coping behavior. Lower levels will more likely result in inhibition or failure and, consequently, perpetuation of the perceived incompetence. Bandura notes, however, that "expectation alone will not produce desired performance if the component capabilities are lacking" (p. 194), and as the preceding chapter stressed, the troubled client may need careful training in any of a series of deficient social skills in order to raise his or her perception of self-efficacy and make action even possible.

INCREASING SELF-EFFICACY. For people whose low levels of self-efficacy are affecting key areas of their life—a common clinical problem—what can most effectively raise their perceived sense of competence? The social learning theory analysis identifies four major sources of information about self-efficacy available to the individual, each of which corresponds to certain clinical procedures. The most powerful of these sources are *performance accomplishments*, that is, feedback from the person's actions that demonstrate the ability to cope. Next in potency are what Bandura calls *vicarious experiences*, in which the individual sees others coping successfully with similar problems. It is also possible to gain a heightened level of self-efficacy through the *verbal persuasion* provided by significant others (including, of course, the therapist), although this source of information is generally weaker in its effects because of the lack of genuine participation by the individual. Finally, certain forms of *emotional arousal* can add to self-efficacy expectations, particularly if the person finds that the aroused emotion in a feared situation is less debilitating than had been anticipated.

Bandura and his associates (1977a, 1980) have conducted a series of studies within the therapeutic setting to determine the generality of self-efficacy theory and to identify the comparative strength of these various approaches to altering the individual's perceptions. Their data substantiate that perceived self-efficacy is closely related to therapeutic gain and, furthermore, changes in concert with a variety of behavioral and other measures. In examining the changes in clients with severely disabling phobias, for example, they found that enactive therapeutic methods, particularly those emphasizing real-life tasks, were most beneficial in increasing self-efficacy. These studies of therapeutic process strongly suggest that the major aim of any intervention must be to heighten perceived self-efficacy, and that methods that stimulate the individual's actual performance accomplish this objective most effectively.

ENACTMENTS AND TASKS. Although these conclusions are generally supportive of such typical behavioral therapy approaches as modeling and desensitization, the implications of the data are much broader. For example, the emphasis in brief therapy on behavior rehearsal and task assignment is supported by these findings. From this perspective, such strategies should not be regarded as simply convenient shortcuts toward change but as critically related to the process of inducing change in the client's sense of competence. Both of these methods are enactive and, when skillfully shaped to the client's immediate needs, can provide the necessary foundation for this key aspect of cognitive change. As later sections of this chapter will describe, tasks are frequently employed in all of the major cognitive therapies.

This is not to say that therapeutic procedures involving verbal persuasion or emotional arousal should not be employed. At many points throughout this work I have suggested ways in which the therapist can employ language or the nuances of the immediate relationship as part of the helping art. It is apparent, however, that the effect of these techniques on a central construct such as self-efficacy is relatively weak, and methods that rely solely on such strategies would be questionable, particularly where the troubled individual is struggling with a problem of some magnitude.

Thus, techniques such as redefinition, relabeling, suggestion, supplying information, and reshaping attribution are best regarded as supplementary to such active strategies as modeling, behavior rehearsal, and task performance. The various forms of emotional arousal—ventilation, catharsis, confrontation—should be seen in a similar light. They form a useful part of the therapeutic repertoire but are most effective when preparatory to, or combined with, the active strategies that can directly foster heightened competence or self-efficacy.

IRRATIONAL BELIEFS

Perhaps the earliest of the distinctly cognitive approaches is Albert Ellis's (1962, 1971) rational-emotive therapy (RET). Ellis contends that certain strongly held beliefs influence the perceptions of the troubled person in a manner likely to either arouse such negative emotions as anxiety and depression or significantly impair the individual's judgment and ability to act. In either case, effective management of even normal problems in living is profoundly affected.

Ellis (1962) characterizes these cognitions as "irrational beliefs" and has identified a set of twelve that he regards as most detrimental as well as most commonly held by troubled people. These include, for example, the belief that "it is a dire necessity for every human being to be loved or approved by virtually every significant other person in his community" (p. 61), that "one should be thoroughly competent, adequate, and achieving in all possible respects, if one is to consider oneself worthwhile" (p. 63), and "the idea that it is awful and catastrophic when things are not the way one would very much like them to be" (p. 69). These three appear to be the most fundamental and pervasive of the irrational ideas. The remainder of the twelve that Ellis identifies, as Lange and Jakubowski (1976) suggest, can probably be considered "'second-order' cognitive reactions after one of the three basic beliefs is operating" (p. 127).

INDUCING CHANGE. The RET approach to cognitive modification includes (1) identifying the irrational assumptions most affecting the client; (2) convincing the client of the potency of these beliefs in his or her life; (3) verbally challenging the logic of the client's irrational belief system; and (4) further exercises and assignments, both in the interview and outside, to develop a more rational belief system. DiLoreto (1971) offers supporting empirical data from a carefully designed controlled study on the efficacy of the RET approach.

Two aspects of RET are particularly worth noting. First, the theoretical principles of the approach are immediately and openly taught to the client, usually in the initial phases of intervention. It is considered essential that the individual have a clear grasp of the RET cosmology in order to be able to examine and change his or her life in accord with these principles. However, perhaps the most unique feature of the RET approach to cognitive change is the frequent use of a technique of direct disputation in relation to the client's irrational beliefs. The therapist persistently exposes and challenges these assumptions, utilizing a combination of probing questions and pointed confrontations, along with a continued teaching of RET theory and philosophy. Walen et al. (1980) offer many examples of this strategy.

CLIENT: But it's awful if I don't get this promotion!

THERAPIST: Well, just how is that awful?

CLIENT: Because . . . then I'll be stuck in the same job and I won't get the extra money nor the prestige that goes with it.

THERAPIST: Look, Jack, that's evidence why it's unfortunate or bad that you don't get the promotion. Because it's bad, it doesn't follow that it's terrible. Now, try again. Can you show me how it's *terrible*?

CLIENT: But I've worked hard for this for a long time. I deserve it!

THERAPIST: Jack, that may be true that you've worked hard. But that's only further evidence that it's unfortunate that you didn't get it. How is that *terrible*?

CLIENT: You mean all those reasons for it being bad don't make it terrible?

THERAPIST: That's right, Jack! Terrible means that you can't live with this or possibly be happy. It means 101 percent bad. Now, how is failing to get the promotion *that* bad? (p. 101)

Walen and colleagues (1980) discuss the disputation method in some detail and provide the practitioner with many useful guidelines for its application. Their discussion is also noteworthy for its examination of many of the nuances of the directive approach in therapy, an often neglected aspect of therapeutic activity.

ASSIGNINGS TASKS. Irrational ideas can also be challenged and altered through homework assignments. Some examples of these were briefly reviewed in Chapter 7 when risk-taking and shame-attacking assignments were discussed. Yet another instance from my own practice involved a young man struggling with a moderate depression as he attempted to work out more adequate personal relationships. Discussion revealed that he was convinced that almost everyone else, unlike him, was happy and contented. This irrational belief had the effect of generating a good deal of inhibiting rumination and self-pity. He was instructed to ask several of his friends and acquaintances whether they were happy and to listen carefully to their replies. The following week he reported his amazement at the amount of discontent this simple question had revealed, placing his own troubles in a much more realistic perspective.

FAULTY THINKING PROCESSES

All human beings are constantly engaged in processing the information received from various external and internal sources, and in the course of such operations errors may arise. Mistakes in judgment then ensue and, from these, maladaptive behaviors may develop. Such writers as Beck (1976), Mahoney (1974), and Raimy (1975) have contributed to the theoretical base and the clinical applications of this approach to cognitive restructuring. Indeed, to many practitioners, cognitive therapy simply means the well-developed (and well-researched) system of therapy originally developed by Aaron Beck and his associates for the treatment of depression (Beck et al., 1979) and later extended to the treatment of both anxiety (Beck & Emery 1985) and personality disorders (Beck, 1990). Without denying the signal contribution made by Beck and his colleagues, I believe it will be instructive to look at the many similar ideas espoused by other clinical writers as this highly useful therapeutic approach has evolved.

Rathjen et al. (1978) suggest that from a clinical perspective the essential question in relation to cognitive processing is "What underlying rules lead to competent and incompetent performance?" (p. 42). Each of us, at any given moment, receives information from many sources—the opinions and actions of others, cues from the immediate physical environment, our own emotional and physiological reactions, and stray recollections of past experiences, to name only a few. These must be interpreted, encoded, evaluated, and, when needed, recalled in order to make a decision or mobilize a particular action. Arriving at a decision or carrying out an action, in turn, provides further information that must be managed in the same way.

Governing this process is a series of underlying rules, often quite idiosyncratic, that are used to organize and simplify what would otherwise be an overwhelming mass of data. The cognitive therapists have identified a number of common errors or of distortions in cognitive processing that may seriously mar its operation, and these are discussed at length by Beck (1976), Beck et al. (1979), Burns and Beck (1978), and Mahoney (1974). A number of the more prominent distortions will be reviewed here.*

1. *Selective inattention.* Although the individual must necessarily simplify many aspects of experience, this aspect of the cognitive process can become skewed and cause the oversight of important cues. For example, nonverbal or contextual qualifications may be disregarded in evaluative feedback from significant others, or the presence of positive statements may be ignored.

2. *Incorrect labeling.* On the other hand, information from the environment may be accurately received but mistakenly categorized or labeled by the person. Nonverbal cues are particularly subject to such misclassification, as they are by their very nature ambiguous ("Did her silence mean consent?"). Individuals may also mislabel their own internal experiences and, as Walen et al. (1980) point out, misidentify anxiety as guilt or vice versa.

3. *Arbitrary inference.* In some instances, of course, this type of faulty thinking may be the classic non sequitur in which the conclusions do not follow from the premises. More commonly, however, individuals may simply reach a conclusion based on scanty evidence or where the available evidence is actually contrary to the conclusions drawn.

4. *Magnification.* Accurate information processing is heavily dependent on the interpretation the person places on an event. A

---

*Although I will emphasize how faulty thinking processes affect troubled individuals, it will be obvious that any of these disortions can be present in the processing operations of quite functional people. The misperceptions and erroneous judgments they promote are simply less disastrous for those of us not already in a stressful situation.

common error is to exaggerate the personal significance of a current or past experience, thus increasing its potential for heightened emotional arousal.

5. *Overgeneralization.* A pernicious tendency in the distressed person is to take a single incident of difficulty or failure as proof of complete personal inadequacy. As in some instances of arbitrary inference, the critical incident may have some relevance to the issue of adequacy, but its utilization as complete proof is not justifiable. This type of fallacious reasoning is particularly likely if the individual has already magnified the importance of the event.

6. *Dichotomous reasoning.* In this type of faulty processing, individuals tend arbitrarily to interpret their experience in an either-or fashion. Thus, one is either good or bad, lovable or unlovable, and events are joyful or catastrophic, with no gradations between.

7. *Misplaced attribution.* Troubled individuals may tend to ascribe responsibility to external sources in the case of success ("I couldn't have done it if she hadn't helped me") and to themselves in the case of failure ("I've ruined it all again"), in both instances significantly impairing their sense of self-efficacy.

EXPLAINING TO THE CLIENT. The cognitive therapists have developed a variety of approaches to altering these faulty thinking processes. As in any therapeutic approach, the development of a common conceptualization (Meichenbaum, 1974) between therapist and client concerning the nature and source of the difficulties is essential. It is little use attempting to work with a client on distorted thinking processes if, say, the client is convinced that her problems are entirely due to her husband's insensitivities or the deprivations of her early life. Piasecki and Hollon (1987) emphasize this early step:

> We typically like to draw the client out about his or her experience of depression and his or her understanding as to why he or she is currently depressed. Typically, the client will discuss perceived inadequacies or overwhelming life events. . . . The information uncovered in this process can then be used to illustrate a cognitive theory of depression. (p. 128)

Similarly, Burns and Beck (1978) present several case illustrations of the cognitive approach to such mood disorders as depression and anxiety, and in each of these the therapist places considerable emphasis on explaining to the client in simple, straightforward terms how behavior and emotion are affected by thoughts. Analysis of several case studies of cognitive therapy (Wells, 1993) found much early emphasis on this sort of clear and detailed explanation of both the nature of the emotions and of what would be required of the client during intervention. These are further clinical examples of the structuring techniques described in Chapter 5 and underscore once again the importance of the information-giving, educational role of the therapist.

UTILIZING TASKS. From such explanations clients often readily grasp the notion that how they are thinking, the manner in which they interpret the experience available to them, can profoundly affect both emotional response and behavior. Like any new level of awareness, gaining such knowledge can induce a degree of change, but the helper is well advised not to rely on this alone. Cognitive therapists reinforce such intellectual changes through a series of observational and performance tasks that capitalize on the findings I have already noted in discussing self-efficacy—that changes in cognitive patterns are most strongly influenced by feedback from actual experience.

Thus, logs and diaries are used as a medium for gathering data on the client's immediate experience and the manner in which he or she is processing this information. The Daily Diary of Dysfunctional Thoughts (described in Chapter 7) is a prime example of this approach, since the client is encouraged to track the occurrence of disturbing cognitions and, in addition, to experiment with substituting more realistic or more positive statements. As therapist and client jointly examine the diary, it is useful (a) to repeatedly ask the client for the *evidence* for any of the automatic thoughts and (b) to have the client rate the *believability* of any of these thoughts on a scale of 0 to 100 percent. The purpose of this process, which is used repeatedly in homework reviews, is not to just to challenge the client's cognitions but, most important, to teach him or her a more realistic and rational method of self-evaluation (Piasecki & Hollon, 1987).

Similarly, Lazarus and Fay (1975) offer many examples of performance tasks designed to challenge negative cognitions in their book *I Can If I Want To*. Although it was written as a popular self-help book, both authors are highly experienced clinicians, and the volume contains many specific illustrations of tasks that can be used to influence faulty thinking processes or crippling beliefs. With the individual fearful of making mistakes, for example, a series of behavioral assignments might be prescribed, including keeping a daily log of errors or efforts to conceal mistakes, deliberately drawing attention to one's mistakes instead of covering them up, and telling friends about major mistakes one has made. Similarly, Burns and Beck (1978) not only give an anxious young man the assignment of attending a social gathering, but also pose several related questions on which he is to gather data while at this event in order to test out his anticipatory apprehensions about how others will respond to him.

These illustrations also epitomize the collaborative, empirical spirit that characterizes the cognitive restructuring approach. In the case described by Burns and Beck, the therapist accepts the shy young man's apprehension that "no one will talk to me," but reframes this as a question that can only be realistically answered by attending the social gathering and tracking the number and amount of conversations he has. In a like vein, the belief that making a mistake would be terrible is not directly challenged by the therapist, nor are its conjectured historical roots examined. Instead, the behavioral assignment of deliberately making a mistake offers the client the opportunity of evaluating the anxiety this raises and, of course, can be accompanied by training in stress management techniques to cope with any actual tensions.

CHALLENGING FAULTY THINKING. At times, moreover, material from the client's diary or log can be reviewed within the therapeutic session and faulty thinking patterns can be directly challenged by the practitioner in a manner analogous to the disputing techniques of the RET advocates. For example, Layden and her associates (1993) illustrate this technique through a dialogue between Aaron Beck and a depressed man who had characterized as "utter disaster" his failing to receive a promotion:

> DR. BECK: On a scale of 0 to 100, how much of a disaster was the loss of this promotion?
>
> PATIENT: Definitely 100. It's a crushing blow. I can't get over it.
>
> DR. BECK: I know it's very upsetting to you, but if you could bear with me for a moment, let's see if we can put this in perspective. You

say that the loss of the promotion is a 100 percent disaster. What rating on a disaster scale would you give to a situation where you were in an accident and everybody in your family died?

PATIENT: That would be 100.

DR. BECK: Is the loss of the promotion as bad?

PATIENT: No. Of course not. I see your point.

DR. BECK: What would you rate the loss of the promotion now?

PATIENT: I'd give it 90.

DR. BECK: OK. That's a start. (Pause) How would you rate the situation where you got into an accident and became paralyzed for life?

PATIENT: I'd give it a 95.

DR. BECK: So the loss of a job is only 5 points less noxious than losing the use of your legs?

PATIENT: Not when you put it that way.

DR. BECK: How would you rate the loss of the promotion now?

PATIENT: Maybe a 75. (pp. 74–75)

Once again the collaborative, empirical spirit of cognitive therapy (Alston, 1993), is clearly exemplified in this dialogue. The client is obviously magnifying the emotional impact of the event, but the therapist does not directly challenge this process. Instead, he gently but persistently leads the client through an examination of other potential life events in order, as he says, to "put this in perspective."

In conclusion, although cognitive therapy for depression is itself a short-term psychotherapy, typically entailing sixteen to twenty weekly sessions (Moretti et al., 1990), its greatest contribution to the field of brief therapy has been an important perspective about human difficulties, and a series of strategies for managing these problems. Both viewpoint and strategy add significantly to the repertoire of the brief therapist working in any number of areas of clinical practice.

SELF-DIALOGUES: NEGATIVE AND POSITIVE

Quite aside from these broader concepts of expectation, belief, and cognitive process, there is no doubt that we all talk to ourselves at many times in our daily lives. Distinctly or vaguely, in fragmentary form or in complete phrases or sentences, words flash through our minds as we engage in our typical activities. Meichenbaum (1974, 1975) argues that behavior is mediated by internal cues from these subvocal dialogues with ourselves. He distinguishes two major aspects of this kind of cognitive mediation, either of which may result in dysfunctional response and, consequently, difficulties in living:

1. *Prevalence of negative self-talk.* Individuals may be habitually producing a series of negative cues in their self-talk that inhibit, block, or disrupt the needed response. In a situation calling for assertive action, for example, the internal dialogue ("I can't do it," "I'll blow it again," "I'm such a fool") may effectively inhibit the desired behavior, or at least arouse emotion with much the same effect. In such instances, therapeutic attention must be directed to reducing the negative self-talk that is resulting in maladaptive behavior or debilitating emotional arousal.

2. *Lack of positive self-talk.* On the other hand, individuals may not be utilizing the kind of positive self-talk ("Try that first and see if it works," "Take it easy, you're doing all right") needed to monitor, guide, and encourage the sequence of steps often involved in complex behaviors. For example, there is evidence (Kendall & Braswell, 1985) that hyperactive children do not provide themselves with the discriminative and self-reinforcing cues necessary for even simple problem-solving tasks. (I will discuss a cognitively oriented therapy for such children a little later in this section.)

REDUCING NEGATIVE SELF-TALK. Certain of the principles of systematic desensitization, a therapeutic procedure well established as an effective intervention with moderate to severe anxiety (Kazdin & Wilson, 1978), have been adapted to the treatment of negative self-dialogues. Meichenbaum (1975) calls this approach *self-instructional training* (SIT) because of its emphasis on the person's learning to guide or instruct himself or herself in a more effective manner.

As in social skill training, clients are asked to identify a series of real-life scenes along a continuum of increasing difficulty or anxiety and to imagine someone (not necessarily themselves) responding to each of these situations in turn. These cognitive rehearsals begin, as in desensitization, with the least demanding situations and progress toward the more difficult, but rather than using the mastery kind of imagery, a *coping* imagery is emphasized. The client is asked to imagine a scene in which anxiety and negative self-statements are usually experienced, and is then coached by the therapist to substitute positive statements, guiding cues, and selected relaxation procedures that will make the experience more manageable. The approach recognizes the reality of anxiety but utilizes cognitive rehearsals, within the therapeutic session, to teach and strengthen coping responses. Homework assignments are given to practice this kind of imagery repeatedly as clients gradually introduce it into their daily life.

The SIT approach can thus lead, as Meichenbaum (1975) points out, to clients viewing anxiety "as positive and not debilitating (i.e., as a cue for employing their coping mechanisms)" (p. 375). Densensitization becomes, in Meichenbaum's words, an "active means of learning coping and self-control skills" (p. 375) rather than a passive procedure for counterconditioning relaxation responses. In addition, the common human tendency to worry is accepted, but reframed and redirected into serving as a useful signal for the activation of coping responses. This is a more realistic goal with many clients than attempting to completely eliminate their tendency toward anxiety or worry. In effect, the client becomes reeducated: worry and tension are transformed into the normal cues needed to mobilize one's coping devices.

Modeling is similarly used in self-instructional training. The model is visualized, in the cognitive rehearsals, as employing coping behaviors to reduce anxiety, rather than mastering a situation in an anxiety-free manner. The therapist coaches the client to visualize the model using guiding self-instruction, relaxation procedures, and self-reinforcement in each of the rehearsed scenes. Additionally, the model may show anxiety in the initial phases of the visualization in order to increase the perceived similarity between model and the observing client.

Throughout the SIT process, whatever the coaching, modeling, or rehearsal procedures employed, there is a consistent emphasis on accepting and utilizing the client's learned pattern of worry and fear as a beginning point for change:

> the client's own maladaptive behavior is the cue, the reminder, to use the cognitive and behavioral techniques. In the past the client's symptoms were the occasion for worry, anxiety, depression and mal-

adaptive behaviors, whereas following self-instructional training what the client says to himself about his symptoms has changed to a more adaptive way of functioning. (Meichenbaum, 1975, p. 378)

TEACHING CHILDREN SELF-CONTROL. Yet another application of self-instructional training can be seen in work with hyperactive children, who, as noted earlier, are often deficient in guiding themselves through even simple problem situations (Meichenbaum, 1979; Kendall & Braswell, 1985). A form of play therapy is used as the medium of the therapeutic encounter, but in contrast to the reflective and interpretive procedures of conventional play therapy, the clinician uses the session as an opportunity to directly reshape the child's self-dialogues.

The therapist and child engage in a series of tasks during the play, whereby the therapist overtly models the kind of guiding self-dialogue that can be used to contain frustration and expedite task accomplishment:

Okay, what is it I have to do? You want me to copy the picture with different lines? I have to go slowly and carefully. Okay, draw the lines down, good; then to the right, that's it; now down some more and to the left. Good, I'm doing fine so far. Remember, go slowly. Now back up again. No, I was supposed to go down. That's okay. Just erase the line carefully. . . . (Meichenbaum, 1979, p. 19)

Following modeling by the adult, the child performs the task with continued guidance from the therapist. Further repetitions by the child encourage first spoken, then whispered self-instruction and, finally, covert self-guidance. The training procedure, emulating the models provided by both desensitization and social skill training, involves a series of tasks of gradually increasing difficulty and complexity. Recognizing the short-attention span and low frustration tolerance of such children, the therapist should keep sessions relatively brief and must provide a good deal of verbal praise and other suitable reinforcers.

Meichenbaum's (1979) review of self-control training with children summarizes the findings of a number of studies supporting the effectiveness of this cognitively oriented approach. An additional controlled study (Kendall & Wilcox, 1980) found significant changes in social adjustment of treated children, with the gains maintained at a one-month follow-up assessment.

APPLICATIONS IN COUPLE THERAPY. Finally, both negative self-dialogues and the lack of positive self-guidance can be particularly disruptive in important interpersonal relationships (Segraves, 1990). With conflicted couples, for example, either of these patterns may be operating. A couple may be functioning in terms of negative stereotypes or cues ("He won't listen," "She doesn't care," "I'll just get hurt again") that disrupt such positive actions as affectional gestures and clear requests. On the other hand, through inadequate learning experiences or long-continued conflict, they may also lack the positive discriminative cues ("She'll enjoy this," or "Try to say it more clearly") necessary for maintaining a constructive relationship. Brief couple therapy methods are discussed more fully in Chapter 10.

FURTHER COGNITIVE CHANGE TECHNIQUES

Two further cognitive change strategies, thought stopping and cognitive rehearsal, are worth examining at greater length. These techniques are quite flexible and can often be combined with other strategies—one of the social skill training approaches, for example—or utilized as a major change component in a single-session intervention.

THOUGHT STOPPING. Wolpe's (1990) thought-stopping technique is particularly useful where an individual is experiencing episodes of ruminative thought that are arousing dysfunctional levels of anxiety or interfering with important activities. Clients typically describe themselves as unaware of the beginnings of these worrisome cycles and express a great sense of helplessness about controlling them.

The possibility of learning this self-management strategy is introduced by the therapist after the need to control worrisome thought cycles has been clearly established and the technique is rehearsed in the therapeutic session, prior to any application in real life. In the rehearsal the therapist instructs the client to consciously begin the cycle of intruding thought and to signal when this is clearly present. At that moment the therapist shouts "STOP!" to the client and then inquires about the effect of this sudden intrusion. Clients, of course, are visibly startled and will almost always report at least a momentary interruption in the ruminative cycle, and the therapist uses this as an opportunity to underscore the possibility of gaining further control. The same sequence is rehearsed several times more within the session, with the client gradually taking over responsibility to say "Stop" at the appropriate moment. It can be helpful to have the client reinforce the use of the "Stop" signal by visualizing a pleasant scene or by verbalizing positive reinforcement. During these latter rehearsals the "Stop" signal is changed from a spoken to a subvocal form, and the client is instructed to practice this covert version at home. Five to ten daily repetitions are prescribed, and after perhaps a week or two of practice, the client is asked to use the procedure when disturbing thoughts intrude in real life.

Some further instructions also seem to help clients use thought stopping effectively. First, I suggest that it should initially be used on an "experimental" basis and the client should not expect the technique to stop all worrisome thoughts immediately. Second, as in stress management training, worrisome thoughts are reframed as positive signals that inform the individual that thought stopping is needed. Third, the client is told that the ruminative cycle will probably return, not too long after a given thought-stopping command, and that it is likely that repeated thought stopping will be needed. Finally, thought stopping is characterized as a way of obtaining at least temporary relief from unwanted worry and is helpful in freeing up energy the client can use in whatever other problem-solving activities have been identified.

COGNITIVE REHEARSAL. There are also instances where a cognitive version of behavior rehearsal can be used to stimulate change. Kazdin (1973, 1974) offers empirical evidence that this approach can alter anxiety reactions or enhance assertiveness, and its effectiveness with even severe phobic conditions has been demonstrated (Bandura et al., 1980). Theoretically, cognitive rehearsal is based on modeling principles but utilizes the individual's own mental images as the source of the modeling demonstration. Thus, individuals contending with difficulties in some aspect of an interpersonal relationship are guided in visualizing themselves or another person coping in a more functional way. Mr. Faber (see Chapter 3), for example, was asked to mentally rehearse a series of scenes in which he interacted with young women in a confident and assured manner. As in behavior enactments, the elements of more adequate performance can be arranged along a logical or emotional hierarchy and rehearsed in their appropriate order.

In employing cognitive rehearsal, the practitioner should keep several clinical considerations in mind. Initially, the scene that the client mentally rehearses should be closely monitored by the clinician. The client should describe aloud the essentials of the scene, or the clinician should literally instruct the client in what to visualize. In addition, as Meichenbaum (1975) suggests in relation to self-instructional training, it is usually beneficial to employ a coping rather than a mastery theme in the visualization. That is to say, clients should imagine themselves meeting with a degree of realistic difficulty within the scene, but overcoming this rather than dealing with the situation without any tension at all. Finally, once a scene has been rehearsed within the session, the client can be given the daily homework task of visualizing a specific number of repetitions. Daily practice will tend to reinforce the effect of the cognitive rehearsal in enhancing self-efficacy and consequently reducing detrimental affect or negative cognition.

OTHER APPROACHES TO TREATING DEPRESSION

Epidemiological studies (Meyers et al., 1984; Robins et al., 1984) reveal that depressive disorders are among the most serious and pervasive of mental health concerns. Whether severe enough to warrant a psychiatric label, feelings of sadness and discouragement are common human emotions frequently encountered in therapeutic practice. The competent brief therapist must be knowledgeable about effective ways of helping in this important area of human concern.

As Edelstein (1990) notes, when psychoanalytic thought was paramount in psychotherapy, it was believed that depression was "the result of early childhood experiences and that the proper treatment was the uncovering of these experiences and resolution of the feelings generated by them" (p. 151). This, of course, called for lengthy and extensive therapeutic contact and, as with most psychoanalytic therapy, little or no research examination of its effectiveness.

During the 1970s and 1980s, extensive psychopharmological

research demonstrated the effectiveness of antidepressant medication in relieving depression. Many depressed individuals have benefited from this approach, and the nonpsychiatric brief therapist should be prepared to make appropriate referrals for evaluation for medication. However, as Becker and co-workers (1987) point out, antidepressants are not the only answer to the treatment of depression:

> These medications are efficient to administer and can be very effective for many patients. However, they can have side effects that some patients are unable to tolerate, and some patients simply do not respond to medications. Therefore, it is important to provide alternative treatment procedures for patients who prefer a nonchemical approach or for whom antidepressants are ineffective. (pp. 13–14)

This position has spurred important inquiry and innovation in both the clinical and empirical arenas. Thus, the National Institute of Mental Health's Collaborative Depression Project (Elkins et al., 1989) compared the effectiveness of one of the best-established antidepressant medications (imipramine) with two specific psychotherapeutic approaches—cognitive therapy and interpersonal psychotherapy—and found both of the therapeutic approaches equivalent in outcome to the medication. Preceding sections of this chapter have discussed cognitive therapy, but an examination of interpersonal psychotherapy as yet another established alternative approach to depression (Klerman et al., 1984) is also useful.

There are many parallels between the development of cognitive therapy and that of interpersonal psychotherapy for depression (IPT). Most obviously, both were designed to be specific therapeutic treatments for depression but, in addition, each approach has been carefully evaluated in a series of research studies during its formative stages. This has encouraged the specification of carefully structured guidelines for therapeutic use, and the major proponents of each method continue this pattern of clinical research in examining new applications.

Like other approaches in this highly emotional area, IPT typically begins by providing the client with information on the nature of depression and assurance that effective treatment is available. With this base of understanding established, Cornes (1990) summarizes the major focus of treatment as follows:

The . . . goal is to help the patient develop more successful patterns for dealing with current social and interpersonal problems that were associated with the onset of depression. The major problem areas that have been associated with the onset of depression are (1) delayed or disorted grief reactions, (2) interpersonal role disputes, (3) role transitions, and (4) interpersonal deficits. . . . This is achieved by determining which of the four common problem areas are present and focusing the therapy around one or two of those problem areas, leading to a more complete mastery of social roles and resolution of interpersonal conflicts. (p. 266)

In contrast to cognitive therapy, IPT does not emphasize the internal processing of the client's world, but focuses strongly on his or her immediate transactions with the people in this world. Both approaches are similar, however, in emphasizing the here-and-now of the individual's life and stressing a cooperative, collaborative approach within the therapeutic alliance. As Cornes (1990) notes, IPT "relies on familiar techniques such as reassurance, clarification of emotional states, improvement of interpersonal communication, and reality testing of perceptions and performance" (p. 275) to achieve its goals. Both operate within a time-limited framework, typically involving twelve to sixteen weekly sessions, especially where the client is seriously depressed.

In effect, IPT affirms the importance of several key areas of interpersonal functioning in generating the complex of emotions and behaviors that we clinically identify as depression. For the eclectic brief therapist, there is also a valuable central lesson to be drawn from the established effectiveness of both IPT and cognitive therapy in dealing with depression, as well as support for the specific techniques and strategies utilized in either method. The commonality in these two approaches is that discouraged, emotionally depleted individuals are provided with a supportive explanatory framework for their difficulties, and firm guidance and direction (both inside and outside the therapy session) in reengaging themselves in their current lives and solving the daily problems that confront them.

10

*Brief Family and Couple Therapy**

"My dear friend Copperfield," said Mr. Micawber, "acci-
dents will occur in the best-regulated families . . ."

—Charles Dickens, *David Copperfield*

There is such a wealth of brief family and couple methods available
in the clinical literature (cf. Gurman, 1985; Wells & Giannetti, 1990,
1993) that this chapter can do justice to only a few of these many
approaches. Therefore, following a brief exposition of family systems
theory, this chapter will describe and clinically illustrate two highly
useful methods of family or couple intervention: (1) the innovative
development of one-person family therapy (Szapocznik et al., 1990)
in the area of family intervention and (2) the structured methods of
communication training in couple therapy, particularly Guerney's
(1977, 1988) relationship enhancement method. Both of these are
well substantiated clinical strategies with a wide range of applications across client problems and populations. Along with these two
specific approaches I will look at the employment of tasks in couple
therapy, as well as identifying a number of specific techniques useful

---

*In consonance with current thinking, the term "couple therapy" will be used to describe
therapeutic intervention with two individuals experiencing difficulties in an intimate
adult relationship. Although historically much of this work has been called "marital therapy," its principles and strategies are applicable whether the couple are conventionally
married or of the same or different genders.

in managing the conjoint interviews most often used in therapy with couples and families.

THE EMERGENCE OF FAMILY SYSTEMS THEORY

Although brief psychotherapy has a lengthy history, dating back to at least the beginning of this century (Wells & Phelps, 1990), there is no doubt that it was profoundly influenced by the family and couple therapy methods that began to develop about 1950. The publication of Jay Haley's classic work *Strategies of Psychotherapy* (1963) highlighted the emergence of an approach that emphasized both brief intervention and a relationship-oriented view of human problems.

AN INTERPERSONAL CONTEXT. Haley argued that an individual's symptoms can only be understood in the context of the key relationships in which that person was involved. He contrasted this viewpoint with more conventional theories:

> One might consider anxious behavior by a patient as a way he defends himself against repressed ideas which are threatening to intrude into consciousness. One could also observe that same patient and notice that his anxious behavior occurs in an interpersonal context and so describe that behavior as a way of dealing with, perhaps of disarming, another person. These two points of view represent astonishingly different theoretical systems. (p. 5)

Further, he contended that brief therapy, specifically designed to bring about changes in immediate relationships within a dyad or within the nuclear family, was the most effective way of responding to a wide array of the problems that people typically brought to therapists.

> a patient's symptoms are perpetuated by the way he himself behaves and by the influence of other people intimately involved with him. It follows that psychotherapy should be designed to persuade the individual to change his behavior and/or persuade his intimates to change their behavior in relation to him. (p. 6)

In *Strategies of Psychotherapy*, and in subsequent volumes (1967, 1973, 1990), Haley was also instrumental in bringing the work of

Milton Erickson, the highly innovative brief therapist, to the attention of a wide audience of mental health professionals in both public and private settings. Although Erickson himself did not practice family therapy per se, his emphasis on a strategic, interactional approach in which the therapist uses directives, reframings, and carefully selected tasks to induce change, has profoundly influenced much current couple and family therapy.

Thus, more than thirty years ago, Haley expressed the two most essential concepts of what we now know as family systems theory: first, that behavior must be understood in relation to its current interpersonal context and second, that problematic behavior can be altered by changing the interpersonal context in which it occurs. The remainder of family systems theory, and the clinical practice of much contemporary family and couple therapy, are nothing more or less than elaborations on these two basic ideas.

INFLUENCE OF GENERAL SYSTEMS THEORY. Family theorists have borrowed a number of organizing concepts from the general systems theory expounded by such writers as von Bertalanffy (1950, 1968). The most important of these is the notion of the family as a system, analogous to the manner in which many physical, mechanical, biological, and physiological entities can be seen to be functioning as systems. In a like manner, the members of a family can be usefully viewed in relation to the basic definition of a system, that is, as a group of elements in continuing, reciprocal interaction.

They can also be meaningfully seen as exhibiting that most basic function of systems—the tendency toward homeostasis or self-regulation that helps to maintain the steady state of the ongoing system. Unlike certain physical and mechanical systems that are closed to outside influence, however, the family must be considered an open system, affected by outside influences, but still striving to maintain its habitual interactions and relationships over time.

CYBERNETICS AND COMMUNICATION THEORY. Similarly, concepts from cybernetics and communication theory (Ruesch & Bateson, 1951: Bateson et al., 1956) have also influenced the thinking of family therapists, and Rosenbaum (1990) points out the differing view of how we know our world that flows from such a framework:

Linear epistemologies consist of discrete elements that are assumed to have existences of their own, independent of the relationships and contexts in which they appear. Causality is linear and unidirectional. One atomistic element acts on the other to produce an effect that starts and stops. In contrast, systemic epistemologies see patterns and relationships that alter in different contexts: there is no ultimate essence or identity separate from how it is framed by the participants. This framing is in turn recursive: the way something is framed acts on the framer to alter the framing. (p. 357)

CHANGING THE INTERPERSONAL CONTEXT. Although a given individual functions in a number of systems at any point in his or her life, the family is regarded as the most important and enduring of these systems. From this perspective the family has both negative and positive potential for any of its members, and clinical approaches have frequently emphasized this duality of meaning.

For example, the highly effective family crisis therapy developed by Langsley and Kaplan (1968) and Langsley et al. (1971) draws major interventive support from the notion that individual crisis is often based on shifts and changes in family structure but, at the same time, the family offers the most viable resource for crisis resolution. As Pittman and his colleagues (1990) suggest, the therapeutic task is to quickly identify why the crisis is happening now and, from this knowledge, prescribe tasks and stimulate interaction that will alter the relationship context and assist in restoring the normal functioning of family members.

ONE-PERSON FAMILY THERAPY: A CASE ILLUSTRATION

One of the most promising innovations in the family therapy field in recent years has been the work of Jose Szapocznik and his colleagues (Szapocznik et al., 1990) at the Spanish Family Guidance Center at the University of Miami in developing the principles of one-person family therapy (OPFT). Employing techniques and strategies derived from both structural and strategic family therapies, these researchers have created, and empirically substantiated, a clinically useful way of working with one individual in relation to problems arising within the family system.

UTILIZATION IN PRACTICE. For the brief therapist with a family orientation, OPFT offers both a theoretical framework and a series of interventive strategies with many applications in practice. Its most obvious application is in situations where the problems experienced by the client are interpersonal in nature and where, as Szapocznik and his colleagues note, "[the] client appears to need the benefits of family therapy but circumstances make seeing the whole family during most therapy sessions impractical or undesirable" (1990, p. 494).

There are also instances, for example, where time limitations make it difficult for the clinician to mobilize the multiperson interviews utilized in conventional family therapy. In other cases, key family members will not make themselves available for interviews, or the individual requesting help is reluctant to directly involve his or her family.

BEGINNING OPFT. An extended case example will illustrate the employment of OPFT in the private practice of brief psychotherapy.

> Sally, a thirty-year-old unmarried woman was referred by her family physician who thought that stress and unhappiness were contributing to the physical symptoms she was experiencing. In the initial interview she was highly distraught and wept profusely, making it difficult to get a clear picture of her current situation.
>
> What eventually emerged during this first session was Sally's distress about the demanding and critical attitude her widowed mother displayed toward her. At the same time, Sally felt that her mother was blatantly favoring a younger sister and that this sister was taking shameless advantage of the situation. These difficulties had become more and more pronounced over the past year, and Sally described a number of examples of the mother's criticism and favoritism. Sally believed she tried hard to please her mother and, when she was criticized by her, Sally's typical reaction was to become upset and cry, usually retiring to her room to recover from her hurt feelings.

It was evident during this beginning session that the pressures of the family situation had reached crisis proportions for Sally, and the therapist initially directed his efforts toward emotional support and stabilization. Along with her descriptions of the unsettling family situation, a clearer picture of Sally herself began to emerge. She was a high school graduate who had worked in a clerical department of a large firm for more than twelve years. She enjoyed her work, carried it out competently, and, during her tenure with the company, had been promoted to positions of increasing responsibility. At the present time she supervised the work of a small staff.

Her major social contacts were with other family members, a few close female friends, and her boyfriend, Tom, whom she had dated for more than two years. Tom was a divorced man, about her own age, who lived in an adjacent neighborhood, and Sally would often spend weekends with him at his apartment. They had talked about marriage but had no specific plans; she explained that Tom had only recently obtained his divorce.

There were a number of ways in which Sally experienced her mother's criticisms: Sally's being overweight, or her desire to have a life of her own, or for not being married, and so on. As Sally described their relationship, her mother was liable to criticize her on both major and minor aspects of her life and it was seldom that she (the mother) recognized the effort Sally put into trying to please her. Looking back, Sally felt that she and her mother had had a good relationship in the past, but this now seemed entirely lost.

DIAGRAMMING THE FAMILY. As Sally described the current strains in her family, the therapist used this information to construct a simple diagram of the current family configuration (Figure 10–1).

This mapping of the family system is shared with the OPFT client as it is done and, as Szapocznik and his colleagues (1990, pp. 99, 503) point out, serves several clinical purposes:

1. It enables the clinician to get a comprehensive picture of the immediate family configuration—who, literally, is living in the home and what the ongoing relationships are between these people.
2. The diagram visually represents the family orientation of the therapy and makes it clear to the client that both problems and solutions will be sought within the family.
3. The clinician may use the construction of the diagram as an opportunity for explanatory statements to the client about the interpersonal nature of the potential interventions.

FIGURE 10–1

Family Diagram: One-Person Family Therapy

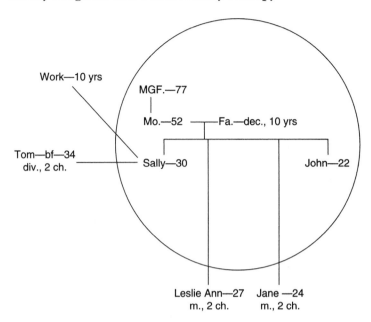

4. Finally, the diagram can clarify important aspects of family relationships that the client is obviously experiencing but may only vaguely or inaccurately perceive.

CURRENT STRESSORS. An especially vexing issue for Sally was her mother's attitude toward Jane, the youngest of her two sisters. Like the other sister, Leslie Ann, Jane was married, had two young children, and lived near the family home. Jane worked part-time, and whenever her regular babysitter was not available, she would bring her children over to have the mother care for them. Sally saw this as an almost outrageous imposition on Jane's part, but she was especially hurt by the way in which her mother went along with Jane's demands. To Sally, this amounted to her mother favoring Jane, as well as manipulation on Jane's part to receive such treatment. Sally had never expressed her feelings about this because she was fearful of provoking her mother, and two or three times she voiced her concern that "she'll disinherit me" if her mother became too angry. The full meaning of this phrase did not become clear until a session or two later in the intervention.

Another critical aspect of the family structure was the presence of the maternal grandfather in the home. He was an elderly man, in his late seventies, and described as quite ill with some sort of incapacitating chronic condition. He was confined to bed, had intermittent difficulty with bladder and bowel functioning, and required a good deal of physical care. This was mainly provided by the mother, who was periodically relieved by Sally in the evenings and on some weekends. The maternal grandfather had previously been in a nursing home, but his care there had not been satisfactory, and sometime during the past year, the mother had moved him into the family home. She and Sally were determined to care for him at home as long as they were able. Mother had had previous work experience as a practical nurse, so these responsibilities were familiar to her. During the first session Sally described this aspect of family life in a matter-of-fact way and did not characterize it as especially stressful to either herself or her mother.

NEGOTIATING A CONTRACT. As much of the foregoing description makes clear, although Sally was quite verbal, she was not a sophisticated person, and this was the first time she had sought out any kind of psychotherapy. She was doing so now upon the recommendation of her family physician, and in the midst of a personal (and family) crisis that was causing her much distress and anxiety.

It was also evident that this was a working-class family that emphasized hard work, close family ties, and daughterly respect for elders—and Sally exemplified all of these virtues. She also was experiencing a good deal of pressure from these same factors, but her essential request in therapy was not how to change her basic attitudes but how to live within them with less personal cost. She had thought of moving out of the family home into an apartment of her own, but she also expressed a good deal of reluctance about taking what seemed to her to be a drastic step. Her greatest concern was to restore the previously positive relationship with her mother, wherever she was living.

Although Sally seemed to be in a crisis state when the initial interview began, she was quite responsive to the practitioner's empathic support during the session and was much more settled by the end of this first interview. The therapist contracted to work with her over four succeeding sessions, spaced at two-week intervals, with the closely related goals of (1) continuing to alleviate her stress and (2) assisting her in improving the relationship with her mother.

ASSIGNING TASKS. Explaining that therapy would involve testing out new ways of acting, the practitioner assigned two initial tasks to Sally. These were both family oriented and were stimulated by the family configuration that had been diagrammed and discussed with Sally earlier in the interview.

One task was aimed at testing out the nature and extent of the negative, critical relationship Sally had described with her mother. She was to request that she and mother do one positive thing together during the next week. The therapist specified that this didn't have to be anything major but must be something positive that both of them would enjoy doing.

The other task was targeted toward the most positive interaction in her current life, her relationship with Tom. Although Sally had indicated that Tom knew how upset she was with things at home, it was also apparent that they had never really discussed this in any depth. Her assignment was to tell Tom, with the same sort of detail and examples that she had given the therapist in this initial session, how unhappy she was at home. Furthermore, she was to ask for his advice about what she should do about these pressures.

The First and Second Interventive Sessions

Let us examine the course of treatment with Sally by dividing the intervention into two segments. During the first four weeks of therapeutic contact, Sally continued to report difficulties with her mother similar to those she had described in the initial interview. Mother continued to criticize her on any number of minor matters, and the relationship was still fraught with tension for Sally.

FOLLOWING UP ON TASKS. When she came in for the first of these two sessions, Sally had not carried out the task that had called for her to request that she and her mother do something positive together. She made some weak excuse about lack of opportunity, but it became evident that she was not sure how to voice such a request. Indeed, Sally was fearful that she would become upset while doing so and would provoke a reciprocal wrath from her mother.

The interviews were being conducted at the beginning of the Christmas shopping season, and requesting that they go out shopping together was identified as a reasonable and nonthreatening request. Some time was spent behaviorally rehearsing how to make such a request, which was helpful in demonstrating to Sally that she could remain calm and also make her request in a clear and positive manner. This task was reassigned at the end of the first interventive session.

By contrast, the task of telling Tom about her difficulties had gone well. It was apparent that they had never talked before in detail about the pressures she was experiencing. Tom was understanding and supportive and encouraged her to continue in therapy to work out the problems. She felt very positive about their relationship, she and Tom had had a good weekend together, and she had started on a diet to lose weight because she wanted to be even more attractive to him. The therapist asked her to continue the diet as her other task for the period between these two sessions.

EXPLORING ALTERNATIVES. There was also discussion in both of these two sessions about the possibility of Sally moving out of the family home and finding an apartment of her own. As she had indicated in the initial interview, she was reluctant to consider this alternative for two major reasons:

1. It was apparently a family rule, not untypical of working-class families, that the adult children remained at home until they married. She had spoken of her fear that the mother might "disinherit" her and said this had happened to her sister Leslie Ann when, prior to her marriage, she had moved out of the family home a few years ago. What "disinheriting" meant was that the mother refused to talk to her daughter or have any contact with her for about a year. This situation eased following Leslie Ann's marriage.

2. The other factor was that, despite the pressures she was experiencing, Sally was comfortable and settled living in the family home. She paid only nominal rent and had recently purchased a large, new car and would find the payments more difficult if she were living in her own apartment. However, several of her women friends were living on their own, and she agreed to an exploratory task in which she would discuss the possibility of sharing an apartment with one of

them. She would also draw up a realistic budget of what she might be able to afford.

In the second of these two sessions, the situation with her mother was still much the same. Sally had again not carried out the task of requesting that the two of them do something positive together outside the home, and the therapist reiterated the importance of her taking this initiative. However, it was also evident that the precarious health of the maternal grandfather was seriously declining. Sally spoke of the demands that this was placing on both her and her mother in taking care of him, and the possibility that he could not survive much longer.

COPING WITH STRESS. The therapist used this as an opportunity to move into some frank discussion with Sally about the pressures that her mother must be experiencing, not only in physically caring for her father but also in knowing that someone she deeply cared for was approaching death. This was done in a nonblaming manner and was largely framed as educational information about the stressful effects caring for a dying parent, and becoming caught up in anticipatory grieving, might be having on the mother. As the same stressors were also affecting Sally, the therapist coached her in some simple stress management techniques she could use to better manage the tensions she was feeling.

Intervention during these first two sessions was based on the therapist's belief that the family was under considerable strain because of such changes as the grandfather's return from the nursing home and the altered (and demanding) role changes this required for both Sally and her mother. As the "one person" (OP) in OPFT, Sally was the potential vehicle through which changes could be made to assist the family to restabilize and thus reduce the discomfort and distress that she was presently experiencing.

EARLY-SESSION ISSUES. During the first few sessions of a brief intervention, it is often the case that nothing particularly different happens and that many of the same difficulties and problems continue unabated. This was certainly the case with Sally, since the criticism from her mother continued unabated. The temptation for the therapist inexperienced in brief intervention is to become alarmed, to think that brief therapy is "not working," to forget about the time limits that have been predicted, and (implicitly or explicitly) to move into non-time-limited therapy. Experienced brief therapists are more used to this period of seeming inactivity, continue to utilize tasks and directives designed to mobilize the client, and hold to whatever time limit has been set.

Similarly, it is also not unusual for clients to fail to comply with tasks in the early phases of therapy. With Sally it might have been better if there had been time in the initial interview to rehearse the request to her mother for positive time together, but this was not done until the first interventive session, after she had failed to carry out the task. When she failed the task a second time, the therapist saw this as affirming the importance of Sally taking this initiative with her mother and reassigned the task one more time.

A Critical Event

In the interval between the second and third sessions, an event took place that represented a turning point in the current relationship between Sally and her mother. A week before the third session, Sally phoned the therapist's answering service with an urgent request for a telephone consultation. Fortunately, the therapist was able to return her call not long after it was placed and found that Sally and her mother had, at Sally's request, been out Christmas shopping together. During this time together the mother had made some critical comment and, Sally, to her own utter amazement, had told her mother that these sorts of remarks deeply hurt her.

As she described this episode on the telephone, Sally was surprised that she had been able to stand up to her mother in this way and was also astonished that her assertiveness had not simply made her mother more angry and critical. The therapist assured her that she had taken an important step in improving her relationship with the mother. An earlier appointment was arranged to help Sally deal with this critical event.

The Final Two Interventive Sessions

The major focus of the third session was concerned with reviewing and strengthening the breakthrough Sally had achieved in her relationship with her mother. She reported that her mother had been apologetic about hurting her with her criticisms and, since that time, their relationship had been much more positive.

REINFORCING ASSERTIVENESS. In further behavioral rehearsal, Sally was coached in assertive ways of telling her mother that her critical remarks were hurtful and unfair. In effect, the rehearsals both supported and refined the response that Sally had already made. In addition, rehearsing such responses further reinforced the permission that the therapist had given Sally to alter certain aspects of her relationship with her mother.

Because Sally was not used to being assertive with her mother, even at this very modest level, she was also given some additional instruction in basic relaxation skills—based on cue words—that she had learned in the previous session. It was pointed out that these could be employed in relieving her overall stress level, but could also be helpful in any future situations where she needed to stand up assertively to her mother's criticisms.

WATCHING FOR RELAPSE. Sally reported, however, that since the episode on the shopping trip, her mother had been markedly more considerate and positive toward her. The therapist acknowledged the relief Sally felt at this change, and praised her initiative in making her feelings clear to her mother.

At the same time, it was pointed out that there were many pressures and problems continuing in the household, and it would not be surprising if her mother were to relapse back to her previous negative attitudes. Since Sally must be prepared for this, another task assigned, prior to the final therapy session, was to watch carefully for indications of such a relapse on her mother's part. If this happened, she was to again, assertively, clarify her feelings to her mother. In effect, relapse was reframed as a helpful signal, rather than an occasion for discouragement.

TERMINATION AND FOLLOW-UP. The final interventive session, two weeks later, was relatively uneventful. The grandfather's health was no better or worse, Sally and her mother were coping with his care adequately, but they were also considering a possible nursing home placement if his condition worsened drastically. The relationship with her mother continued to be positive, although Sally assured the therapist that she had been diligently watching for signs of her mother returning to her critical ways. None had occurred.

Follow-up telephone contacts at six months and one year found the improved situation continuing. When the therapist asked Sally for feedback on anything she saw as having been helpful in the therapeutic intervention, she was not able to identify any specific technique. What was important, she said, was that she learned "I had to do it myself," in managing her difficulties, and it was evident that she had found that she could, indeed, do so.

BRIEF COUPLE THERAPY

For hundreds of years people have sought assistance for difficulties in their marriages, and other intimate relationships, from members of the clergy, or respected friends, relatives, and other community figures, but it was not until the early decades of this century that this sort of helping became professionalized. The history of marital therapy has been recounted by such writers as Broderick and Schrader (1981) and Nichols and Everett (1986) and will not be reviewed here. The two theoretical frameworks contributing most significantly to contemporary practice in couple therapy are strategic psychotherapy (Fisch et al., 1982; Haley, 1976; Madanes, 1984) and social learning theory (Jacobson & Holtzworth-Monroe, 1986; Whisman & Jacobson, 1990). They share the two features common to almost all such therapies:

1. An interventive focus on the dyadic relationship, rather than either of its individual members
2. A predominant use of the conjoint interview, in which the couple are seen together (although individual interviews may be utilized for strategic purposes)

In addition, both the strategic and behavioral approaches have heavily emphasized the employment of task and homework assignments in stimulating change. Dorothy Freeman (1982, 1990) has combined these two approaches, along with material drawn from the family life cycle framework (Carter & McGoldrick, 1988), into a vigorous, eclectic approach that is well suited to brief contact. The brief therapist can utilize concepts drawn from these various frameworks to identify a number of potential entry points for intervention.

DEVELOPMENTAL CRISES. The family life cycle postulates a series of stages in family development, each of which presents certain unique problems to the marital couple. Haley (1973) discusses a simplified but clinically useful version of this framework:

1. Early marriage
2. Entry of the first child
3. Parenting
4. The child-leaving stage
5. Retirement and old age

Although couples may present for marital therapy at any of these stages, I have found that the parenting and child-leaving stages predominate in practice and offer certain characteristic problems. Thus, in their efforts to deal with the multiple demands of raising a family, couples in the parenting stage can easily move into rigid, child-oriented roles that obscure (or even deny) their relationship as a marital pair. At the child-leaving stage, on the other hand, partners who have successfully managed (or at least, survived) the demands of parenting can become anxious as they are faced with the uncertainties of becoming a couple once again.

Surveying the problems typical of the stage of family life cycle with which a couple are contending offers a current and practical means of assessing their particular version of these difficulties. At times, simply identifying and normalizing these common hazards in a given stage of the family life cycle can be helpful. Many couples genuinely believe that the problems they are experiencing are uniquely theirs and are relieved to discover they are common to the stage.

Finally, a common emphasis across all of the brief approaches to couple therapy is that of enhancing communication between the partners, and this important area of practice is considered at length in the next section.

TRAINING COUPLES IN COMMUNICATION SKILLS

Undoubtedly the best substantiated of the various communication training approaches currently available is the relationship enhancement (RE) method developed by Bernard Guerney and his associates (Guerney, 1988; Snyder & Guerney, 1993) at Pennsylvania State

University. This comprehensive and highly structured method actually trains couples in a cluster of relevant skills, including not only communicative but also negotiating, problem-solving, generalizing, and maintenance skills. The discussion in this section will focus mainly on a simplified adaptation (Wells & Figurel, 1979) to brief therapy of training in basic communicative skills.*

IDENTIFYING COMMUNICATION PROBLEMS. It is not at all uncommon for one or both of a distressed couple, at some point in the initial interview, to state, "Our problem is that we can't communicate." Sometimes this is simply a cliché, at other times the speaker means something altogether different, but in many instances communication represents a distinct and genuine area of difficulty within a troubled relationship.

> Janet and Bob, a couple in their early thirties, applied for counseling at a family service agency at the point where their marriage was seemingly at an end. Both were in touch with lawyers, and active planning was under way regarding separation and divorce.
>
> They agreed that their ten-year marriage had reached a crisis following an episode a few months earlier in which Bob believed his wife had been unfaithful to him with an acquaintance of the family, but they had been literally unable to discuss this issue together as it aroused such strong emotion in each of them. Whenever they tried, Bob would become angry and accusatory, Janet would become tearful and confused, and their attempt to talk about the subject would rapidly break down.
>
> Exploration of their marital history and current areas of functioning revealed few other areas of conflict. Their present marital adjustment was no better or worse than that of most couples in this stage of the family life cycle, with the exception of their complete inability to deal with the possibility that Janet had been sexually unfaithful. Even with encouragement and support from the therapist,

---

*Training workshops in RE methodology are offered regularly by Guerney and his associates. I have attended two such workshops over the years and profited greatly from them. Further information on workshop schedules may be obtained from Bernard G. Guerney, Jr., Individual and Family Consultation Center, Department of Human Development and Family Studies, Pennsylvania State University, University Park, PA 16802.

efforts to talk about the incident during the initial interview were futile. However, they agreed to defer their divorce planning for a five-week period while they received communication training.

This couple represents a dramatic illustration of communication problems, and the consequences of their difficulties—the break-up of their marriage—are much more severe than commonly encountered. Typically, couples with communication problems are having difficulties talking in a meaningful way about a wide range of areas in their marriage. Their communicative attempts may break down in anger and frustration, as was the case with Bob and Janet, but they are as likely to simply become mired in digressions, vagueness, blaming statements, mind reading, and the like. The end result is not necessarily divorce but, just as sadly, a distant and frustrating relationship that continues through the years, with neither partner receiving the satisfaction and intimacy that is potentially there.

THE COMMUNICATIVE DYAD. As Guerney (1988) has repeatedly emphasized, an adequate approach to communication training must attend to both sides of the communicative interaction. This comprises, on the one hand, a *speaker* who is specific, emotionally expressive, and nonblaming in his or her statements and, on the other hand, a *listener* who comprehends the important emotion and content of the speaker's utterances and, furthermore, communicates this understanding back to the speaker for confirmation. The goal of training is to develop the abilities of each spouse in both of these roles but, as we shall see, the process of training focuses on each skill separately until facility is attained in each area.

PREPARING FOR TRAINING. As in all skill-building approaches, training begins with relatively simple and undemanding topics. Typically, communication training is identified as needed in the initial interview and, following a brief explanation of the method, the therapist gives the couple a homework assignment asking each of them to identify a series of current topics that are relevant to their marriage.

Each is to prepare a list of three topics that are relatively easy to discuss, three topics that are moderately challenging, and three topics that are intensely emotional and difficult to discuss. Having topics identified in advance helps in structuring the process and, on occasion, avoids spouses' differing perceptions of levels of difficulty. If the husband, for example, lists the disciplining of the children as an easy topic, but the wife considers this to be moderately difficult, then it is best to simply not use this topic in the early stages.

The couple are instructed that they will literally engage in a dialogue, beginning with one of the easy topics, while the therapist will coach each of them in the skills involved. Before actually beginning the first dialogue, the roles of both speaker and listener are clearly described, and guidelines are identified for each role. The speaker guidelines are as follows:

1. Expresses his or her feelings in the topic area
2. Avoids making blaming and attacking statements
3. Does not ask questions of the listener
4. Keeps his or her statements short—two or three sentences before pausing for listener feedback

The listener guidelines are similarly clear and concise:

1. Reflects back the feelings he or she hears the speaker expressing
2. Suspends judgment about the validity of the speaker's feelings
3. Does not ask questions of the speaker
4. Keeps reflections short—typically one or two sentences

The speaker and listener guidelines may be written down and given to the spouse who is assuming a particular role in an initial dialogue. In explaining the guidelines, the therapist should acknowledge that this type of structured conversation will feel very awkward to the couple at first but that the therapist will coach them in their initial efforts so as to help them develop the needed skills.

COACHING INITIAL DIALOGUES. As a coach, the clinician should sit at a close but equal distance from the partners as they face each other and begin a dialogue on a selected topic. Initially there may be some need to keep the couple talking to each other rather than to the therapist, which is usually accomplished by a firm directive ("Talk to him, not to me"). On the other hand, one or the other may break out of his or her role, and similar directives ("Don't ask questions, just reflect back her feelings" or "Stop now so that your listener can respond") are used to maintain the structured separation of the roles.

Since the beginning topics are not controversial areas in the couple's life, strong emotions are not usually aroused, and this, of course, provides opportunity to learn the principles of clear expression and responsive listening in a minimally conflicted atmosphere. Despite this, a speaker may still use phrasing that is blaming or a listener may become judgmental in responding. The therapist must remain highly alert and assist the couple in reframing such common difficulties. The following is typical of a beginning dialogue:

HUSBAND (AS SPEAKER): You know, I've been feeling an awful lot of pressure lately on my job. There's times when I just get sick and tired of the same old routine, day after day.

WIFE (AS LISTENER): Then it's probably about time you began to think of—

THERAPIST: (Interrupts) Remember now, just reflect back his feeling.

WIFE: Oh, okay, uhm, you're feeling pressured about your job and all.

HUSBAND: Yeah. There's times I wonder if it will ever get any better. I start to think what else I could do and I just don't know—what else am I qualified for? What else could I find—

THERAPIST: (Simultaneously) Get the feeling in.

HUSBAND: (Continues)—that I'd really like? But I'm also feeling disgusted with myself for giving up too easy.

THERAPIST: Good.

WIFE: You don't know what to do but you're also angry with yourself in some ways for giving up.

THERAPIST: That's good.

HUSBAND: Yeah, I'm pretty disgusted, and the pressure gets bad at times, and I don't know whether you've ever really understood that at all.

THERAPIST:(Interrupts) Can you stop? The last part of that statement was getting into blaming your wife—can you rephrase so it isn't blaming her?

HUSBAND: I don't know what you mean.

THERAPIST: There's something real important you want from her—can you express that?

HUSBAND: Oh, I see what you mean. (To wife) Yeah, I'm pressured, but it would really help if I knew you were backing me up.

THERAPIST: Nice.

WIFE: You're really feeling pressured.

THERAPIST: (To wife) And you'd feel good if you knew I was with you—add that.

WIFE: And you want me with you.

THERAPIST: Good.

Throughout the dialogue, the therapist directly guides each spouse in the role each is taking as speaker or listener. For example, when the wife begins a response in a blaming manner ("it's . . . about time"), the therapist interrupts this immediately and reminds her of the listener's basic responsibility to reflect the speaker's feelings. When the husband ends a statement with an implied attack ("whether you've ever really understood"), the trainer immediately stops the dialogue and asks him to rephrase his statement. When he has difficulty doing this, the therapist offers him a positive reframing that he can substitute in his original statement. Throughout the ongoing dialogue, the therapist rewards the participants with brief verbal interjections ("Good," "Nice") as they meet speaker or listener guidelines; this reinforcement is given irrespective of whether the clients matched the guideline on their own, or did so in response to a therapist directive.

REINFORCING EARLY GAINS. It is critically important for the therapist to stay keenly alert to the statements and responses of both participants, especially during the early dialogues in the easier topic areas. If they do not begin to develop good expressive and responsive skills in these less conflicted areas, it is much less likely that they will be able to communicate effectively as they move to the more difficult and emotionally loaded topics.

Thus, as the above dialogue illustrates, the couple's early efforts are frequently stumbling and marked by frequent corrective interruptions by the trainer. At the same time, the clinician maintains a highly supportive and encouraging atmosphere, explicitly rewarding every instance in which speaker and listener meet the expectations of their roles. These initial dialogues should not last too long—two or three minutes usually—because the topics being discussed do not lend themselves to lengthy discussion and, in addition, most couples find it a strain to meet the unfamiliar requirements of the speaker and listener roles. The practitioner can utilize the interval between dialogues to offer the couple further support ("It's usually very awkward and difficult as you start") and to ask them to review what they have experienced and learned in the preceding segment.

When the dialogue resumes, the spouses usually reverse roles so that, in relation to the dialogue noted above, the wife is now the speaker and the husband is learning the listener role. The topic may well be the same area they had previously considered or another topic selected from their joint list. In an hour-long therapy session, it is possible to guide the couple through several repetitions on easy topics, with each receiving feedback and reinforcement from the trainer in both speaker and listener roles.

ASSIGNING A TASK. Their homework assignment is to take further topics at the easy level and to practice dialogues, alternating in the speaker and listener roles. They are cautioned against moving into more demanding topics until their skills are more established, but are assured that they will be advancing into these areas as the training sessions progress. As a safeguard against possible difficulties in the practice sessions, the couple should be asked to pay particular attention to any problems they experience when the therapist is not there to coach them. This reframes the potential difficulties as useful learning and, furthermore, underscores the overall goal of the couple developing a self-sustaining level of communicative skill.

TRANSITION TO HARDER TOPICS. Moving to the next level of difficulty usually takes place without undue strain because the couple have now incorporated a reasonable degree of skill from the earlier stages. A difference that is often evident, however, is that the medium level topics are usually more meaningful, and the couple will consequently need longer dialogues in order to develop a given topic. The same structuring into separate speaker and listener roles is observed, and the therapist continues to monitor the dialogue closely. If either participant lapses from the expectations of the designated role, the therapist immediately responds with corrective feedback or suggested rephrasings. It is perhaps even more important as they make the transition to a new level for the trainer to continue the explicit reinforcement of successful effort that permeated the earlier dialogues.

SWITCHING SPEAKER AND LISTENER ROLES. As the couple progress, especially into the intense level topics, they are taught a structured method of changing speaker and listener roles during the course of an ongoing dialogue, rather than staying in one role until a given dialogue ends. By this point in the training, the couple are talking about areas of their relationship that have been the subjects of quarrels and disputes, and the emotional content is high. It can be difficult for a listener to maintain a highly responsive role in such an area for a lengthy period of time; similarly, a speaker who has been openly expressive may develop a strong need to know what the other person feels about the feelings he or she has disclosed.

When that happens, the spouse who wants to switch roles indicates this desire, the speaker makes a concluding summarizing statement, and the listener reflects back the emotion in this statement. Once this is done, the couple then reverse their roles and the dialogue continues. The trainer points out that this method of switching builds in a degree of closure before the roles are changed. In addition, this provision moves the couple much closer to a method of continuing dialogues in intensely emotional areas that will be usable in the daily course of their lives once the communication training has concluded.

> Janet and Bob, the couple described earlier, received training over four weekly sessions, beginning with less demanding topics in their lives. By the fifth session their skills had developed sufficiently that they were able to move into dialogue concerning the suspected incident of infidelity that had previously been impossible for them to discuss. They used this area as one of their intense level topics and, with support from the trainer (but only minimal guidance), were able to sustain a lengthy dialogue on this emotionally charged topic.
>
> As speaker, Bob was able to express that beneath his anger was a sense of deep dismay and hurt at even the possibility that his wife would be unfaithful. For her part, Janet was able to move past her

previous confused tearfullness to relate her husband's accusations to the shame she had felt as an adolescent when her parents' unjustly accused her of sexual misbehavior. As listeners, both were able to respond fully to the other's emotions and, as they found themselves moving to a deeper level of understanding, they mutually agreed to cancel their plans for divorce.

BEYOND COMMUNICATION TRAINING. Several options are possible as communication training is concluded. For a number of couples the training is sufficient to enable them to resolve their difficulties on their own.

In an initial session with one couple, the wife described their marriage as lacking "emotional intimacy" but could not specify any critical areas of difficulty. Her husband agreed with her but had no notion of what either of them might do differently. The therapist suggested two further sessions concentrating on communication training and described this as a method of enhancing their skills in expressing and responding to emotions. The couple worked diligently on the in-session training and homework assignments and quickly gained facility in the basic skills. A later follow-up found both satisfied with what they saw as a renewal of their marriage.

With some couples the training can be utilized in further sessions of conjoint therapy, which focus on specific areas of difficulty. Conjoint therapy designed to assist them in negotiating or problem solving becomes much more productive in the context of their heightened expressive and listening skills.

STIMULATING CHANGE THROUGH TASKS

Tasks are essential in brief couple therapy if the therapist is to help the partners find new solutions to the life stage they are experiencing, or move past the repetitive and dissatisfying interactions that have brought them to therapy. Although sharing similarities with one-to-one psychotherapy, identifying tasks in conjoint therapy, and motivating the couple to perform them, confronts the therapist with some unique considerations.

For example, tasks should frequently involve both members of the dyad, but this can be difficult early in therapy because of problems in communication and cooperation—the very problems, of course, that made therapy necessary.

> Tom and Alice, a couple in their early thirties, were experiencing difficulties in sexual functioning and, as a consequence, had not made love together for more than two years. An early assignment was for them to experiment with the initial level of sensate focus exercise derived from Masters and Johnson's (1970) sexual therapy. The exercise was described to them in detail and they agreed that they would attempt it twice in the week before their next therapy session.
>
> When they arrived at the next session they reported that they had not attempted the exercise at all. Each had waited for the other to take the initiative in suggesting when they should carry out the assignment, with the not-surprising result that they never got started.

It was possible to use this failure to examine the nature and effect of their communicational difficulties and also the exquisite sensitivity to anticipated rejection that had built up over their long sexual hiatus.

INCREASING POSITIVE PERCEPTIONS. As Whisman and Jacobson (1990) note, "most couples present for therapy at a time when both spouses are deriving little satisfaction from their relationship and are focusing most of their attention on perceived deficits in the other" (p. 330). They recommend behavior exchange strategies in which each spouse is encouraged to identify (and initiate) behaviors that would result in a more pleasing relationship with the other.

As a prelude to this sort of exchange, I have found it helpful to instruct each spouse to carefully observe her or his partner and, over the course of the following week, note even the *smallest* actions that are in any way pleasing to them. I ask the couple to place a sheet of paper in a prominent place, on the refrigerator, for example, where each can record these behaviors on a day-by-day basis.

This task is accompanied by a straightforward explanation about how easily distressed couples can neglect the positive aspects that may well still remain in their relationship. It is also important to emphasize that these positives may be very slight, at this point, but can help in the process of rebuilding their marriage.

ENHANCING SEXUALITY. The sensate focus tasks employed in sexual therapy (Masters & Johnson, 1970; Beck, 1990) can be readily adapted to assisting troubled couples in enhancing their sexual relationship even where the difficulties fall far short of a specific sexual dysfunction. There are two distinct levels of sensate focus assignment:

1. Initially, the couple's intimate contact is limited to touching and caressing exercises, specifically nonsexual, in order to learn ways of reducing the tension and anxiety that has permeated their sexual interaction. Additionally, this assignment enables the couple to reexperience the affectionate behaviors that characterized their early relationship before it became specifically sexual. Freeman (1990) uses an even more focused variation of this level as the initial task assignment in her work with a naive, frightened young couple who had been unable to consummate their marriage:

> They were specifically asked to avoid any sexual contact during the coming week. I suggested that they could share and show any affection that they wished to show each other spontaneously, and they might talk together briefly about our meeting. I also asked that they try to avoid "stewing" over their problem. I thought it would be good, however, if they could talk a little together about the parental attitudes toward sex they had mentioned, and about any concerns or experiences they had had in their teens. (p. 31)

There is an intriguingly paradoxical quality to this assignment as Freeman instructs the couple, who are having difficulty achieving satisfactory sex, *not* to have sex. But this injunction is, in effect, permission to enjoy themselves sensually, without feeling that they must achieve any specific result.

2. The initial level of sensate focus may be followed by an assignment in which more explicit sexual touching is prescribed, but, as in the previous level, the couple are to refrain from orgasmic release. Instead, their focus is on learning ways of increasing sensuality and arousal that are sensitive to their individual needs. Both of these early assignments encourage the development of open verbal communication within a relaxed and nondemanding atmosphere.

REDUCING OVERINVOLVEMENT. At any stage of the life cycle it is possible for the couple to become so enmeshed within the troubled confines of their relationship that they isolate themselves from needed outside interests and satisfactions. Freeman (1990), in a brilliant three-session intervention, used direct suggestion with a couple in the parenting stage:

> To Mrs. Martin I indicated that a constant diet of home duties and the company of young children week in and week out wasn't very stimulating, nor was this in the best interests of the children. She said she'd like an afternoon off, but had been too discouraged to even think about it. At this Mr. Martin said he'd be glad if she got a sitter and went out, and at the same time perked herself up a bit. (p. 81)

When initially giving a couple the task of going out together socially, it is often advisable to keep this assignment very limited. For example, the therapist may ask them to take only a twenty-minute walk together, twice a week, since an attempt at a whole evening out may simply break down in quarreling or dissatisfaction.

TECHNIQUES IN FAMILY AND COUPLE THERAPY

A number of techniques useful in facilitating the engagement phase of brief psychotherapy were described earlier. These were divided into relationship-building, information-gathering, and management (or survival) techniques, and their employment during the engagement process was described and illustrated. The therapist continues to utilize many of these same techniques as therapy proceeds—the employment of periodic summaries, for example, or the continued use of reframing are especially important techniques. A number of other tactics, which are especially suited to use in the conjoint interview, can also be identified.

EQUALIZING. In this reframing maneuver, the therapist will summarize the discussion between a couple in such a way as to highlight similarities in their feelings, behaviors, attitudes, or personal style. Equalizing is usually employed to dilute combative interaction between a couple by emphasizing similarities in goals; it can also be used to promote hope in the more distant couple as unacknowledged but meaningful commonalities are identified.

MOBILIZING COMPETENCY. At a point where one spouse is struggling to express an important feeling or to understand a significant issue, the therapist directs the other spouse to "help" his or her partner with this matter. The purpose of this technique is usually to encourage the "helping" spouse to move from a typically critical or passive response toward the other to a more positive role.

THERAPIST PROCESSING. This is a therapeutic technique where the clinician "interprets for a spouse what the partner has said" (Ables & Brandsma, 1977). This may be done where the spouse is having difficulty understanding the other, or where the partner's statement includes a mix of positive and negative. In the latter instance, the therapist's interpretation would likely be a reframing that highlighted the positive elements in the partner's statement.

Processing is highly useful in moving past potentially explosive interactions early in therapy, but it should not become the primary technique because it is dependent, of course, on the therapist's acting as a conduit, so to speak, between the couple. If the clinician finds herself frequently processing couple statements in this manner, she should move to structured communication training, as this will provide the couple with the listener and speaker skills that therapist processing is providing for them.

INDIRECT CHALLENGING. In this technique, questions about one spouse are deliberately addressed to the other spouse. Thus, a husband may be asked to describe his wife's depression, or a wife may be queried about pressures the husband is experiencing on his job. The tactic is not designed to gain factual information so much as to stimulate the nonquestioned spouse to amplify on his or her feelings and thoughts in the area of focus.

CAROMING. This is a technique in which a therapist statement about a particular family member—and usually of a challenging nature—is directed to other family members. The caromed statement is often couched to the other family members as an "informational" addition to their understanding. In a family session, for example, Minuchin challenges the mother's overprotectiveness by addressing a statement to the father and children:

MINUCHIN: Carlo, you have a lovely wife. You children have a lovely mother. But I think she can be a problem to children growing up. (Minuchin et al., 1978, p. 291)

GAMBITING. In this maneuver, the therapist offers a complimentary statement, then a challenging one, so that accepting the compliment implies accepting the challenging statement. Pairing praise and challenge together also helps to make the challenging statement appear less critical. For example:

MINUCHIN: This always happens. When you are very sensitive to the pains of the younger kids, then there is the problem of how to become the mother of older children. (Minuchin et al., 1978, p. 287)

DIPLOMATING. This is a therapeutic strategy whereby an apparently unnegotiable (or highly emotional) issue is deliberately set aside while other, less volatile issues are dealt with and resolved. The objective is to create skills in problem solving and good will that will enhance the later work on the more difficult area. It is a tactic frequently employed in diplomatic and labor-management negotiations, hence the label.

GRANDMOTHERING. The title for this technique comes from Minuchin's comment that he learned the tactic from his grandmother. It involves making a challenging statement about one person's behavior—often phrased in very blunt terms—but placing responsibility for these actions on another family member. For example, in order to challenge a daughter's behavior, Minuchin addresses himself to the mother:

MINUCHIN: Margherita, you do so many things for your daughter that she becomes an extremely childish, incompetent person. (Minuchin et al., 1978, p. 313)

Like all of the conjoint therapy techniques that this section has identified, grandmothering gives the therapist further flexibility in managing the often complex interactional dynamics of the conjoint interview. Without skill in such maneuvers, therapists can be overwhelmed by the demands of multiperson interviews and not fully utilize this powerful mode of therapeutic intervention.

FINAL WORDS: THE INTERPERSONAL CONTEXT

This chapter has examined a number of key facets in the application of the principles and strategies of brief psychotherapy to family and couple intervention. Both one-person family therapy and structured communication training are especially useful as brief therapeutic strategies: the former because it offers the therapist a guiding framework for promoting family change without necessarily having to mobilize and engage the entire family; the latter because of its emphasis on teaching couples an essential interpersonal skill in an economical and focused manner.

Although family and couple approaches have been separately considered in this chapter, the reader will note that many of the case illustrations considered throughout this book were concerned with interpersonal issues and problems. This highlights the fact that effective brief therapy is consistently targeted toward the current meaningful relationships of the troubled person, and whether or not one is explicitly offering family or couple therapy, these important contexts of living must be considered and supported.

11

Innovation, Evaluation, and the Future of Brief Therapy

HURRY UP PLEASE IT'S TIME
—T. S. Eliot, *The Waste Land*

This concluding chapter discusses several areas particularly germane to the clinical practice of brief psychotherapy, which have been suggested but not fully considered in preceding chapters. It begins with a closer look at single-session intervention, an innovation in brief therapy that brings together, in a focused way, many of the most important principles of time-limited intervention. This is followed by consideration of how evaluative procedures, throughout the treatment process, strengthen the clinical practice of brief therapy. Finally, a concluding section attempts some predictions concerning the future of brief psychotherapy.

SINGLE-SESSION PSYCHOTHERAPY

There have been references throughout this book to the intriguing work, in both community mental health and managed health care settings, involving the deliberate use of very brief intervention. The practice of single-session therapy (SST) brings together two aspects of clinical practice and research that have long been known:

1. A significant number of clients—anywhere from 25 to 50 percent, depending on the setting—do not continue contact for more than one session (cf. Garfield, 1986).

2. Over the years, a number of clinical research studies have identified clients who have shown meaningful improvement following a session or two of therapy (e.g., Endicott & Endicott, 1963; Malan et al., 1975; Schorer et al., 1968; Sloane et al., 1975)

INITIAL FORMULATION. In a ground-breaking article published in 1981, Bernard Bloom reviewed these frequent references in the clinical literature to significant change taking place in a single therapeutic session, and went on to recount his own experience in deliberately employing what he called "focused single-session psychotherapy" in series of cases in a community mental health center. He used a format in which the client was seen for a two-hour session, and structured the interview as follows:

> the contractual agreement I made with each client was that I was assuming that a single appointment would be sufficient. If, at the conclusion of the interview, we both felt that another appointment was necessary, we would schedule it for the following week. If not, I would give the client my card and invite him or her to call me if there was a need to get in touch with me for any reason—with a problem or a progress report. Finally, I said that if the client did not contact me in a couple of months, I would call to see how he or she was getting along. (p. 181)

GUIDELINES FOR PRACTICE. In this context of positive expectation and careful attention to follow-up, Bloom identified a number of specific guidelines for conducting single-session therapy (SST):

1. Identify a focal problem
2. Do not underestimate clients' strengths
3. Be prudently active
4. Explore, then present interpretations tentatively
5. Encourage the expression of affect
6. Use the interview to start a problem-solving process
7. Keep track of time
8. Do not be overambitious
9. Keep factual questions to a minimum
10. Do not be overly concerned about the precipitating event

11. Avoid detours
12. Do not overestimate a client's self-awareness (i.e., don't hesitate to state what may seem obvious)

POTENTIAL CLIENTELE. There was little interest in SST, aside from an occasional article in the clinical journals (e.g., Rockwell & Pinkerton, 1982), until three psychologists at the Kaiser Permanente Medical Center, Moshe Talmon, Michael Hoyt, and Robert Rosenbaum, conducted a clinical trial of fifty-eight cases of SST at that organization. In several reports of their work (Hoyt et al., 1992; Rosenbaum et al., 1990; Talmon, 1990) they have identified five major categories of patients most likely to benefit from SST:

1. Patients who come to solve a specific problem for which a solution is in their control.
2. Patients who essentially need reassurance that their reaction to a troubling situation is normal.
3. Patients seen with significant others or family members who can serve as natural supports and "co-therapists."
4. Patients who can identify (perhaps with the therapist's assistance) helpful solutions, past successes, and exceptions to the problem.
5. Patients who have a particularly "stuck" feeling (e.g., anger, guilt, grief) toward a past event. (Hoyt et al., 1992, p. 62)

PREPARING FOR SST. These categories offer a useful framework for making a tentative identification of potential clients for whom SST might be feasible. This preliminary assessment can be done during a telephone contact, prior to the first session, in which the needed information can be obtained. If it seems possible that SST might be sufficient, this contact can also be used to suggest a preliminary task for the client, designed to focus and expedite the anticipated single session. Two types of tasks predominate:

1. A monitoring assignment concerned with gaining more specific data on some aspect of the problem the client has identified
2. A task designed to focus or define what the client most wants to get from the therapeutic contact by writing a brief statement of his or her goals

DURATION AND PROCESS. As Hoyt and his colleagues (1992) point out, the SST interview is longer than the conventional therapeutic interview, allowing about an hour and a half for an individual, and up to two hours for a couple or family. The process of the single session is not unlike any first session, and the stages outlined earlier for the initial interview are a useful guideline. The difference, of course, is that in the latter half of the session, the SST practitioner assists the client to move into a problem-solving process, and tasks must be identified for the client to carry out prior to whatever follow-up contact is arranged.

Structuring SST: The PLISSIT Model

Annon's (1976) PLISSIT model for brief therapy has proven to be a useful schema for quickly identifying an appropriate level of practitioner activity in conducting SST. This framework is especially compatible with such very abbreviated therapy, since it suggests that intervention should be attempted at the simplest possible level before turning to more complex procedures. The PLISSIT acronym stands for four potential levels of therapist activity, each of which may be complete in itself:

P = permission
LI = limited information
SS = specific suggestions
IT = intensive therapy

Along with its usefulness in organizing SST intervention, Annon's model is a useful reminder that therapeutic intervention need not be extensive or complex to be helpful, and for that reason alone it is worth examining.

PERMISSION (P). At this most basic level the practitioner, as a socially sanctioned authority figure, offers the individual permission to act or feel in a certain way. Typically, this involves a behavior the person is already engaged in, or something he or she wants to do but needs support to carry out. For example, the vacillating parent is supported in taking a firm stand with an unruly adolescent. A key maneuver in Minuchin's work with anorectic adolescents and their families was to redefine the adolescent's refusal to eat as "rebelliousness" and to sanction the parents' taking a united stand against this behavior (Minuchin et al., 1978).

At a verbal level, moreover, the clinician can often effectively restructure detrimental beliefs and attitudes through permission-giving intervention. In the chapter on behavior enactment (Chapter 6) this approach was illustrated in an account of what was essentially a single-session intervention designed to help hospitalized patients talk to their physicians about their medical condition. It was pointed out that it was helpful in the preparatory phases to shape certain of the patient's beliefs through such therapist statements as "You have a right to such information," "You have to take responsibility to get it," "You often have to teach your doctor how to talk to you," and so on. Therapist activity of this sort constitutes a type of cognitive restructuring—in effect, a mild exhortation designed to counter some of the more common beliefs that can impede patient activity, or a reframing ("You have to teach your doctor . . .")–designed to increase confidence.

At this level the clinician does not attempt to explore the client's belief system in any depth, but simply assumes that if the person is having difficulty in a given area of life, then it is likely that some of the more common human trepidations will be affecting functioning. Thus, individuals who need to act assertively are troubled by notions of what others may think of them, parents struggle with high expectations of themselves or worry about the adverse consequences of taking a firmer stand with their children, couples are affected by sexual taboos that inhibit freer communication or detract from enjoyment of intimacy, and so on.

None of these factors is critically dependent on a highly refined "diagnostic" assessment on the clinician's part so much as on an imaginative and empathic knowledge of the human condition—what Schulman (1979) has called "preparatory empathy." Similarly, the individual client scarcely needs to "work through" these common roadblocks in some elaborate therapeutic process. For many people it is enough to have the clinician point out how prevalent such beliefs are and directly or indirectly give permission to discard or surmount them.

LIMITED INFORMATION (LI). If necessary, the therapist can offer the client factual information on some key aspect of the problem. For example, people with medical difficulties are frequently able to manage the accompanying stress better if knowledge of the extent or prognosis of their condition is made available to them. Annon characterizes the information-giving function as "limited," because the therapist provides only the information most specific and relevant to the targeted problem.

Insufficient attention has been paid to how providing accurate and timely information to a client constitutes a potent method of cognitive change. This important educational function of the therapist has at least three major areas of application:

1. *Beliefs based on erroneous or fallacious information.* In a number of instances the therapeutic task is to supply the information that will correct of modify inaccurate beliefs. These are frequently based on early experiences in the individual's family of origin or may be characteristic of the social or cultural milieu in which she or he was reared.

2. *Beliefs based on a lack of information.* In their development of brief sexual therapy, Masters and Johnson (1970) identified the absence of accurate information about human sexuality as one of the major contributors to sexual dysfunction. Such beliefs as "Women have a lower sexual drive than men," "Masturbation can have detrimental physical effects," and "Older people have no interest in sex" are all untrue, yet are held by many people. Masters and Johnson bluntly characterize the source of these beliefs as "ignorance," and a significant component of their sexual therapy methodology is devoted to the necessary reeducation.

Sexuality, of course, is a particularly troublesome area. Considering the lack of sexual education provided to most people and the general taboo against open discussion of sexual matters, it is not surprising to find widespread misinformation. Yet there can be significant gaps in other life areas that can act in a similar way to promote or perpetuate human difficulty. Many young parents, for example, lack information on effective child-rearing practices and normal childhood development. Some honestly believe that a child should be fully toilet-trained by twelve months; some have little or no appreciation of the important developmental differences between girls and boys. Others have scant knowledge about the expectations and demands of such intimate relationships as marriage.

3. *Beliefs based on lack of interpersonal feedback*. It is not at all unusual, or pathological, for people to act in ways that are detrimental to their interpersonal relationships, but to be quite unaware of their impact on others. An SST case conducted by Michael Hoyt is a clear example of the therapeutic relevance of this kind of information giving:

> A patient complained of people not liking him, but not knowing why. As he sat down in the therapist's office, he commented: "I guess you're a psychologist because you couldn't get into medical school, huh?" and smiled. The therapist stopped him, saying, "What effect do you think it had on me to start our meeting with that comment?" The patient said he didn't understand. The therapist decided to go along with the patient's ploy of innocence (avoiding the discussion of whether or not it was "unconscious") by explaining that sometimes a person had an interpersonal style that annoys other people without realizing it, but that once they know about it, then they are responsible for what they do. He repeated the comment and asked the patient if there were other times the patient could think of when his "jokes" might have been misunderstood. The patient quickly learned about his counterproductive behavior and began to modify it. (Rosenbaum et al., 1990, p. 175)

This case is an excellent illustration of what Bloom (1981) meant by his admonition not to overestimate the client's self-awareness. Therapists must stay alert to these blind spots in the client's self-knowledge, even in situations where the missing information might appear to be glaringly obvious to everyone except the client.

SPECIFIC SUGGESTIONS (SS). At this level the client is given some specific directions to manage the problem. This can include, for example, brief instruction in relaxation methods, training in empathically responding to the feelings of a troubled significant other, or (as in the following case) directions on how to talk to a partner about a sexual difficulty one is experiencing:

> Mr. Z., a twenty-seven-year-old divorced man, had experienced problems with erection in the few intimate relationships he had entered since the breakup of his marriage. He was now dating a young woman to whom he was deeply attracted but he hesitated to

begin a sexual relationship with her for fear the same difficulties would appear. He was seen for a single session and coached in how to tell his partner, in a nondefensive manner, that he might experience problems with erection, although he still very much wanted to make love with her.

He recontacted the therapist a few weeks later to report that his woman friend had been accepting and understanding of his explanation, and they had begun a sexual relationship. Some erectile problems were apparent, however, but his partner was willing to enter brief sexual therapy with him to deal with these. A further appointment was arranged with the couple to consider this new level of treatment.

The intervention at the specific suggestion level, in the first contact with this client, was considered to be complete in itself. It responded to his most immediate concern about the relationship and enabled him to move past the impasse he was experiencing. In this particular case, resolving the impasse opened up the possibility of intervention at a different level, but this is not necessarily the objective of any specific episode of SST.

In what might have become a failed couple therapy case, specific suggestions—in the form of skill training in initiating conversations—became a way of providing a helpful intervention to a distressed marriage:

> Mrs. K. appeared alone for the initial interview, her husband having reneged on his agreement to accompany her. They had been married almost ten years, had two children, and were experiencing the isolation and distance not uncommon in the parenting stage. Mrs. K.'s main complaint was that her husband seldom talked to her.
>
> The therapist contracted to work with her on this difficulty and used the latter part of the first interview to teach her—via behavioral rehearsal—some basic conversational skills. These included the use of open-ended questions and simple emphatic responses. Her task was to experiment with these skills in initiating conversations with her husband.

In a subsequent follow-up session further behavioral rehearsal refined these skills in the light of the increased responsiveness she was eliciting from her husband. A telephone contact several months later found Mrs. K. reporting the marriage as much improved.

INTENSIVE THERAPY (IT). Finally, where SST is judged insufficient to respond to the client's request for service, short-term therapy may be offered or, in other instances, open-ended treatment may be appropriate. In the clinical research conducted by Hoyt and his colleagues, they report that 58.6 percent of their sample of fifty-eight clients chose to complete their therapy in one session. Obviously, more studies are needed across a variety of settings to better determine the applicability of SST.

The advent of experimentation with such very brief therapy has raised questions for many therapists about how such abbreviated contact can fit into the overall context of professional practice. Moshe Talmon's response to the blunt question "How are we to make a living providing successful SST?" places this issue in an instructive context:

> When you recall that the majority of people with psychological problems never go to see a therapist, you realize that there are many, many more people who can be helped by us. If being helped by a therapist is less expensive, more positive, and a safer experience than many of us were led to believe, then we are more likely to have our satisfied SST customers return for a checkup, another brief therapy, or even extended treatment sometime down the road—as well as referring many more patients to us. (Hoyt et al., 1992)

This section on SST is not intended to advocate the exclusive, or even predominant employment of such highly abbreviated methods of psychotherapy. Yet there are certainly situations where such brevity is appropriate, and this discussion, and the categories suggested by Hoyt and his colleagues (1992), will assist the practitioner in deciding when to employ SST.

Evaluation and Follow-up

Practice has suffered because individual clinicians have not been encouraged to build sound evaluative measures into their ongoing work. Properly utilized, objective outcome evaluation becomes a part of responsible practice and a potentially valuable source of personal feedback for every clinician, but its demands must be scaled down and shaped to meet the realities of daily practice. Implicit in the model of brief treatment outlined in this book are some ways of achieving a suitable compromise between methodological rigor and practice reality.

For example, the efforts of the brief therapist to negotiate clear and specific goals with the client around one or two major problems often makes the need for elaborate evaluation instruments unnecessary. It should be apparent at termination or follow-up whether the goals of intervention have been achieved. Recent work by Rudolph (1993) has also highlighted the importance in many cases of conducting a midpoint evaluation as a way of reconfirming the contract and the projected time limits. Short-term treatment, which usually concentrates on immediate, practical objectives concerned with daily living, should similarly assist in evaluating the progress and outcome of service. Has the client found a job? Has the move to a new apartment taken place? Is the client now able to obtain dates with women? These questions should be readily answerable from observation or from client self-report.

There are times, however, when more intangible effects must be measured or when client reports and clinical judgment need corroboration. Walter Hudson (1982) has developed a series of clinically oriented scales that assist greatly in this task. The Hudson Scales, explicitly designed for the exigencies of clinical practice, measure client status in five major areas that constitute frequent goals of clinical intervention:

1. Depression
2. Self-esteem
3. Marital adjustment
4. Sexual adjustment
5. Parent-child relationships

Each scale is relatively short (twenty-five items) and can be completed by the typical client in five or ten minutes. The results can be immediately graded by the clinician and a score, ranging from 0 to 100, calculated. For each scale, Hudson's validation work suggests a clinical cutting point of 30—that is, client scores between 30 and 100 represent clinically significant degrees of difficulty within the given area. As Hudson points out, the clinical cutting point provides a useful diagnostic criterion—the client who scores 50 on the depression scale, for example, is showing a moderate degree of clinically significant depression. This feature makes the results of any of the scales easily comprehensible to both clinician and client, and the scales are quite sensitive to the changes sought in treatment. I have found most clients perfectly willing to use these measures and, as might be expected, highly interested in the results. Hudson's discussion of the scales in his monograph *The Clinical Measurement Package* (1982) offers many suggestions on their adaptation to practice, as well as complete versions of each scale.*

FOLLOW-UP CONTACT. Closely related to the issue of ongoing outcome assessment is the consistent employment of follow-up interviews as an integral part of clinical practice. The model of short-term treatment presented in this book has placed considerable emphasis on the need for a follow-up interview with every client. This interview is initiated by the therapist and is usually scheduled two to six months after the termination of the intervention. Unfortunately, most clinicans never see their clients following active treatment unless the client returns to seek further help. Yet systematic follow-up can provide important benefits to both clients and clinicians.

I noted briefly in an earlier chapter that there is some suggestive empirical evidence (Liberman, 1978) that in conjunction with an active, task-oriented approach, significant gains can take place following the actual cessation of intervention. Building in the routine use of follow-up contact allows for the encouragement of such gains, and from a client perspective is a needed safeguard following any type of intervention–whether brief or lengthy, limited in focus or wide-ranging in scope. Has the client made meaningful gains that can endure past the immediate influence of the therapist-client relationship?

*The Hudson Scales, along with many other clinically relevant measures, are reviewed in Corcoran and Fischer's *Measures for Clinical Practice* (1987). The interested reader should consult this highly useful volume for a much wider range of information on outcome evaluation measures than can be covered in this section.

STRUCTURING FOLLOW-UP. The client should be aware of the follow-up interview at an early stage of intervention. Mention of this practice can be included in the therapist's initial explanation of treatment, and it is helpful if, from time to time during intervention, the client is reminded that follow-up will occur at a specified interval following termination. This will make it clear that the follow-up session is not an intrusion into the client's private life or undertaken merely to satisfy the helper's curiosity, but is an integral part of the helping process. I do not attempt to set a specific date for the follow-up interview but usually indicate to the client that I will be in touch after a designated interval to arrange this session. The time preceding this contact should be clarified as offering the client an opportunity to test out and integrate the learning or change that has taken place during intervention.

In order to maintain a positive expectation about this process the follow-up session is characterized as "a chance to check on your progress" rather than an opportunity to determine whether the client's problems have returned. Similarly, a therapist may want to allow clients the freedom to initiate an interview prior to the actual follow-up session, but what is said about this too should be positively phrased. Thus, my preference is to say, "Call me if you have any questions," rather than the more negative "Call me if you have any problems." The essential message concerning the clinician's availability is clear but does not create needless anticipation of difficulty.

FEEDBACK FROM CLIENTS. Maluccio (1979) provides a fascinating account of a series of follow-up interviews with clients seen at a family service agency. He also interviewed the practitioners who had seen these clients and in some cases found an almost alarming discrepancy between the client's evaluation of service and the helper's perceptions. Generally the clients were highly positive about the help they had received, and they tended to evaluate this in terms of enhanced relationships, better job functioning, improved emotional and social life, and so on. The clinicans, none of whom apparently conducted follow-up interviews as part of their practice, were often still concerned about the conflicted or depleted state in which the client had entered treatment, and their judgments were biased by this more gloomy recollection. Without the salutary effect of hearing the client's realistic evaluation of improved functioning through follow-up contact, the practitioners were unable to appreciate either the tangible gains or the realistic limitations of their work.

A further benefit for the practitioner lies in the informative feedback the follow-up session can provide concerning the impact of various therapeutic techniques. It is extremely useful during the follow-up to ask the client specifically to evaluate the procedures used during intervention. What was most helpful? What aspects of therapy were not beneficial? What was gained from any aspect of treatment that can continue to be utilized in life? The therapist should emphasize that this sort of evaluation is an integral part of his or her own professional growth. Some clients can give only a very general assessment of treatment procedures, but on occasion, client feedback can be highly illuminating.

A thirty-two-year-old school teacher had been seen in a time-limited series of sessions that had focused on her difficulty in handling a lingering depression, related to unresolved grief around the death of her father. In a follow-up interview one year after termination she reported that her emotional and social functioning was quite satisfactory.

When asked to evaluate treatment, she identified an interview in which the therapist had utilized an experiential enactment technique as having been particularly helpful. The practitioner also thought that this procedure had been a turning point and saw the enactment (a variant of the "empty chair" technique) as forcing the client to recontact and face the submerged and evaded emotions that were preventing her from resolving her feelings about the deceased parent. The client, on the other hand, identified *the therapist's supportiveness* during the enactment as the most meaningful element in enabling her to cope with her grief.

Other clients may not be so dramatic in their recollections but can still provide the practitioner with an important source of feedback on treatment strategy. Along with this, of course, there is opportunity within the follow-up interview to negotiate a further helping contract if this proves necessary. Although the outcome studies of brief intervention are generally encouraging, there will be those who need (or want) further help. Follow-up interviews provide the client with this needed safeguard.

BRIEF THERAPY AND THE FUTURE OF CLINICAL PRACTICE

In the nearly one hundred years of its existence, psychotherapy has undergone a considerable metamorphosis (Freedheim, 1992). Until World War II it was largely conducted in private practices and exclusive clinics and was not readily available to the general public. In the past forty years a number of comprehensive federal legislative initiatives, including the Community Mental Health Act of 1963 and the Health Maintenance Organization Act of 1973, have made psychotherapeutic services vastly more affordable and accessible across the nation. During this same period of time, the waning of psychoanalytic dominance and the development of such major innovations as behavior therapy and family therapy—both emphasizing a here-and-now problem focus and the employment of action-oriented strategies—have provided a fertile ground for the growth of brief therapeutic methods.

CLIENTELE AND PROVIDERS. These significant changes during the past forty years have resulted in a radical democratization of the clientele of psychotherapy. In this regard, the development of a variety of brief therapeutic methods has made psychotherapy both accessible and meaningful to clients across a wide socioeconomic spectrum. There has also been a democratization in its providers, with psychologists, social workers, and psychiatric nurses all recognized as legitimate practitioners of psychotherapy. This latter change stands in stark contrast to the situation at the beginning of this era when, as May (1992) points out, psychotherapy was tenaciously defended as an exclusively "medical" prerogative and nonmedical practitioners risked "being declared outlaws" (p. xxiii).

Brief psychotherapy has become the treatment of choice in the variety of managed health care settings that are developing across this country. If a federally funded national health insurance program becomes a reality, and includes coverage for outpatient psychotherapy, there is little doubt that this will further spur the utilization of short-term methods. There are powerful social and political forces impelling these major changes in the structure and organization of health and mental health services (VandenBos et al., 1992), and the implications for psychotherapeutic practice are many.

PRACTICE DILEMMAS. Major changes in how clinical services will be delivered loom ahead. For example, Nicholas Cummings (cited in Adams, 1987, p. 20) has predicted that by 1995 half of the private practices in the United States will no longer exist; other writers have suggested even more drastic reductions. As third-party payers at a variety of levels become the dominant source of remuneration for psychotherapeutic services, and place conditions and restrictions on the services they will support, it will no longer be possible for many private therapists to survive.

Clinics and agencies, both public and private, are experiencing the same pressures. Discussion in earlier writing (Wells & Phelps, 1990), has suggested certain of the dilemmas this may raise:

> Those therapists who choose to restrict their practice to the economically affluent will be continuing a form of practice not unlike that which existed prior to the advent of the community mental health movement in the 1960s. In addition to limiting long-term therapy to an elite clientele, it also requires a much smaller population of therapists. . . . Many clinicians will literally become employees of one or other type of service-providing organization, whereas even those who maintain a semblance of independence will find significant aspects of their practice governed by their relationship to an external source of remuneration. (pp. 22–23)

THREATS TO THERAPEUTIC INTEGRITY. Brief psychotherapy has been criticized, sometimes by characterizing it as "Reagapeutics" (Good, 1987) and attempting to connect it to the politically conversative decade of the 1980s (Goleman, 1981). Such criticism is misplaced, as brief therapy's most significant development took place long before this time. Others (Meyer, 1993) simply wax nostalgic for the days when therapists felt unrestricted in their practice.

However, there are dangers inherent in a movement toward utilizing brief therapeutic methods simply as a response to the demands and mandates of third-party payers, or on the basis of purely financial interests on the part of the therapist. Again, Cummings (1993), a long-time advocate of brief methods, forthrightly states the case:

> the current emphasis on efficiency is neither a movement nor a school of brief therapy, but it is a shifting of the control of the psy-

chotherapeutic process from the practitioner to those who administer America's health industry. The resulting demand for greater efficiency is in lieu of the professions having taken the responsibility and leadership for doing this themselves. (p. 493)

Stern (1993) sounds a similar alarm and speaks of the threat to therapeutic integrity, which he defines as "the establishment and maintenance by a competent therapist of the conditions necessary for successful therapeutic work" (p. 163). Both of these writers highlight the need for therapists—and their professional organizations—to reexert therapeutic control, not through denying the efficiency and efficacy of brief psychotherapy, but by integrating it into the mainstream of therapeutic education and practice. The more fully psychotherapists across all of the helping professions recognize the legitimacy as well as the utility of brief psychotherapy, the more likely they are to retain control of its implementation.

References

Ables, B. S., & Brandsma, J. M. (1977). *Therapy with couples*. San Francisco: Jossey-Bass.

Adams, J. (1987). A brave new world for private practice. *Family Therapy Networker, 11*, 19–25.

Alberti, R. E., & Emmons, M. L. (1990). *Your perfect right: A guide to assertive living* (6th ed.). San Luis Obispo, CA: Impact.

Alston, B. A. (1993). Brief cognitive psychotherapy of panic disorder. In R. A. Wells & V. J. Giannetti (Eds.), *Casebook of the brief psychotherapies* (pp. 65–75). New York: Plenum.

American Psychiatric Association. (1987). *Diagnostic and statistical manual of mental disorders* (3rd ed., rev.). Washington, DC: Author.

Andrews, G., & Harvey, R. (1981). Does psychotherapy benefit the neurotic patient—a reanalysis of the Smith, Glass and Miller data. *Archives of General Psychiatry, 38*, 1203–1208.

Annon, J. S. (1976). *Behavioral treatment of sexual problems: Vol. 1. Brief therapy*. New York: Harper & Row.

Austad, C. S., & Berman, W. H. (1991). Managed health care and the evolution of psychotherapy. In C. S. Austad, & W. H. Berman (Eds.), *Psychotherapy in managed health care: The optimal use of time and resources* (pp. 3–18). Washington, DC: American Psychological Association.

Austad, C. S., Sherman, W. O., Morgan, T., & Holstein, L. (1992). The psychotherapist and the managed care setting. *Professional Psychology: Research and Practice, 23*, 329–332.

Azrin, N. H., & Besalel, V. A., (1980). *Job club counselor's manual: A behavioral approach to vocational counseling*. Baltimore: University Park Press.

Baekland, F., Lundwall, L., & Kissin, B. (1975). Methods for the treatment of chronic alcoholism: A critical appraisal. In R. J. Gibbins, Y. Israel, H. Kalant, R. E. Popham, W. Schmidt, & R. G. Smart (Eds.), *Research advances in alcohol and drug problems* (Vol. 2, pp. 247–327). New York: Wiley.

Bandler, R., & Grinder, J. (1976). *The structure of magic: A book about language and therapy*. Palo Alto, CA: Science and Behavior Books.

Bandler, R., Grinder, J., & Satir, V. (1976). *Changing with families* (Vol. 1). Palo Alto, CA: Science and Behavior Books.

Bandura, A. (1969). *Principles of behavior modification*. New York: Holt, Rinehart and Winston.

Bandura, A. (1977a). Self-efficacy: Toward a unifying theory of behavioral change. *Psychological Review, 2,* 191–215.

Bandura, A. (1977b). *Social learning theory*. Englewood Cliffs, NJ: Prentice-Hall.

Bandura, A. (1986). *Social foundations of thought and action: A social cognitive theory*. Englewood Cliffs, NJ: Prentice-Hall.

Bandura, A., Adams, N. E., Hardy, A. B., & Howells, G. N. (1980). Tests of the generality of self-efficacy theory. *Cognitive Therapy and Research, 4,* 39–66.

Barten, H. H. (1969). The coming of age of the brief psychotherapies. In L. Bellak & H. H. Barten (Eds.), *Progress in community mental health* (pp. 3–28). New York: Grune & Stratton.

Bateson, G., Jackson, D. D., Haley, J., & Weakland, J. (1956). Toward a theory of schizophrenia. *Behavioral Science, 1,* 251–264.

Beck, A. T. (1976). *Cognitive therapy and the emotional disorders*. New York: International Universities Press.

Beck, A. T., & Emery, G. (1985). *Anxiety disorders and phobias: A cognitive perspective*. New York: Basic Books.

Beck, A. T., Freeman, A., & Associates (1990). *Cognitive therapy of personality disorders*. New York: Wilford.

Beck, A. T., Rush, A. J., Shaw, B. F., & Emery, G. (1979). *Cognitive therapy of depression*. New York: Guilford.

Beck, D. F., & Jones, M. A. (1973). *Progress on family problems*. New York: Family Service Association of America.

Beck, J. G. (1990). Brief psychotherapy for the sexual dysfunctions. In R. A. Wells & V. J. Giannetti (Eds.), *Handbook of the brief psychotherapies* (pp. 461–491). New York: Plenum.

Becker, R. E., Heimberg, R. G., & Bellack, A. S. (1987). *Social skills training treatment for depression*. Elmsford, NY: Pergamon.

Benson, H. (1974). Your innate asset for combatting stress. *Harvard Business Review, 52,* 49–60.

Benson, H. (1975). *The relaxation response.* New York: Morrow.

Bergin, A. E., & Lambert, M. J. (1978). The evaluation of therapeutic outcomes. In S. L. Garfield & A. E. Bergin (Eds.), *Handbook of psychotherapy and behavior change,* (2nd ed., pp. 139–190). New York: Wiley.

Beutler, L. E. (1984). *Eclectic psychotherapy: A systematic approach.* New York: Pergamon.

Bloom, B. L. (1981). Focused single-session therapy: Initial development and evaluation. In S. H. Budman (Ed.), *Forms of brief therapy* (pp. 167–216). New York: Guilford.

Bloom, B. L. (1992). *Planned short-term psychotherapy: A clinical handbook.* Boston: Allyn & Bacon.

Bolter, K., Levenson, H., & Alvarez, W. (1990). Differences in values between short-term and long-term therapists. *Professional Psychology, 21,* 285–290.

Brehm, S. S. (1976). *The application of social psychology to clinical practice.* Washington, DC: Hemisphere.

Broderick, C. B., & Schrader, S. (1981). The history of professional marriage and family therapy. In A. S. Gurman & D. P. Kniskern (Eds.), *Handbook of family therapy* (pp. 5–35). New York: Brunner/Mazel.

Brown, E. (1976). Divorce counseling. In D. H. L. Olson (Ed.), *Treating relationships* (pp. 399–429). Lake Mills, IA: Graphic Press.

Budman, S. H., & Gurman, A. S. (1983). The practice of brief therapy. *Professional Psychology, 14,* 277–292.

Budman, S. H., & Gurman, A. S. (1988). *Theory and practice of brief therapy.* New York: Guilford.

Budman, S. H., Hoyt, M. F., & Friedman, S. (Eds.). (1992). *The first session in brief therapy.* New York: Guilford.

Burgoyne, R. W., Staples, F. R., Yamamoto, J., Wolkon, G. H., & Kline, F. (1979). Patient requests of an outpatient clinic. *Archives of General Psychiatry, 36,* 400–403.

Burns, D. D., & Beck, A. T. (1978). Cognitive behavior modification of mood disorders. In J. P. Foreyt & D. P. Rathjen (Eds.), *Cognitive behavior therapy: Research and application* (pp. 109–134). New York: Plenum.

Caplan, G. (1964). *Principles of preventive psychiatry.* New York: Basic Books.

Carkhuff, R. R. (1969). *Helping and human relationships* (Vols. 1 and 2). New York: Holt, Rinehart and Winston.

Carter, E. A., & McGoldrick, M. (1988). *The family life cycle: A framework for family therapy* (2nd ed.). New York: Gardner.

Chesney, M., & Shelton, J. L. (1976). A comparison of muscle relaxation and electromyogram biofeedback treatments for muscle contraction headaches. *Journal of Behavior Therapy and Experimental Psychiatry, 7,* 221–226.

Corcoran, K. J., & Fischer, J. (1987). *Measures for clinical practice.* New York: Free Press.

Cornes, C. (1990) Interpersonal therapy of depression (IPT). In R. A. Wells & V. J. Giannetti (Eds.), *Handbook of the brief psychotherapies* (pp. 261–276). New York: Plenum.

Corsini, R. J. (1966). *Roleplaying in psychotherapy.* Chicago: Aldine.

Cotton, D. H. G. (1990). *Stress management: An integrated approach to therapy.* New York: Brunner/Mazel.

Cummings, N. A. (1977a). The anatomy of psychotherapy under national health insurance. *American Psychologist, 32,* 711–718.

Cummings, N. A. (1977b). Prolonged (ideal) versus short-term (realistic) psychotherapy. *Professional Psychology, 8,* 491–501.

Cummings, N. A. (1991). Brief intermittent therapy throughout the life cycle. In C. S. Austad & W. H. Berman (Eds.), *Psychotherapy in managed health care: The optimal use of time and resources* (pp. 3–18). Washington, DC: American Psychological Association.

Cummings, N. A. (1993) Empowering the psychotherapist to heal rapidly [Review of *Expanding therapeutic possibilities: Getting results in brief psychotherapy*]. *Contemporary Psychology, 38,* 492–493.

Cummings, N. A., & Follette, W. T. (1968). Psychiatric services and medical utilization in a prepaid health plan setting: Part II. *Medical Care, 6,* 31–41.

Cummings, N. A., & Follette, W. T. (1976). Brief psychotherapy and medical utilization. In H. Dorken & Associates (Eds.), *The professional psychologist today: New developments in law, health insurance and health practice* (pp. 165–174). San Francisco: Jossey-Bass.

Cummings, N. A., & VandenBos, G. R. (1979). The general practice of psychology. *Professional Psychology, 10,* 430–440.

Curran, J. P., & Monti, P. M. (1982). *Social skills training: A practical handbook for assessment and treatment.* New York: Guilford.

Davenloo, H. (Ed.). (1978). *Basic principles and techniques of short-term dynamic psychotherapy.* New York: SP Medical and Scientific Books.

de Shazer, S. (1985). *Keys to solution in brief therapy.* New York: Norton.

DiLoreto, A. O. (1971). *Comparative psychotherapy: An experimental analysis.* Chicago: Aldine-Atherton.

Dobson, K. S. (1989). A meta-analysis of the efficacy of cognitive therapy for depression. *Journal of Consulting and Clinical Psychology, 57,* 414–419.

Duncan, B. L., Solovey, A. D., & Rusk, G. S. (1992). *Changing the rules: A client-directed approach to therapy*. New York: Guilford.

Dunlap, K. (1932). *Habits: Their making and unmaking*. New York: Liveright.

D'Zurilla, T. J., & Goldfried, M. R. (1971). Problem-solving and behavior modification. *Journal of Abnormal Psychology, 78*, 107–126.

Edelstein, M. G. (1990). *Symptom analysis: A method of brief therapy*. New York: Norton.

Elkins, J., Shea, J. T., Watkins, S. D., Imber, S. M., Sotsky, J. F., Collins, D. R., Glass, D. R., Pilkonis, P. A., Leber, W. R., Docherty, J. P., Fiester, S. P., & Parloff, M. B. (1989). National Institute of Mental Health Treatment of Depression Collaborative Research Program: General effectiveness of treatments. *Archives of General Psychiatry, 46*, 971–982.

Ellis, A. (1962). *Reason and emotion in psychotherapy*. New York: Lyle Stuart.

Ellis, A. (1971). *Growth through reason*. North Hollywood, CA: Wilshire.

Endicott, N., & Endicott, J. (1963). "Improvement" in untreated psychiatric patients. *Archives of General Psychiatry, 9*, 575–585.

Epstein, L. (1980). *Helping people: The task-centered approach*. St. Louis: Mosby.

Epstein, L. (1992). *Brief treatment and a new look at the task-centered approach*. New York: Macmillan.

Epstein, N. B., Bishop, D. S., Keitner, G. I., & Miller, I. W. (1990). A systems therapy: Problem-centered systems therapy of the family. In R. A. Wells & V. J. Giannetti (Eds.), *Handbook of the brief psychotherapies* (pp. 405–436). New York: Plenum.

Erickson, M. H. (1967) Deep hypnosis and its induction. In J. Haley (Ed.), *Advanced techniques of hypnosis and therapy: Selected papers of Milton H. Erickson, M.D.* (pp. 7–31). New York: Grune & Stratton.

Ewing, C. P. (1978). *Crisis intervention as psychotherapy*. New York: Oxford University Press.

Ewing, C. P. (1990). Crisis intervention as brief psychotherapy. In R. A. Wells & V. J. Giannetti (Eds.), *Handbook of the brief psychotherapies* (pp. 277–294). New York: Plenum.

Eysenck, H. J. (1952). The effects of psychotherapy: An evaluation. *Journal of Consulting Psychology, 16*, 319–324.

Fensterheim, H., & Baer, J. (1975). *Don't say yes when you want to say no*. New York: McKay.

Fisch, R., Weakland, J., & Segal, L. (1982). *Tactics of change*. San Francisco: Jossey-Bass.

Fischer, J. (1976). *The effectiveness of social casework.* Springfield, IL: Thomas.

Fisher, S. G. (1980). The use of time-limits in brief psychotherapy: A comparison of six-session, twelve-session, and unlimited treatment for families. *Family Process, 19,* 25–36.

Fisher, S. G. (1984). Time-limited brief therapy with families: A one-year follow-up study. *Family Process, 23,* 101–106.

Fishman, D. B., & Franks, C. M. (1992). Evolution and differentiation within behavior therapy: A theoretical and epistemological review. In D. K. Freedheim (Ed.), *History of psychotherapy: A century of change* (pp. 159–196). Washington, DC: American Psychological Association.

Fodor, I. G. (1987). Moving beyond cognitive-behavior therapy: Integrating gestalt therapy to facilitate personal and interpersonal awareness. In N. S. Jacobson (Ed.), *Psychotherapists in clinical practice* (pp. 190–231). New York: Guilford.

Follette, W. T., & Cummings, N. A. (1967). Psychiatric services and medical utilization in a prepaid health plan setting. *Medical Care, 5,* 25–35.

Frank, J. D. (1968). The role of hope in psychotherapy. *International Journal of Psychiatry, 5,* 383–395.

Frank, J. D. (1969). Common features account for effectiveness. *International Journal of Psychiatry, 7,* 122–127.

Frank, J. D. (1974). *Persuasion and healing* (2nd ed.). Baltimore: Johns Hopkins University Press. (Original work published 1961)

Frank, J. D. (1978). Expectation and therapeutic outcome: The placebo effect and the role induction interview. In J. D. Frank, R. Hoehn-Saric, S. D. Imber, B. L. Liberman, & A. R. Stone (Eds.), *Effective ingredients of successful psychotherapy* (pp. 1–34). New York: Brunner/Mazel.

Frank, J. D. (1979). The present status of outcome studies. *Journal of Consulting and Clinical Psychology, 47,* 310–316.

Freedheim, D. K. (Ed.). (1992). *History of psychotherapy: A century of change.* Washington, DC: American Psychological Association.

Freeman, D. R. (1982). *Marital crisis and short-term counseling.* New York: Free Press.

Freeman, D. R. (1990). *Couples in conflict: Inside the counseling room.* Milton Keynes, England: Open University Press.

Friedman, S., & Fanger, M. T. (1991). *Expanding therapeutic possibilities: Getting results in brief psychotherapy.* Lexington, MA: Lexington Books.

Freudenberger, H. J., & North, G. (1985). *Women's burnout.* New York: Doubleday.

Garfield, S. L. (1980). *Psychotherapy: An eclectic view.* New York: Wiley.

Garfield, S. L. (1986). Research on client variables in psychotherapy. In S. L. Garfield & A. E. Bergin (Eds.), *Handbook of psychotherapy and behavior change.* (3rd ed., pp. 213–256). New York: Wiley.

Garfield, S. L. (1989). *The practice of brief psychotherapy.* New York: Pergamon.

Garfield, S. L., & Bergin, A. E. (Eds.). (1986). *Handbook of psychotherapy and behavior change* (3rd ed.). New York: Wiley.

Garfield, S. L., & Kurtz, R. (1977). A study of eclectic views. *Journal of Consulting and Clinical Psychology, 45,* 78–83.

Garvin, C. D. (1990). Short-term group therapy. In R. A. Wells & V. J. Giannetti (Eds.), *Handbook of the brief psychotherapies* (pp. 513–536). New York: Plenum.

Giannetti, V. J. (1990). Brief treatment and mental health policy. In R. A. Wells & V. J. Giannetti (Eds.), *Handbook of the brief psychotherapies* (pp. 79–90). New York: Plenum.

Gibbons, J. S., Bow, I., Butler, J., & Powell, J. (1979). Client's reactions to task-centered casework: A follow-up study. *British Journal of Social Work, 9,* 203–215.

Gittellman, M. (1965). Behavior rehearsal as a technique in child treatment. *Journal of Child Psychology and Psychiatry, 6,* 251–255.

Golan, N. (1974). Crisis theory. In F. J. Turner (Ed.), *Social work treatment: Interlocking theoretical approaches* (pp. 420–456). New York: Free Press.

Goldberg, I. D., Krantz, G., & Locke, B. Z. (1970). Effect of a short-term outpatient psychotherapy benefit on the utilization of medical services in a prepaid group practice medical program. *Medical Care, 8,* 419–428.

Goldfried, M. R., & Davison, G. C. (1976). *Clinical behavior therapy.* New York: Holt, Rinehart and Winston.

Goldfried, M. R., & Goldfried, A. P. (1975). Cognitive change methods. In F. H. Kanfer & A. P. Goldstein (Eds.), *Helping people change* (1st ed., pp. 89–116). New York: Pergamon.

Goldstein, M. J., Rodnick, E. H., Evans, J. R., May, P. R. A., & Steinberg, M. R. (1978). Drug and family therapy in the aftercare of acute schizophrenics. *Archives of General Psychiatry, 35,* 1169–1177.

Goleman, D, (1981). Deadlines for change: Therapy in the age of Reagonomics. *Psychology Today, 15,* 60–69.

Good, P. R. (1987). Brief therapy in the age of Reagapeutics. *American Journal of Orthopsychiatry, 57,* 6–11.

Greene, M. (1978). Some recent contributions to a noneclectic approach. *Clinical Social Work Journal, 6,* 171–187.

Grier, W. H., & Cobbs, F. R. (1968). *Black rage*. New York: Basic Books.

Guerney, B. G., Jr. (1977). *Relationship enhancement: Skill-training programs for therapy, problem prevention and enrichment*. San Francisco: Jossey-Bass.

Guerney, B. G., Jr. (1988). Family relationship enhancement: A skill training approach. In L. A. Bond & B. M. Wagner (Eds.), *Families in transition: Primary prevention programs that work* (pp. 99–134). Newbury Park, CA: Sage.

Guerney, B. G., Jr., Stollak, G., & Guerney, L. (1971). The practicing psychologist as educator: An alternative to the medical practitioner model. *Professional Psychology, 2*, 276–282.

Gurman, A. S. (Ed.). (1985). *Casebook of marital therapy*. New York: Guilford.

Haley. J. (1963). *Strategies of psychotherapy*. New York: Grune & Stratton.

Haley, J. (1967). Commentary on the writings of Milton H. Erickson, M.D. In J. Haley (Ed.), *Advanced techniques of hypnosis and therapy: Selected papers of Milton H. Erickson, M.D.* (pp. 530–549). New York: Grune & Stratton.

Haley, J. (1973). *Uncommon therapy: The psychiatric techniques of Milton H. Erickson, M.D.*. New York: Norton.

Haley, J. (1976). *Problem-solving therapy*. San Francisco: Jossey-Bass.

Haley, J. (1990). Why not long-term therapy? In J. K. Zeig & S. G. Gilligan (Eds.), *Brief therapy: Myth, methods and metaphors* (pp. 3–17). New York: Bruner/Mazel.

Haley, J., & Hoffman, L. (1967). *Techniques of family therapy*. New York: Basic Books.

Hammond, J., Hepworth, D. H., & Smith, V. (1977). *Improving therapeutic communication*. San Francisco: Jossey-Bass.

Hansell, N. (1973). *A primer of mental health advances* (six audiotape cassettes). Elgin, Il: New Orient Media.

Hansell, N. (1975). *The person-in-distress*. New York: Behavioral Publications.

Hatcher, C., & Himelstein, P. (1976). *The handbook of gestalt psychology*. New York: Aronson.

Hawton, K. (1991). Sex therapy. *Behavioral Psychotherapy, 19*, 131–136.

Heitler, J. B. (1976). Preparatory techniques in initiating expressive psychotherapy with lower-class, unsophisticated patients. *Psychological Bulletin, 83*, 339–352.

Hepworth, D. H. (1979). Early removal of resistance in task-centered casework. *Social Work, 24*, 317–323.

Hepworth, D. H., & Larsen, J. A. (1990). *Direct social work practice: Theory and skills* (3rd ed.). Homewood, IL: Dorsey.

Herzberg, A. (1941). Short treatment of neurosis by graduated tasks. *British Journal of Medical Psychology, 19*, 36–51.

Hollin, C. R., & Trower, P. (Eds.). (1986). *Handbook of social skills training* (Vols. 1 and 2). Oxford: Pergamon.

Holmes, T. H., & Rahe, R. H. (1967). The social readjustment rating scale. *Journal of Psychosomatic Research, 11*, 213–218.

Holtzworth-Monroe, A., Jacobson, N. S., DeKlyen, M., & Whisman, M. A. (in press). The relationship between behavioral marital therapy outcome and process variables. *Journal of Consulting and Clinical Psychology*.

Howard, K. I., Kopta, S. M., Krause, M. S., & Orlinsky, D. E. (1986). The dose-effect relationship in psychotherapy. *American Psychologist, 41*, 159–164.

Hoyt, M. F. (1990). On time in brief therapy. In R. A. Wells & V. J. Giannetti (Eds.), *Handbook of the brief psychotherapies* (pp. 115–143). New York: Plenum.

Hoyt, M. F. (1985). Therapist resistances to short-term dynamic psychotherapy. *Journal of the American Academy of Psychoanalysis, 13*, 93–112.

Hoyt, M. F. (1987). Resistances to brief therapy. *American Psychologist, 42*, 408–409.

Hoyt, M. F. (1993). Two cases of brief therapy in an HMO. In R. A. Wells & V. J. Giannetti (Eds.), *Casebook of the brief psychotherapies* (pp. 235–247). New York: Plenum.

Hoyt, M. F., Rosenbaum, R., & Talmon, M. (1992). Planned single-session psychotherapy. In S. H. Budman, M. F. Hoyt, & S. Friedman (Eds.), *The first session in brief therapy* (pp. 59–86). New York: Guilford.

Hudson, W. W. (1982). *The clinical measurement package: A field manual*. Homewood, IL: Dorsey.

Imber, S. D., & Evanczuk, K. J. (1990). Brief crisis therapy groups. In R. A. Wells & V. J. Giannetti (Eds.), *Handbook of the brief psychotherapies* (pp. 565–582). New York: Plenum.

Jackson, D. D. (Ed.). (1965). *Communication, family and marriage*. Palo Alto, CA: Science and Behavior Books.

Jacobson, E. (1929). *Progressive relaxation*. Chicago: University of Chicago Press.

Jacobson, G. (1965). Crisis theory and treatment strategy: Some sociocultural and psychodynamic considerations. *Journal of Nervous and Mental Disease, 141*, 209–218.

Jacobson, N. S., & Holtzworth-Monroe, A. (1986). Marital therapy: A social learning–cognitive perspective. In N. S. Jacobson & A. S. Gurman (Eds.), *Clinical handbook of marital therapy* (pp. 29–70). New York: Guilford.

Jakubowski-Spector, P. (1973). Facilitating the growth of women through assertive training. *The Counseling Psychologist, 4,* 75–86.

Jayarante, S. (1978). A study of clinical eclecticism. *Social Service Review, 52,* 621–631.

Kanfer, F. H. (1979). Self-management: Strategies and tactics. In A. P. Goldstein & F. H. Kanfer (Eds.), *Maximizing treatment gains: Transfer enhancement in psychotherapy* (pp. 185–224). New York: Academic Press.

Kazdin, A. E. (1973). Covert modeling and the reduction of avoidance behavior. *Journal of Abnormal Psychology, 81,* 87–95.

Kazdin, A. E. (1974). Effects of covert modeling and model reinforcement on assertive behavior. *Journal of Abnormal Psychology, 83,* 240–252.

Kazdin, A. E., & Wilson, G. T. (1978). *Evaluation of behavior therapy: Issues, evidence and research strategies.* Cambridge, MA: Ballinger.

Keilson, M. V., Dworkin, F. H., & Gelso, C. J. (1979). The effectiveness of time-limited psychotherapy in a university counseling center. *Journal of Clinical Psychology, 35,* 631–636.

Kendall, P. C., & Braswell, L. (1985). *Cognitive-behavioral therapy for impulsive children.* New York: Guilford.

Kendall, P. C., & Wilcox, J. E. (1980). Cognitive-behavioral treatment for impulsivity: Concrete versus conceptual training in non-self-controlled children. *Journal of Consulting and Clinical Psychology, 48,* 80–91.

Klerman, G. L., Weismann, M. M., Rounsaville, B. J., & Chevron, E. S. (1984). *Interpersonal psychotherapy of depression (IPT).* New York: Basic Books.

Koss, M. P. (1979). Length of psychotherapy for clients seen in private practice. *Journal of Consulting and Clinical Psychology, 47,* 210–212.

Koss, M. P., & Butcher, J. N. (1986). Research on brief psychotherapy In S. L. Garfield & A. E. Bergin (Eds.), *Handbook of psychotherapy and behavior change* (3rd ed., pp. 627–670). New York: Wiley.

Lambert, M. J., Shapiro, D. A., & Bergin, A.E. (1986). The effectiveness of psychotherapy. In S. L. Garfield & A. E. Bergin (Eds.), *Handbook of psychotherapy and behavior change* (3rd ed., pp. 157–211). New York: Wiley.

Lange, A. J., & Jakubowski, P. (1976). *Responsible assertive behavior: Cognitive/behavioral procedures.* Champaign, IL: Research Press.

Langsley, D. G. (1978). Comparing clinic and private practice of psychiatry. *American Journal of Psychiatry, 135,* 702–706.

Langsley, D. G., & Kaplan, D. K. (1968). *The treatment of families in crisis.* New York: Grune & Stratton.

Langsley, D. G., Machotka, P., & Flomenhaft, K. (1971). Avoiding mental hospital admission: A follow-up study. *American Journal of Psychiatry, 127,* 1391–1394.

Lansky, M. R., & Davenport, A. E. (1975). Difficulties in brief conjoint treatment of sexual dysfunction. *American Journal of Psychiatry, 132,* 177–179.

Layden, M. A., Newman, C. F., Freeman, A., & Morse, S. B. (1993). *Cognitive therapy of borderline personality disorder.* Boston: Allyn & Bacon.

Lazare, A., Cohen, F., Jacobson, A., Williams, R., Mignone, R., & Zisook, S. (1972). The walk-in patient as "customer": A key dimension in evaluation and treatment. *American Journal of Orthopsychiatry, 42,* 872, 883.

Lazare, A., Eisenthal, S., & Wasserman, L. (1975). The customer approach to patienthood. *Archives of General Psychiatry, 32,* 553–558.

Lazare, A., Eisenthal, S., Wasserman, L., & Harford, I. (1975). Patient requests in a walk-in clinic. *Comprehensive Psychiatry, 16,* 467–477.

Lazarus, A. A., & Fay, A. (1975). *I can if I want to.* New York: Morrow.

Lennard, H. J., & Bernstein, A. (1960). *The anatomy of psychotherapy.* New York: Columbia University Press.

Leventhal, T., & Weinberger, G. (1975). Evaluation of a large-scale brief therapy program for children. *American Journal of Orthopsychiatry, 49,* 119–133.

Levy, R., & Shelton, J. (1990). Tasks in brief therapy. In R. A. Wells & V. J. Giannetti (Eds.), *Handbook of the brief psychotherapies* (pp. 145–163). New York: Plenum.

Lewis, M. S., Gottesman, D., & Gutstein, S. (1978). The course and duration of crisis. *Journal of Clinical and Consulting Psychology, 47,* 128–134.

Liberman, B. L. (1978). The role of mastery in psychotherapy: Maintenance of improvement and prescriptive change. In J. D. Frank, R. Hoehn-Saric, S. D. Imber, B. L. Liberman, & A. R. Stone (Eds.), *Effective ingredients of successful psychotherapy* (pp. 35–72). New York: Brunner/Mazel.

Linehan, M. M., & Egan, K. J. (1978). Assertion training for women. In A. S. Bellack & M. Hersen (Eds.), *Research and practice in social skills training* (pp. 237–271). New York: Plenum.

London, P. (1986). *The modes and morals of psychotherapy* (2nd ed.). Washington, DC: Hemisphere.

Lorion, R. P. (1978). Research on psychotherapy and behavior change with the disadvantaged. In S. L. Garfield & A. E. Bergin (Eds.), *Handbook of psychotherapy and behavior change* (2nd ed., pp. 903–938). New York: Wiley.

Lorion, R. P., & Felner, R. D. (1986). Research on mental health interventions with the disadvantaged. In S. L. Garfield & A. E. Bergin (Eds.), *Handbook of psychotherapy and behavior change* (3rd ed., pp. 739–775). New York: Wiley.

McCary, J. (1973). *Human sexuality: A brief edition*. New York: Van Nostrand.

McFall, R. M., & Lilliesand, D. V. (1971). Behavior rehearsal with modeling and coaching in assertive training. *Journal of Abnormal Psychology, 77*, 313–323.

McFall, R. M., & Twentyman, C. T. (1973). Four experiments on the relative contribution of rehearsal, modeling and coaching to assertion training. *Journal of Abnormal Psychology, 81*, 199–218.

Madanes, C. (1984). *Behind the one-way mirror: Advances in the practice of strategic therapy*. San Francisco: Jossey-Bass.

Maguire, L. (1991). *Social support systems in practice: A generalist approach*. Silver Spring, MD: National Association of Social Workers Press.

Maguire, L. (1993). Brief social support interventions with adolescents. In R. A. Wells & V. J. Giannetti (Eds.), *Casebook of the brief psychotherapies* (pp. 91–108). New York: Plenum.

Mahoney, M. J. (1974). *Cognition and behavior modification*. Cambridge, MA: Ballinger.

Mahoney, M. J., & Arkoff, D. B. (1978). Cognitive and self-control therapies. In S. L. Garfield & A. E. Bergin (Eds.), *Handbook of psychotherapy and behavior change* (2nd ed., pp. 689–722). New York: Wiley.

Malan, D., Heath, E., Bacal, H., & Balfour, F. (1975). Psychodynamic changes in untreated neurotic patients. II: Apparently genuine improvements. *Archives of General Psychiatry, 32*, 110–126.

Maluccio, A. (1979). *Learning from clients*. New York: Free Press.

Mann, J. (1973). *Time-limited psychotherapy*. Cambridge, MA: Harvard University Press.

Mann, J., & Goldman, R. (1982). *A casebook in time-limited psychotherapy*. New York: McGraw-Hill.

Marks, I. (1978). Behavioral psychotherapy with adult neurosis. In S. L. Garfield & A. E. Bergin (Eds.), *Handbook of psychotherapy and behavior change* (2nd ed., pp. 493–548). New York: Wiley.

Marmor, J, (1979). Short-term dynamic psychotherapy. *American Journal of Psychiatry, 136,* 149–155.

Masters, W. H., & Johnson, V. (1966). *Human sexual response.* Boston: Little, Brown.

Masters, W. H., & Johnson, V. (1970). *Human sexual inadequacy.* Boston: Little, Brown.

May, R. (1992). Foreword. In D. K. Freedheim (Ed.), *History of psychotherapy: A century of change* (pp. xx–xxvii). Washington, DC: American Psychological Association.

Meichenbaum, D. H. (1974). *Cognitive behavior modification.* Morristown, NJ: General Learning Press.

Meichenbaum, D. H. (1975). Self-instructional methods. In F. H. Kanfer & A. P. Goldstein (Eds.), *Helping people change* (pp. 357–392). Elmsford, NY: Pergamon.

Meichenbaum, D. H. (1979). Teaching children self-control. In B. B. Lahey & A. E. Kazdin (Eds.), *Advances in clinical child psychology* (Vol. 2, pp. 1–33). New York: Plenum.

Meyer, W. S. (1993). In defense of long-term treatment: On the vanishing holding environment. *Social Work, 38,* 571–578.

Meyers, J. K., Weismann, M. M., Tischler, G. L., Holzer, C. E. III, Leaf, P. J., Orvaschel, H., Anthony, J. C., Boyd. J. H., Burke, J. D., Jr., Kramer, M., & Stolzman, R. (1984). Six-month prevalence of psychiatric disorders in three communities. *Archives of General Psychiatry, 41,* 959–967.

Minuchin, S. (1974). *Families and family therapy.* Cambridge, MA: Harvard University Press.

Minuchin, S., & Silverman, C. (1981). *Family therapy techniques.* Cambridge, MA: Harvard University Press.

Minuchin, S., Rosman, B., & Baker, L. (1978). *Psychosomatic families: Anorexia nervosa in context.* Cambridge, MA: Harvard University Press.

Moreno, J. L. (1959). *Psychodrama.* New York: Beacon House.

Morretti, M. M., Feldman, L. A., & Shaw, B. F. (1990). Cognitive therapy: Current issues in theory and practice. In R. A. Wells & V. J. Giannetti (Eds.), *Handbook of the brief psychotherapies* (pp. 217–237). New York: Plenum.

Morrison, J. (1993). *The first interview.* New York: Guilford.

Naar, R. (1990). Psychodrama in short-term psychotherapy. In R. A. Wells & V. J. Giannetti (Eds.), *Handbook of the brief psychotherapies* (pp. 583–600). New York: Plenum.

Nezu, A. M. (1989) *Problem-solving therapy for depression.* New York: Wiley.

Nicholas, R. A., & Berman, J. S. (1983). Is follow-up necessary in evaluating psychotherapy? *Psychological Bulletin, 93,* 261–278.

Nichols, W. C., & Everett, C. (1986). *Family therapy: An integrative approach.* New York: Guilford.

Norcross, J. C. (Ed.). (1986). *Handbook of eclectic psychotherapy.* New York: Brunner/Mazel.

Orlinsky, D. E., & Howard, K. I. (1986). Process and outcome in psychotherapy. In S. L. Garfield & A. E. Bergin (Eds.), *Handbook of psychotherapy and behavior change* (3rd ed., pp. 311–381). New York: Wiley.

Pacoe, L. V., & Greenwald, M. A. (1993). Brief treatment of anxiety disorders. In R. A. Wells & V. J. Giannetti (Eds.), *Casebook of the brief psychotherapies* (pp. 129–141). New York: Plenum.

Parad, H. J. (Ed.). (1965). *Crisis intervention: Selected readings.* New York: Family Service Association of America.

Parad, H. J., & Parad. L. J. (1968). A study of crisis-oriented planned short-term treatment, Parts I and II. *Social Casework, 49,* 346–355 and 418–426.

Patterson, C. H. (1989). Foundations for a systematic eclectic psychotherapy. *Psychotherapy, 26,* 427–435.

Phelps, P. A. (1993). The case of oppositional cooperation. In R. A. Wells & V. J. Giannetti (Eds.), *Casebook of the brief psychotherapies* (pp. 287–302). New York: Plenum.

Piasecki, J., & Hollon, S. D. (1987). Cognitive therapy for depression: Unexplicated schemata and scripts. In N. S. Jacobson (Ed.), *Psychotherapists in clinical practice: Cognitive and behavioral perspectives* (pp. 121–152). New York: Guilford.

Pittman, F. S. (1987). *Turning points: Treating families in transition and crisis.* New York: Norton.

Pittman, F. S., Flomenhaft, K., & DeYoung, C. D. (1990). Family crisis therapy. In R. A. Wells & V. J. Giannetti (Eds.), *Handbook of the brief psychotherapies* (pp. 297–324). New York: Plenum.

Rabkin, R. (1977). *Strategic psychotherapy: Brief and symptomatic treatment.* New York: Basic Books.

Raimy, V. (1975). *Misunderstandings of the self: Cognitive psychotherapy and the misconception hypothesis.* San Francisco: Jossey-Bass.

Rapoport, L. (1970). Crisis intervention as a mode of treatment. In R. W. Roberts & R. H. Nee (Eds.), *Theories of social casework* (pp. 152–171). Chicago: University of Chicago Press.

Rathjen, D. P., Rathjen, E. D., Hiniker, A. (1978). A cognitive analysis of social performance: Implications for assessment and treatment. In J. P. Foreyt & D. P. Rathjen (Eds.), *Cognitive behavior therapy: Research and application* (pp. 33–76). New York: Plenum.

Reid, W. J. (1975). A test of the task-centered approach. *Social Work, 22*, 3–9.

Reid, W. J. (1978). *The task-centered system.* New York: Columbia University Press.

Reid, W. J. (1985). *Family problem solving.* New York: Columbia University Press.

Reid, W. J., & Epstein, L. (1972). *Task-centered casework.* New York: Columbia University Press.

Reid, W. J., & Shyne, A. W. (1969). *Brief and extended casework.* New York: Columbia University Press.

Ripple, L., Alexander, E., & Polemis, B. (1964). *Motivation, capacity amd opportunity.* Chicago: University of Chicago Press.

Robins, L. N., Helzer, J. E., Weisman, M. M., Orvaschel, H., Gruenberg, E., Burke, J. D., & Regier, D. A. (1984). Lifetime prevalence of specific psychiatric disorders in three sites. *Archives of General Psychiatry, 41*, 949–958.

Rockwell, W. J. K., & Pinkerton, R. S. (1982). Single-session psychotherapy. *American Journal of Psychotherapy, 36*, 32–40.

Rose, S., (1977). *Group therapy: A behavioral approach.* Englewood Cliffs, N. J.: Prentice-Hall.

Rose, S. D. (1990). Social skill training in short-term groups. In R. A. Wells & V. J. Giannetti (Eds.), *Handbook of the brief psychotherapies* (pp. 537–550). New York: Plenum.

Rosen, J. C., & Wiens, A. N. (1979). Changes in medical problems and the use of medical services following psychological intervention. *American Psychologist, 34*, 420–431.

Rosenbaum, R. (1990). Strategic psychotherapy. In R. A. Wells & V. J. Giannetti (Eds.), *Handbook of the brief psychotherapies* (pp. 351–403). New York: Plenum.

Rosenbaum, R., Hoyt, M. F., & Talmon, M. (1990). The challenge of single-session therapies: Creating pivotal moments. In R. A. Wells & V. J. Giannetti (Eds.), *Handbook of the brief psychotherapies* (pp. 165–189). New York: Plenum.

Rudolph, B. A. (1993). The importance of the midpoint review in time-limited therapies. *Professional Psychology: Research and Practice, 24*, 346–352.

Ruesch, J., & Bateson, G. (1951). *Communication: The social matrix of psychiatry.* New York: Norton.

Ryan, W. (1969). *Distress in the city.* Cleveland: Case Western Reserve University Press.

Salter, A. (1949). *Conditioned reflex therapy.* New York: Creative Age.

Satir, V. (1964). *Conjoint family therapy*. Palo Alto, CA: Science and Behavior Books.

Schorer, C., Lowinger, P., Sullivan, T., & Hartlaub, G. (1968). Improvement without treatment. *Diseases of the Nervous System, 29,* 100–104.

Schulman, L. (1979). *The skills of helping*. Itasca, IL: Peacock.

Schulman, L. (1981). *Identifying, measuring and teaching helping skills*. New York: Council on Social Work Education.

Schwartz, W. (1979). Foreword. In L. Schulman, *The skills of helping* (pp. vi–ix). Itasca, IL: Peacock.

Scott, W. O., Baer, G., Kristoff, K. A., & Kelly, J. (1984). The use of skills training procedures in the treatment of a child-abusive parent. *Journal of Behavior Therapy and Experimental Psychiatry, 15,* 329–336.

Segraves, R. T. (1990). Short-term marital therapy. In R. A. Wells & V. J. Gianetti (Eds.), *Handbook of the brief psychotherapies* (pp. 437–459). New York: Plenum.

Shapiro, A. K., & Morris, L. A. (1978) Placebo effects in medical and psychological therapies. In S. L. Garfield & A. E. Bergin (Eds.), *Handbook of psychotherapy and behavior change* (2nd ed., pp. 369–410). New York: Wiley.

Shelton, J. L. (1973). Murder strikes and panic follows: Can behavioral modification help? *Behavior Therapy, 4,* 706–708.

Shelton, J. L. (1975). The elimination of persistent stuttering by the use of homework assignments involving speech shadowing. *Behavior Therapy, 6,* 392–393.

Shelton, J. L. (1979). Instigation therapy: Using therapeutic homework to promote treatment gains. In A. P. Goldstein & F. H. Kanfer (Eds.), *Maximizing treatment gains: Transfer enhancement in psychotherapy* (pp. 225–245). New York: Academic Press.

Shelton, J. L., & Ackerman, J. M. (1974). *Homework in counseling and psychotherapy*. Springfield, IL: Thomas.

Sledge, W. H., Moras, K., Hartley, D., & Levine, M. (1990). Effect of time-limited therapy on patient dropout rates. *American Journal of Psychiatry, 147,* 1341–1347.

Sloane, R. B., Staples, F. R., Cristol, A. H., Yorkston, N. J., & Whipple, K. (1975). *Psychotherapy versus behavior therapy*. Cambridge, MA: Harvard University Press.

Smith, J. C. (1990). *Cognitive-behavioral relaxation training: A new system of strategies for treatment and assessment*. New York: Springer.

Smith, M. J. (1975). *When I say no I feel guilty*. New York: Dial Press.

Snyder, M., & Guerney, B. G., Jr. (1993). Brief couple/family therapy: The relationship enhancement approach. In R. A. Wells & V. J. Giannetti (Eds.), *Casebook of the brief psychotherapies* (pp. 221–234). New York: Plenum.

Stampfl, T. J., & Levis, D. J. (1967). Essentials of implosive therapy: A learning-theory-based psychodynamic behavior therapy. *Journal of Abnormal and Social Psychology, 72,* 496–503.

Stern, S. (1993). Managed care, brief therapy, and therapeutic integrity. *Psychotherapy, 30,* 162–175.

Stevenson, I. (1959). Direct instigation of behavioral changes in psychotherapy. *Archives of General Psychiatry, 61,* 99–117.

Strong, S. R., & Claiborn, C. (1982). *Change through interaction.* New York: Wiley.

Sullivan, H. S. (1953). *The interpersonal theory of psychiatry.* New York: Norton.

Sullivan, H. S. (1954). *The psychiatric interview.* New York: Norton.

Szapocznik, J., & Kurtines, W. M. (1989). *Beyond family therapy: Breakthroughs in the treatment of drug abusing youth.* New York: Springer.

Szapocznik, J., Kurtines, W. M., Perez-Vidal, A., Hervis, O. E., & Foote, F. H. (1990). One-person family therapy. In R. A. Wells & V. J. Giannetti (Eds.), *Handbook of the brief psychotherapies* (pp. 493–510). New York: Plenum.

Talmon, M. (1990). *Single-session therapy: Maximizing the effect of the first (and often only) therapeutic encounter.* San Francisco: Jossey-Bass.

Treadway, D. C. (1985). Learning their dance: Changing some steps. In A. S. Gurman (Ed.), *Casebook of marital therapy* (pp. 155–175). New York: Guilford.

Truax, C. B., & Carkhuff, R. R. (1967). *Toward effective counseling and psychotherapy.* Chicago: Aldine.

Truax, C. B., & Mitchell, K. M. (1971). Research on certain therapist skills in relation to process and outcome. In A. E. Bergin & S. L. Garfield (Eds.), *Handbook of psychotherapy and behavior change* (1st ed., pp. 299–344). New York: Wiley.

Turner, R. M. (1992). Launching cognitive-behavioral therapy for adolescent depression and drug abuse. In S. H. Budman, M. F. Hoyt, & S. Freidman (Eds.), *The first session in brief therapy* (pp. 135–155). New York: Guilford.

VandenBos, G. R., Cummings, N. A., & DeLeon, P. H. (1992). A century of psychotherapy: Economic and environmental influences. In D. K. Freedheim (Ed.), *History of psychotherapy: A century of change* (pp. 65–102). Washington, DC: American Psychological Association.

Vattanno, A. (1978). Self-management procedures for coping with stress. *Social Work, 23,* 113–120.

von Bertalanffy, L. (1950). The theory of open systems in physics and biology. *Science, 3*, 23–29.

von Bertalanffy, L. (1968). *General sysytems theory: Foundation, development, applications*. New York: Braziller.

Wachtel, P. L. (1977). *Psychoanalysis and behavior therapy: Toward an integration*. New York: Basic Books.

Walen, S. R., DiGuiseppe, R., & Wessler, R. L. (1980). *A practitioner's guide to rational-emotive therapy*. New York: Oxford University Press.

Waxenberg, B. (1973). Therapist's empathy, regard and genuineness as factors in staying in or dropping out of short-term, time-limited family therapy. *Dissertation Abstracts International, 34*, 1288B.

Weinberger, G. (1971). Brief therapy with children and their parents. In H. H. Barten (Ed.), *Brief therapies* (pp. 196–211). New York: Behavioral Publications.

Weisman, A. (1976). Industrial social work. *Social Casework, 57*, 50–54.

Wells, R. A. (1980). Engagement techniques in family therapy. *International Journal of Family Therapy, 2*, 79–94.

Wells, R. A. (1992). Planned short-term treatment for persons with social and interpersonal problems. In K. Corcoran (Ed.), *Structuring change: Effective practice for common client problems* (pp. 292–307). Chicago: Lyceum.

Wells, R. A. (1993). Clinical strategies in brief psychotherapy. In R. A. Wells & V. J. Giannetti (Eds.), *Casebook of the brief psychotherapies* (pp. 3–17). New York: Plenum.

Wells, R. A., & Figurel, J. A. (1979). The techniques of structured communication training. *Family Coordinator, 28*, 273–281.

Wells, R. A., Figurel, J. A., & McNamee, P. (1977). Communication training vs. conjoint marital therapy. *Social Work Research and Abstracts, 13*, 31–39.

Wells, R. A., & Giannetti, V. J. (Eds.). (1990). *Handbook of the brief psychotherapies*. New York: Plenum.

Wells, R. A., & Giannetti, V. J. (Eds.). (1993). *Casebook of the brief psychotherapies*. New York: Plenum.

Wells, R. A., & Phelps, P. A. (1990). The brief psychotherapies: A selective overview. In R. A. Wells & V. J. Giannetti (Eds.), *Handbook of the brief psychotherapies* (pp. 3–26). New York: Plenum.

Whisman, M. A., & Jacobson, N. S. (1987, November). *Homework compliance in behavioral marital therapy: Client, therapist, and outcome variables*. Paper presented at the annual meeting of the Association for the Advancement of Behavior Therapy, Boston.

Whisman, M. A., & Jacobson, N. S. (1990). Behavioral marital therapy.

In R. A. Wells & V. J. Giannetti (Eds.), *Handbook of the brief psychotherapies* (pp. 325–349). New York: Plenum.

White, R. (1963). *Ego and reality in psychoanalytic theory*. New York: International Universities Press.

Whitehead, A., & Mathews, A. (1986). Factors related to successful outcome in the treatment of sexually unresponsive women. *Psychological Medicine, 16*, 373–378.

Wolpe, J. (1969). Foreword. In C. M. Franks (Ed.), *Behavior therapy: Appraisal and status* (pp. iv–ix). New York: McGraw-Hill.

Wolpe, J. (1990). *The practice of behavior therapy* (4th ed.). New York: Pergamon.

Wolpe, J., & Lazarus, A. A. (1966). *Behavior therapy techniques*. Oxford: Pergamon.

Wood, K. (1978). Casework effectiveness: A new look at the research evidence. *Social Work, 23*, 437–459.

Worchel, J. (1990). Short-term dynamic psychotherapy. In R. A. Wells & V. J. Giannetti (Eds.), *Handbook of the brief psychotherapies* (pp. 193–216). New York: Plenum.

Worchel, J. (1993). Pathological mourning in short-term dynamic psychotherapy. In R. A. Wells & V. J. Giannetti (Eds.), *Casebook of the brief psychotherapies* (pp. 197–218). New York: Plenum.

Yapko, M. D. (1992). Therapy with direction. In S. H. Budman, M. F. Hoyt, & S. Freidman (Eds.), *The first session in brief therapy* (pp. 156–180). New York: Guilford.

Zuk, G. (1978). Values and family therapy. *Psychotherapy: Theory, Research, and Practice, 15*, 48–55.

Index